IT'S AN
EMOTIONAL GAME

IT'S AN EMOTIONAL GAME

LEARNING ABOUT LEADERSHIP
FROM THE EXPERIENCE OF FOOTBALL

Lionel F. Stapley

KARNAC

LONDON   NEW YORK

First published in 2002 by
H. Karnac (Books) Ltd.
6 Pembroke Buildings, London NW10 6RE
A subsidiary of Other Press LLC, New York

British Library Cataloguing in Publication Data

A C.I.P. for this book is available from the British Library

   ISBN 1 85575 990 X

Edited, designed, and produced by The Studio Publishing Services Ltd,
Exeter EX4 8JN

Printed in Great Britain

10 9 8 7 6 5 4 3 2 1

This book is dedicated to:

Alan and the other team members.

With thanks for providing the opportunities for learning about teams.

ABOUT THE AUTHOR

Lionel F. Stapley has an MSc in Organisation Development and his PhD was awarded for research concerning a psychodynamic explanation of culture and change. He is a Fellow of the Chartered Institute of Personnel and Development (FCIP) and of the institute of Management (FIMgt); and a member of the International Society for the Psychoanalytic Study of Organisations (ISPSO).

In his current roles as an organisation consultant and Director of OPUS (An Organisation for Promoting Understanding of Society) he is very much concerned with individual, group and societal dynamics. In this work he is greatly influenced by a systems psychodynamic frame of working; the Group Relations approach; and, a commitment to learning from experience. He has also worked in the football industry for over six years. This has included a three-year spell working with manager; work with individual players suffering from minor psychological problems and management coaching with a growing number of professional footballers who are coming to the end of their playing careers.

He is the author of *The Personality of the Organisation; A Psychodynamic Explanation of Culture and Change*, London: Free Associations (1996); and a co-editor with Laurence Gould and Mark Stein of *Systems Psychodynamics of Organisations; Integrating Group Relations, Psychoanalytic and Open Systems Theory*, New York: Other Press (2001).

CONTENTS

viii CONTENTS

PREFACE

T eams have always been an important aspect of our lives in a whole range of situations. This is especially so in the work place where they are becoming increasingly important as a result of the way that information technology and other changes are re-shaping the formal structures and strategies of organizations. One of the effects of these changes is that those faced with the task of managing and leading teams have never experienced as great a challenge as they do today. Of these managerial and leadership roles, few can be as demanding or rewarding as that of a football manager, which is the setting for this book.

Over a period of three years I worked in a continuing consultancy relationship with the manager of a professional football team. From this privileged position I was afforded access to the manager and team at all times, which permitted observation and involvement in all aspects of their work. I joined them in the dressing room when they reported for a match; was present through pre-match, half-time and post-match activities; travelled to occasional away matches and infrequently attended training sessions. Consultancy was mainly with the manager in a one-to-one role consultancy mode, sometimes with individual players—as dictated by needs—

and through occasional workshops with the whole team. Since then I have worked with a growing number of professional footballers providing 'management coaching' to prepare them to take up a role as football managers. It is this experience that will provide the research and background of case material used to illustrate the complicated issues dealt with in this volume.

In general terms, the book seeks to offer *an analysis of management and leadership of teams* in, what is regarded by many, as the highly demanding, anxiety provoking and emotional environment of professional football. More specifically, it looks at that aspect of leadership by the football manager that concerns the struggles associated with his process of managing the boundary between what is inside and what is outside: between what is in the manager's mind and what is happening in the external environment, especially what is in other peoples' minds. In particular, it explores the impact of individual dynamics from the perspectives of both the manager and the team as a whole. In doing so, it looks at the complex interplay of individual and task boundaries and the effect on other team members of the desires of both the leader and other team members.

Essentially, though, this is a book about the largely emotional inner struggles experienced by managers when leading teams.

- It is about the manager's struggles to understand the dynamics that are creating the difficulty of implementing procedures.
- It is about developing a culture that will help to create a team that performs to its fullest potential.
- It is about playing with anxiety in all senses of the term.
- It is about the manager or leader developing an ability for self-awareness and self-control by adopting a reflective approach. A need which is particularly relevant in regard to emotions.

I feel sure that the football manager whom I worked with would be the first to say that his emotional involvement with the team and team behaviour was the biggest difficulty with which he had to struggle to gain self-awareness and self-control. Indeed, there were many occasions when he would quote, in a defensive sort of way, that old football cliché, *'It's an emotional game'*. Football certainly is an emotional game as is the management and leadership of any team. And, this, above all is at the heart of this book.

At this early stage, I want to introduce a procedure that will help all managers and leaders if they wish to gain a deeper understanding of some of the problems associated with their relationships and relatedness to other team members:

- The starting point is *self-awareness*. Through a process of reflecting on our behaviour we can develop our self-awareness. This can lead to:
- *Self-control*. A necessary process in our interactions with others is the need for self-control. This can lead to:
- *Awareness of others*. Without awareness of others we can have no real relationships.

It is through self-awareness, leading to self-control, that we can achieve the ability to be aware of and understand others. It should then be possible to have a real and meaningful relationship. However, as will be shown throughout the book, there will still be many situations when the way that our emotions and phantasies— what I shall refer to as our relatedness to others—will come into the equation. At these times, we shall require an even higher degree of self-awareness if we are to get the best out of other team members.

I should also like to take this early opportunity to say that there are no easy solutions, even though many readers have in the past— and probably will in the future—sought such solutions. There have been many publications which have tried to demonstrate how managers and leaders can develop a 'winning' or 'successful' team. Indeed, with so much good advice available, one is almost bound to ask, why, then, do we still find it so difficult? And, why do we still frequently fail in our endeavours to create successful teams? At one level, managers and leaders clearly understand that the findings presented by many of these authors are sensible and important. For example, that negative feedback is de-motivating and that participation of other team members in decision making is important. However, when it comes to the realities of life, when managers are striving to get the best out of other team members and things are not going well, that clarity of understanding may temporarily be forgotten. For example, during the course of a football match when things are not going as planned, the anxiety may reach such a level that clarity of thinking becomes difficult, if not impossible. At this stage, negative feedback and authoritarian leadership may frequently prevail.

There is nothing new about books telling leaders and managers how they ought to proceed if they want to develop a 'winning' team; they have quite a long history. However, only in recent years have they become so popular, with large numbers of leaders and managers avidly buying and reading them for advice and comfort when feeling uncertain about how to handle the problems they encounter in trying to build and lead an effective team. Indeed, the last decade may be seen as the age of the 'quick-fix'. One of the factors that encourages this approach is that many people tend to believe that times are changing fast and that research is constantly yielding new knowledge, so they feel the need to rely on experts. And, of course, the management gurus are more than happy to provide a ready supply of material to be consumed by managers and leaders. This eagerness to seek 'expert' advice can best be understood within the context of the belief that there are no limits to what people can achieve when they try hard enough and apply themselves in 'scientific' ways. It seems that a reliance on science as the source of progress has replaced an older trust in the wisdom inherent in tradition.

However, there are other important reasons why, during the last few decades, many leaders have sought out and come to trust the advice and recommendations found in leadership and team-building books and articles. One is the great appeal of the 'how-to' approach of many of these publications, as if life were a game that could be played 'by the rules'. This is exemplified by the 'do-it-yourself' industry. Furthermore, there is a bias in our society toward the idea that there is only one right way to do something, while all others are wrong. Thus, if we have proved something is 'right' and if we then follow this way, achieving our goal is a fairly simple process. Therefore, when things become difficult or complex, leaders and managers tend to believe that it must be because they have not used the correct approach, because if they had, things would go easily and successfully.

It is this double-edged conviction on which the 'how-to' manuals base their claim and of course the successes we have when following such instructions which buttress these claims. In fact, to be fair, the 'how-to' movement has shown us that there often is a right way of doing things, which indeed is fairly easy to apply successfully. However, this is most valid when applied to the making of objects, particularly when all that is needed is the correct assembly of existing pieces. The problem is that in our society, which in many respects has had its greatest success in mass-producing machinery, people are tempted to believe that the same principles, which are so eminently successful in the engineering field, should also be applicable to human relations and human development.

Books often tell managers and leaders 'how to be' with their team. For example:

- to be understanding;
- to be participative;
- to encourage conflict; to state but a few.

As statements of what are good practices in teams they are valuable. But as much as we want to be very good, if not great leaders, it is practically impossible to sustain such positive attitudes in crisis situations, when our emotions stir us strongly because we lose patience with what other team members are doing or are determined not to do. We cannot understand what makes them so obstinate. We find ourselves unable to be positive when they badly hurt our feelings, or when they embarrass us, destroy our dreams, or lose their tempers and show their rage by hitting or kicking out at opponents or the authorities, literally or figuratively. While sometimes we can take it all in good humour and retain our self-control, there are other moments when we are simply fed up with other team members' behaviour, even though it may be typical of what happens from time to time.

Anyone who has watched or played a game of football will be aware that it is an unendingly varied and complicated game. Indeed, one of its attractions may be the fact that it encourages and permits many differing views as to which players should play and how the team should play; it seems that the options are endless. But even football offers only an extremely simplified metaphor for the intricacy of human interaction. Each football match starts afresh and in exactly the same way. The rules are identical for both teams; they are unchangeable, clearly understood, and freely agreed upon by the players, who, under the authority of the referee must strictly obey them. And finally, the desired outcome and the reaching of that objective are also clear; the scoring of more goals than the opposition.

Experience has shown that none of this holds true for what happens between the leader and the other individual team members. Anything that occurs in their relationship is affected by a long and complicated history. Each interaction begins differently from all preceding ones. There are no agreed-upon rules, although as will be discussed, leaders often try to impose rules which the players, because of their seemingly weak position, may not be able to resist. But such forced agreements only interfere with the team members' ability to cope with the problem situation in a way that is constructive to them. This is why, in this book, I do not seek to offer definite answers but to suggest approaches that can promote the ability of the manager or leader and other team members to be spontaneous and very much themselves in all that happens between them. In doing so, this will encourage team members to develop the ability to cope with reality successfully on their own terms.

Using football as a metaphor for human relations may be slightly banal and oversimplified, but it can illustrate the fact that in a complex interaction we can never plan more than a few moves in advance. Each move must depend on the response to the preceding one. Thus it is very important to assess correctly the ever-changing overall situation: an appropriate first move can at best give only an indication of what the right reply to the first countermove by the opposition team may be. To gain an understanding of these dynamic situations requires considerable skill and use of methodologies which will help allow us to penetrate these processes. For many years, those working in a systems psychodynamic manner in organizations, will have been aware of the sort of issues raised in the preceding paragraphs. In more recent times, others have helpfully provided a complementary approach using other qualitative methodologies.

Faced with the predominant theory of science that requires empirical confirmation and validation, I feel obliged to acknowledge the criticism that psychoanalytic theory is a purely subjective approach. However, far from apologizing, I would submit that this is one of the only ways we can gain an understanding of processes of human behaviour. *By the term 'processes of human behaviour' we mean; 'dynamic phenomena that exist in a state of flux and which are characterized by spontaneity, freedom, experience, conflict and movement'.*

Only in the most general of terms, could such processes be the subject of confirmation and validation. After all, each of us is unique and each interaction is also unique. To make things even more difficult, we also need to study the emotionality involved in the interactions between leader and other team members: and, surely, it can hardly be contestable that feelings influence our behaviour. In addition, as will become clear later in the book, we also need to study how unconscious phenomena affect the leader and other team members.

The way in which leaders interact with other team members powerfully influences how they will develop and what they will achieve. It is understandable, then, that leaders seek the advice of experts, particularly when they cannot decipher the meaning of other team members' behaviour or are anxious about results, when they are uncertain whether or how to act, or when their efforts to correct other team members' behaviour makes the team unhappy and arouses their resistance. However, to develop the insights and attitudes which will further the development of both leader and other team members, as persons, while advancing the intimacy of their relations, I have found that it is of prime importance to avoid thinking that one knows the right answers, obvious though these may appear to be, before one has carefully examined what is involved in the situation for *each* party.

To achieve this we need to consider that:

- My reality, or reality from my perspective, may be totally different from that of other team members.
- My 'obvious right answer' may not be at all 'obvious' or 'right' to other team members.
- Furthermore, one should not attempt to understand other team members independently from oneself.

If we make a serious effort at understanding ourselves in the context of a given situation, trying to see how we have contributed to it— willingly or unwillingly, consciously or unconsciously—then our view of the matter is nearly always altered, as is our manner of handling it. In other words, if we are able to adopt a reflective approach, using the procedure detailed above, we may have a deeper understanding of the situation.

It is said that the good football players are those who are not affected by their mistakes. No one is perfect and we all make mistakes. Where we differ, though, is in our reactions to having made mistakes and this is the essential element in determining the success of individuals and ultimately teams. Those team members with a high level of self-esteem will, most likely, be able to maintain performance in spite of setbacks. Those with a low level of self-esteem are likely to be crippled by doubts and a lack of confidence. This is so for all sports players and for members of teams in all manner of settings.

For everyone who is a member of a team, anywhere, *it's an emotional game*. Every team member in every team is positively or negatively affected by their emotions. This means that emotions are a matter requiring considerable understanding and attention by the manager or leader if they are to 'get results through other people'. This raises questions such as:

● How does the manager or leader gain an understanding of the emotional state of each of the other team members at any given time?
● What are the implications for the manager or leader if they are to gain an understanding of the emotional state of other team members?

These, and other questions, will be addressed throughout the book, but let me set the scene for what is to follow by clearly and emphatically stating my belief that the manager or leader cannot begin to understand the emotional state of other team members if they are not aware of their own emotionality.

Being a manager in any organization is a difficult job. Being a football manager is a very difficult job. Quite often the difficulty of the work results in the manager becoming angry, frustrated, worried, and even being in a position of not knowing where to turn to next; what on earth can they do to move things forward. Sometimes even the whole world seems against them. The Chairman or other Board members are being difficult for any one of a number of reasons—money, success, or personal preferences about players or team selection; the coaching staff don't want to listen, they want to adopt their own ways of working regardless of what you want; the physiotherapist doesn't seem to understand that you want players back in the team—yesterday; the players are all walking around and looking at you as if you are an alien, and while they do as you tell them, they appear to be grudging and sullen. We can equally say of management, *it's an emotional game.*

Little wonder then, that as a manager or leader, you may be totally engrossed in yourself. Totally absorbed with what you can do to get yourself out of this ghastly situation and make life better for yourself. So you think long and hard and come up with a solution which you are confident will solve the problems. Having come up with your decision you then tell the other team members what you have decided and demand their support. You are beginning to feel a bit better now because you have worked out some of your own problems and seemingly found a way forward. But!

Many leadership books tout the sort of 'visionary' role of leaders, where, like Moses descending from the mountain-top, the leader unveils the new order. For their part in this scenario, dependent followers are supposed to stop wandering around aimlessly. Instead, they dutifully applaud, thank the leader profusely, and line up behind the leader's vision. Most writing concentrates on the inspirers and transformers, and seems to suggest that leadership exists only at the very top and that it is only colourful personalities who make good copy. Although the top leader is critical to the success of the organization, can set its tone and sometimes transform its values, such leaders, working alone, achieve nothing. Leaders achieve results by working with and through people and exist at all levels of the organization.

Management is about 'getting results through other people'. It's not about how happy and content the manager or leader is, they don't go out on the pitch and get results—'the team' do that; it's not about the manager or leader making decisions—it's about the decisions that 'the team' make: these are the things that matter. An important part of the manager or leader's job is ensuring that they do everything possible to ensure that 'the team' will want to go and win games.

The players—'the people you get results through'—will also be suffering many of the same feelings that you, the manager or leader, are experiencing. They too will, from time to time, be angry, frustrated, worried, and even be in a position of not knowing where to turn to next and what on earth they can do to move things forward. Unfortunately, they are not so fortunate as the manager or leader, they do not have the same power. They perhaps have little or no control over their destiny. In such circumstances life can seem pretty desperate, with little or no hope of any desirable change and no one to take forward their ideas for improvement. Of course, one way they can deal with this is by taking revenge.

If, as a manager or leader, you are so pre-occupied with yourself that you are not able to think of others you are not doing your job. You will not be able to do your job if you are solely and continually thinking of yourself. To move forward from this position, you need to have an intimate knowledge of yourself: you need to understand yourself inside out. You need to understand what makes you angry and what you do when you become angry. It's no good getting angry and blaming it on a team member when your anger is about your own failings. If you adopt that sort of behaviour, sooner or later no one is going to play for you. So the key to beginning to be successful is knowing yourself.

Until you know yourself, that is, until you have sufficient self-awareness to develop self-control you will never be able to have a true awareness of others. At the end of the day, having an awareness of others, 'the team', the people who get results for you, is all important. You need to understand their anger and concerns in order to help them feel that even at the darkest hour there is hope and something to look forward to. In essence, that is possibly the most important element of the manager or leader's job.

If you are serious about gaining a deeper understanding of some of the problems associated with your relationships and relatedness to other team members you need to work at the difficult but challenging process referred to earlier.

- Starting with *self-awareness*. Leading to:
- *Self-control*. Leading to:
- *Awareness of others*.

It is through self-awareness, leading to self-control that we can achieve the ability to be aware of and understand others. It should then be possible to have a real and meaningful relationship. However, as will be shown throughout the book, there will still be many situations when the way that our emotions and phantasies—

what I shall refer to as our relatedness to others—will come into the equation. At these times, we shall require an even higher degree of self-awareness if we are to get the best out of other team members.

Emotional development is needed if the feelings of others are to be recognized and respected. Most stereotypes are based on ignorance or the wish to scapegoat others who are different in some way. Familiarity with those different from yourselves is necessary if these labels are to be overcome, with opportunity to explore mutual feelings in some depth. Before you can relate at an emotional level with others, understand what they are feeling, and identify with those feelings (that is, empathize) there is a need to be self-aware, in touch with and understanding your own feelings. You also need to be sensitive to the non-verbal cues that indicate how others are feeling. This includes tone and volume of voice, eye contact, facial expression, posture and gestures. It is recognized that it is not what is said but how it is said that really matters. If a large percentage of an emotional message is communicated non-verbally then skill in interpreting these signals is essential if misunderstandings are to be avoided.

If we are to truly participate with other team members we need to communicate understanding and acceptance of the other team members at the emotional level, feeling with them. In effect, we need to communicate at three levels as below:

- what we hear (what the other team members say);
- what we see (the non-verbal cues that the other team members give us); and
- what we feel (the expressed feelings of other team members).

If, as is frequently the case, we solely rely on communication at the level of what people say, we shall miss a vast amount of what is being communicated with a belief that one can control one's life sufficiently to make its attainment possible.

Let none of us be under any illusion that this is anything but hard work. Like the football manager described in this book, all of us must struggle to understand ourselves better, not the least because our efforts to achieve greater clarity about ourselves make it possible for us to achieve clarity in our relation to other team members, with a consequent enrichment of our life. Such understanding of ourselves around some issue of leadership cannot be handed to us by someone else, no matter how great their expertise may be; it can be achieved only by ourselves, as we struggle to remove whatever has obscured this understanding from our consciousness. Only our own efforts to achieve such higher comprehension lead to permanent personal growth of both the leader and other team members. All that any book can do—including this one—is to address some of the overall problems of leadership: their origin, significance, meaning, and particularly, possible ways of thinking about them.

How to use this book

It is not unreasonable to say that this book starts where many others leave off. It does not seek to offer 'quick-fixes' but seeks to explore some of the less obvious ways that individual and group behaviour affects team dynamics and performance. None of these behaviours will be new to the reader, indeed, I feel sure that all will identify with most of the behaviour and dynamics referred to. They are, though, generally speaking the more difficult issues not usually referred to in books. The approach taken to dealing with these issues in this book is based on what I consider to be the most successful way of helping others with effective leadership: namely, inducing you to develop your own insights about leadership and attitudes appropriate not only to your task but also to the person you are and to other team members; inducing you to strive to reach an understanding and an attitude which are at the same time of individual and mutual benefit to both the manager or leader and to other team members.

Many practising managers and leaders may experience a degree of anxiety and a certain uneasiness as they approach some of the experiences referred to in this book. For some it may indeed be quite threatening and uncomfortable reading; just as the actual experience of exploration was, on many occasions, for the football manager. His experience and that of his team members, as referred to here, is unique and will not be repeated, but the learning gained from *his approach to developing a deeper understanding* will hopefully act as encouragement and guidance for others.

To be of greatest value the reader should try to apply the

material to their own experiences of either managing or leading or of being managed or led. Having done so, they should then reflect on the feelings and emotions that were energized by them at that time and on how they dealt with them. I feel sure that once readers are able to reflect on their past or current experiences they will be pleasantly surprised at how 'live' these experiences can be. To simply read this book without trying to apply it to your own experience will be helpful but nowhere near as helpful as if you are able to apply the material to your own experience.

Organization of book

The book is organized so that the early chapters mainly deal with dynamics concerning the leader and their desires. Early middle chapters deal with what happens when these desires are frustrated and the ways that we react to these situations. Later middle chapters relate to issues of authority, discipline and punishment, and explore ways of ensuring that agreed decisions and aims are achieved. In the last chapter I move to an exploration of the sort of management and leadership behaviour that I feel is necessary in a society where we value and respect all team members. A brief description of each chapter follows:

Chapter 1

'Leaders and teams: understanding self and others', sets the scene by relating to the incredible complexity faced by managers and leaders of teams. It describes something of what it's like to be a manager or leader and highlights the importance of self-reflection as a means of developing an awareness of the emotion aroused in both managers and other team members. Unlike mending a motor car, where we may make an error that can be corrected, when managing or leading a team we may face untold misery if our actions misfire. Topics covered in this chapter include: an exploration of what is involved in learning about yourself; the dynamic nature of both environmental conditions and of other team members; what we mean by leadership; the need for leadership if teams are to be creative; and the need for reflection as a key ingredient in various important aspects of teams (e.g., empathy, unconscious processes, feelings, values, and identification).

Chapter 2

'Motivation of the leader in the context of the team', seeks to answer important questions about why people do things. Why are we motivated to do anything? What is motivation? Why do some people work hard at many different tasks and persist in the face of difficulties while others are rather lazy, have few interests and tend to quit in the face of frustration? Topics covered in this chapter include: the self—who are the individuals that call themselves manager, leader or team member; how by understanding boundaries such as the skin boundary or the body–mind boundary, we can understand ourselves; leadership in the context of relationships; motivation as desires—all behaviour having something to do with satisfaction of desires; how achievement of desires leads to knowledge of our world; the emotions evoked by football, especially the highs and the lows of elation and anxiety; lack of 'self-perception' arising out of emotional overload; the participation of others in the achievement of our desires; and how we learn to avoid dissatisfaction as a result of not achieving our desires.

Chapter 3

'Managing aggression in the leader and other team members', commences by exploring the derivation of our aggressive desires and explains how, under the stresses and strains of life, we regress to the more primitive forms of behaviour that we adopted as infants. Topics covered in the chapter include: how various factors, especially personality, will induce aggressive behaviour in managers and leaders; how other team members are affected in the same way; the need for participation and consultation of other team members as a means of providing opportunities for all to satisfy their desires; an awareness that we cannot do anything without being in some way destructive to somebody else's desires, and the realization that in doing so, this may well result in some sort of harm or loss to self; the different versions of aggressive behaviour adopted by managers and other team members; and learning how to avoid aggressive behaviour.

Chapter 4

'Defence mechanisms—coping with failure', continues on the theme of what happens when we fail to achieve our desires. Having, in the last chapter, explored one reaction, aggression, I now look at some of the many other devices and methods that we adopt as a means of coping with anxiety. Topics covered in this chapter include: how we develop a repertoire of coping mechanisms based on our experience through life; how the threat of loss or actual loss can have the same effect—both inducing anxiety; coping by regression to childlike behaviour, such as the use of magic, wishful thinking, and the development of phantasy solutions; how our previous experience and mental strength effect our means of coping; how the amount of support available and our previous experience of failure effect our means of coping; how we use regression as a means of coping with anxiety and the effect this has on unconscious processes; and an explanation of various defence mechanisms used in everyday life.

Chapter 5

'Authority—who does what', explores one of, if not perhaps, the most important concept for any manager to understand, namely, authority. At the heart of many organizational difficulties lies a problem regarding a lack of clarity about issues of authority. Topics covered by this chapter include: an explanation and differentiation of authority, influence and authoritarianism; how managers and leaders abuse their authority; the sources of authority; why it is important that authority relations are clarified and why there is a need for clarity in the manager or leader's role; how getting results through other people concerns the exercise of authority by all team members; how the emotions of other team members will have an effect on the exercise of authority; the manager's authority in developing a vision; bonding; and delegation of authority.

Chapter 6

'Leaders and discipline', carries forward the exploration and discussion about authority by relating to the important issues concerning how managers and leaders ensure that decisions, when agreed, are carried out in a disciplined way. Such are the potential difficulties and misunderstandings surrounding discipline, it is perhaps no surprise that this is the longest chapter in the book. When our desires are not met, many of us frequently respond at an emotional level, with some sort of punitive action. It is easy to lay the blame elsewhere and not take the responsibility for our own actions. However, it is argued that 'discipline' should be regarded as 'instruction' and that what we should seek is self-discipline. Topics covered in this chapter include: the constant and important need for managers and leaders to provide exemplary role models for other team members; how trust in managers and leaders is necessary if other team members are to seek to emulate them; helping other team members by 'being there' for them; participation and consultation as a means of self-discipline in other team members; the vital leadership task of setting boundaries; being aware of our own emotion so that we don't blame others; dealing with breakdowns in discipline; the essential management skill of developing 'emotional distance'; how phantasies and emotions affect our relatedness to others; the need for empathy and self-awareness; the need for the manager or leader to provide containment; and the difficult and slow process of personal change.

Chapter 7

'Why punishment does not achieve discipline', continues to look at discipline and takes the exploration and discussion forward by taking a detailed look at punishment. It is accepted that most managers or leaders will have given the odd 'slap-down' to other team members when they are exasperated. However, this may lead to rationalization of other harsher types of punishment. It is argued that there is no place for punishment in team development. Punishment may make us obey orders, but the best it will do is to teach us obedience to authority, it will never result in self-discipline. Topics covered in this chapter include: how and why we need to make the vital distinction between firmness and punishment; why the manager or leader needs to have sufficient self-awareness of aspects of their personality, which may effect the way they manage; the need for a sufficient degree of self-awareness that will lead to self-control of the emotions, which might otherwise lead to punishing behaviour; why punishment does not work and the negative effects of punishment; the need for self-discipline if we are to get results through other people; how the 'clamour of the emotions can negatively affect managerial actions; how our own previous experience may lead us to consider that punishment is helpful; dealing with indiscipline; the need for praise; and how self-reflection can lead to an understanding of the negative effects of punishment.

Chapter 8

'Leadership re-defined': in this chapter, the last, the various concepts and notions referred to in the previous chapters, are pulled together to provide a different way of viewing leadership; one which concerns the manager or leader providing the sort of environment which will encourage all team members to develop as autonomous individuals. It is suggested that those much envied and admired, so-called charismatic leaders, are those that provide the sort of environment that encourages other team members to admire and respect them and to seek to emulate them. As a result, other team members identify with them. One of the key reasons why they do so, is the high degree of self-awareness of these leaders which enables them to obtain a high degree of awareness of others; particularly, an awareness of other team member's emotions—the capacity for a high degree of empathy. Topics covered in this chapter include: an exploration of the authority, responsibility, and accountability of managers and leaders in the context of other team members; an exploration of the distinction between 'teams' and 'single-leader work groups'; the need for managers to have a high degree of self-awareness of their emotions; the need for expression of emotions; the appropriate use of emotions; self-awareness as a means of avoiding the development of phantasies in our relatedness to others; how self-awareness can help us cope with anxiety; what is meant by the concept of a 'facilitating environment' and the links with maturity and health of all team members; scapegoating; the way that aggression and disaffection can occur in the wrong sort of environment; how hope, optimism, and a desire for competence need to be encouraged; and how managers and leaders can provide a 'facilitating environment', by making themselves available to other team members for their containment.

Acknowledgements

Most importantly, I should wish to express my thanks to Alan and the other team members for allowing me the privilege of being with them on so many private occasions and for the pleasure of working with them. And, to those I have subsequently worked with in the 'management coaching' role. I am grateful to them all for providing the opportunities for learning about the management and leadership of teams. I feel sure that their learning and development will have made it all worthwhile. But more than this, I feel sure that they would also have a genuine desire that others might also learn from the experience referred to here.

I should also wish to acknowledge the huge impact that psychoanalytic writers such as Melanie Klein [see for example (1975)], Donald Winnacott [see for example (1965a & 1965b)], Otto Kernberg [see for example (1966)], Bruno Bettleheim [see for example (1988)], and Donald Fairbairn [see for example (1952)], have had in influencing this book. Much of the theory is based on their work concerning infant development and I hope that I have in some way added to and enriched this by applying their theoretical endeavours to my work as an organization consultant. I would also wish to acknowledge the work of Daniel Goleman (1995) which I have found both illuminating and encouraging.

Who is this book for?

Essentially, this is a book for managers and leaders of teams at all levels of organizations and institutions, be they Chief Executives who are leading senior management teams; middle or junior managers who are heading up work teams; or, project managers who are heading up less permanent teams. More than this, though, it is a book for all those many interested and sophisticated members of teams everywhere, who are interested in the sort of management and leadership that they could not perhaps espouse but will know and admire when they get it.

It will also be required reading for all those who are interested in the theory and practice of working with groups, teams and organizations, as well as those who have a serious interest in the education of organizational behaviour and organizational development: MBA and other management students; managers; consultants; personnel and training professionals; and, researchers in group and organizational behaviour. It is anticipated, therefore, that this volume could be profitably utilized in a variety of management programmes and courses, and in both undergraduate, graduate, and, post-graduate course offerings in management, organizational behaviour, organization development, psychology, and social science departments.

In addition, this book will be essential reading for all who are concerned in any way with the management and leadership of football teams, at whatever level, anywhere in the world. Or, for that matter, anyone concerned with management and leadership in any team sports. It will also provide huge benefits to all team players, by greatly adding to their knowledge of the dynamics that they are helping to create. And, not least, it will add to the pleasure and excitement of those many interested and sophisticated followers of the game of football, or any other team sport, throughout the world.

CHAPTER ONE

Leaders and teams: understanding self and others

I n this opening chapter I want to introduce the reader to some of the complexities faced by managers or leaders of teams. In later chapters many of these matters will be looked at in greater detail, in a search for a deeper understanding. However, at this stage, I am concerned with helping the reader to concentrate their attention on what it's like to be a manager or leader of a team and to get in touch with the feelings associated with the various memories of events that will be provoked into their thoughts.

How very complicated are the manager or leader's feelings when they are baffled by the problem of how to deal with team members in a difficult situation. Here they have to act and yet find it incredibly complex and often beyond their emotional resources, to conduct themselves in a manner which meets their own needs and at the same time helps other team members in a way that will encourage their development and help them to gain a positive view of themselves and of the world. Other activities, such as not knowing how to fix our motor car when it won't start, pose no such challenge to our self-esteem. But, when we are unable to find, on our own, the 'right' answers to questions of team-management, we often feel that we are inadequate leaders. It is for this reason that we may approach the advice we find in this book with both anxiety and uneasiness.

The greater our perplexity and need, the greater also is the pressure to find a solution right away. The more perturbed we are, the less we are able to reflect and to weigh things carefully and the more we are likely to turn to a book, especially one by a highly regarded manager or leader, because we wish to be instructed by an authority. This willingness as leaders to trust what we are told has much to do with our desire to do right by our team and relatively little to do with the correctness of the instructions these books offer. Otherwise there would have to be widespread agreement concerning which of the many thousands of books to follow and which to reject—an agreement that hardly exists. This pressure also poses a further problem, the more we want such advice, the less we like it, because our need for it is the consequence of our being confronted by a problem which, deep down, we feel we should be able to cope with on our own.

Even assuming that we have the time to refer to our favourite book, which in most instances is highly unlikely, can it really be helpful? While the situation and the behaviour of a manager or leader in it may have features in common with those an author describes and even when the problem we are facing is a common one, each of us is a unique individual. Even though some of us may have had the same parents or were brought up in the same street, or went to the same school or the same work place, each of us will have had a life experience different from anyone else. In all manner of ways, rather like our fingerprints or DNA, there is something quite unique about all of us. Thus, no author of a book written for managers or leaders in general can know and weigh all the factors involved in our particular predicament. We are quite ready to believe that the advice given may apply to most situations, but we are uneasy because we cannot be certain that it is appropriate to ours. We also know that nothing is at stake for the giver of such advice if it backfires, while untold misery may be the consequence for the leader and other team members if his implementation is erroneous or inappropriate, or if the advice or our understanding of it is incomplete.

If we are following instructions for getting our car started or putting together a pre-fabricated piece of furniture, we can make a dreadful error without grave consequences. If we so desire, we can put the instructions away and forget the whole thing; we can perhaps ask for better instructions; no matter what happens we shall not be any worse off than before. However, this is clearly not the case with a team. In managing or leading a team, it is much more difficult to undo the damage that is the consequence of bad timing, of unclear or misunderstood advice, or of advice that is entirely off the mark. Here we are dealing with human processes which, as were described in the Foreword, are dynamic and spontaneous. We know that since we began to follow the advice, things have happened between us and other team members to change the original situation; what we cannot do is retrace our steps, or start again where we began. In managing or leading the team we have to live with the consequences of our actions—good or bad.

Leadership and learning

At this point, it may be helpful to refer to different types of learning. The distinctions between 'knowing about' and 'knowledge of acquaintance' made by William James, are particularly relevant. The former type of knowledge we could refer to as cognitive knowledge; this can be communicated through words and written text which may be understood in the same way. This is rather like the directions for 'do-it-yourself' or the construction of a motor car engine. The latter presents a totally different problem. Knowledge of human behaviour cannot be communicated as if it were an extraneous, objective entity; it cannot be learned from a textbook. Learning by experience—acquiring knowledge of acquaintance—starts with oneself. As a prerequisite about knowing more about the roles and relationships in which I am involved and about managing myself in them, I have to learn more about me.

A further helpful distinction is that made by Daniel Goleman (1995) between 'cognitive intelligence' and 'emotional intelligence', which (he says) include self-control, zeal, and persistence, and the ability to motivate oneself. Goleman states that those who are at the mercy of impulse—who lack self-control—suffer a moral deficiency: The ability to control impulse is the basis of will and character. As will be shown in the next chapter, without emotional learning we shall not be able to harmonize our thoughts and emotions. The result may be that the power of our emotions may disrupt thinking and perception. That's why, when we are emotionally upset we sometimes say, 'we just can't think straight'.

Developing self-awareness

What usually does help a manager or leader in such situations is to reflect on how it was when they wished to behave or actually did behave much as other team members are now doing. All of us will recall the many times when we exhausted our manager or leader's patience, wanted to defy them or actively did so, and objected silently or openly to the way they managed us. If we can truly remember these situations, we will also recall how deeply painful they were for us as team members, how anxious and insecure we were behind our show of defiance and argumentativeness, and how we resented our manager or leader's failure to realize all this because they were so wrapped up in their annoyance.

Understanding our own feelings or emotions can be highly relevant to gaining an understanding of others. For example, a set of circumstances surrounding the signing of a new player proved highly valuable for the manager's future relationship with his team. For many weeks the manager had pursued a player whom he badly needed to improve his team. After much effort he realized his desire and obtained the agreement of the player to sign—a deal which they then shook hands on. The manager went to the Chairman to update him on the good news and to inform him of the financial implications. The response was less than enthusiastic and it was far from being certain that the 'deal' would be confirmed. At best, it would mean waiting several days for the Board to make a final decision. I saw the manager just after this event and his emotional state is well summarized in his comments which were something like: 'I can't speak at the moment Lionel, I just can't think straight, I need some time to clear my head'. On reflection, it was clear that his anger and frustration about not being able to sign the player were such that they prevented any semblance of thought or perception. For the manager, this experience, difficult as it was, proved to be one of the most valuable in relating to players who were in the middle of similar experiences. It was something that the manager could call upon to get in touch with the feelings of others.

If we really get in touch with our memories and more importantly our feelings regarding our own experiences as team members, this will help develop self-control and make us patient and understanding. Also, this should lead us to realize that despite the seeming obstinacy of other team members, they may now be suffering just as we suffered then. If we really want to work with them and provide them with the support they require, we need to have a deep understanding of what other team members are experiencing. However, for this to happen we have to relive such experiences in our mind; merely reading about them will not re-create them in us, because it is the very specifics of our experience which makes it vivid enough to be not just remembered, but relived with feeling.

What is really required is empathy, which builds on self-awareness. By getting in touch with our own feelings we are enabled to have a greater awareness of the feelings of others. There is no way that managers or leaders can convince their team members that they are empathic when they don't really give a damn. As Goleman (1995) says, the emotional notes and chords that weave through people's words and actions—the telling tone of voice or shift in posture, the eloquent silence or telltale tremble—are all non-verbal signals that the manager does truly understand where the team member is at. For all rapport, the root of caring, stems from emotional attunement, from the capacity for empathy. The capacity to know how another feels is important in all management situations. Where it is seen to be absent there will be a lack of trust. To gain an understanding of the feelings of others we need to go beyond the words to read the non-verbal communications. Frequently a team member will say something like 'I'm all right'; the skilled manager will pick up the contrary messages in the tone of voice, gestures, facial expressions, and the like. If the manager or leader is very skilled they will also take in and experience the feelings of other team members. Remember, communication needs to be at three levels.

A dynamic process

Anyone with a basic knowledge of football will be aware that if the team tries to follow their predetermined plans irrespective of the opposition's countermoves, it will soon be beaten. In the same way, managers or leaders who try to follow a preconceived plan, based on explanations they received or advice they were given for dealing with other team members, will also be beaten. In order to be effective, managers or leaders need to continually and flexibly adapt their procedures to the responses of other team members and reassess the ever-changing overall situation as it develops. In a sense, this is not really different from the contingency approach to leadership developed by Lawrence and Lorsch (1967). Not only are circumstances changing, but we also have a team of unique individuals. Not all team members are highly skilled and experienced, not all team members want a high degree of freedom and autonomy, some preferring, instead, to be told what to do (at least, until they have the confidence and trust to participate).

In football it soon becomes obvious that it is a blunder to try to follow one's own plan without giving the most careful considera-tion to the opposition's plan and to their reactions to your own team's moves. For any football manager watching the team play, situations will arise that require changes to the pre-conceived plan. For example, where an opposing player is clearly getting the better of his marker and creating havoc, something has to be done to counter this position. In like manner, a marketing team faced with the opposition taking a big portion of the business must do something to counter the position. Consideration of other team members' intentions and reactions is also crucial to the manager or leader's actions. But, this is even more complicated by the fact that other team members, when in disagreement with the manager or leader, may often hide their true feelings out of their fear about the way the manager or leader may react, in which case the leader is often stymied.

In working with the football team there were many occasions when the team would clearly disagree with the manager but not voice their disagreement. For example, on several occasions the team would come into the dressing room at half time looking and feeling downcast after struggling to come to grips with a better organized or more motivated opposition. From the manager's viewpoint, at the boundary, he would be in a position to make judgements about what was required to gain a tactical advantage. Having made up his mind he would then, with a lot of passion and enthusiasm, say something like, 'Listen up, this is what we're going to do, we're going to change the formation' (or whatever). On nearly every occasion there was not a single member of the team who voiced any sort of opposition to this change, but, the non-verbal signals were deafening—no way, did they agree with this!

Having worked with the players for some considerable time, the manager was not blind to this disagreement. But, the decision had been made without taking into consideration the views of the other team members or without floating it as a way forward. Having announced the plan there was no going back, as this would have been seen to be a weakness and, perhaps more pertinently, the manager firmly believed that this was the right way to go. In their downcast state team members required support and containment for what they were doing. To put a new proposal at that stage simply made them more anxious, thus achieving the reverse of what was intended. Another result of this sort of activity was to provide the players with a rationalization for losing. It wasn't said but it might as well have been: 'We wanted to win but the manager messed up'.

There are few situations, other than perhaps those in the most automated situations, such as an assembly line, where the manager or leader can have total control over the actions of other team members. Even in closed systems, such as prisons, it is clear that there is no such thing as total control. Being a dynamic process, which we will recall is characterized by 'spontaneity, freedom, experience conflict, and movement', the most the manager or leader can normally do is to agree the direction the team will take. After this, events associated with the task will dictate what is required. For example:

- in football a player may be injured or sent off which will dictate a change; or
- in the business world a change of interest rates may also dictate a change.

It is likely to be very rare circumstances which permit the manager or leader to make the required decisions. Sometimes, such as at half-time there may be an opportunity for the manager to make or influence decisions. Although, as the example above shows us, there may be more important things to do than make decisions. On more frequent occasions, team members—those that achieve the results—need to provide the necessary leadership.

The leader and leadership

Football is a good example of the need for all team members to exercise leadership. It has been said by many managers that once the team goes out on the field they are out of the manager's control. In many ways this is true and should be true. Watching various managers constantly hectoring, demanding, urging, imploring, and threatening their players during a game seems rather like the worst of back seat drivers criticizing you every inch of the journey. All of us know just how frustrating that can be and that it eventually leads to anger. If that does happen, if the players become angry as a result of the manager's actions, there is a good chance that they will lose self-control and very likely lose the match—the reverse of what was intended. So, how does the manager maintain control once the players are on the pitch? Firstly, as a rather simplistic starting point, the manager or leader needs to work extremely closely with the captain—the manager's representative on the field. The captain needs to work intimately with the manager and to develop shared thoughts and feelings about the game. In addition, the whole team needs to have a clear idea about what is required of them as individual players and as team members—they need to know the boundaries. It is rather like an army which learns its basic drill that can then be carried out automatically while they are fighting a battle. If they did not learn that drill they would be a shambles—as is the case with some teams.

I also want to advance the important notion that, among other things, the good manager or leader is one who encourages leadership in other team members. The better the leader or manager is in fulfilling this aim—the more successful will be the team. It is my contention that this is what makes the difference, this is what makes a great team and consequently, a great leader. For the leader or manager who feels the demands to succeed lying heavily on their shoulders there will be many times when the temptation to 'take control' and to impose a solution will be exceedingly strong. It is the great manager or leader who has the self-awareness and the self-control to withstand these many pressures, to be aware of and understand the needs, emotions and desires of other team members, and thus, to be able to encourage them to provide leadership.

What do we mean by leadership? It seems that the essential point, for this discussion, is that *leadership always involves attempts on the part of the leader (influencer) to affect (influence) the behaviour of a follower* (see for example, Tannenbaum et al., 1961). To do so, involves the use of power which is potential for influence. As Miller (1985) explained, 'every act is a political act' and every leadership act being an attempt to influence; be that by persuasion, manipulation, request or cajoling, requires the use of power. In an ideal situation, we want to encourage all players to take a leadership role and to constantly attempt to influence their team mates to do better. To achieve this aim, the team members must feel empowered to act, they must feel that they can at times cajole or push their team mates without fear of recriminations either from them or from the manager.

Seen in a different light, the very act of leadership may be thought of as managing a boundary between what is inside and what is outside. It requires the manager to re-examine the boundary between inside and outside and to take a different and riskier stance towards the environment. Thus, if we take another look at the manager's decision making activities at half time referred to above; the management activity required concerns self-awareness of both their own views about what needs to be done (what is inside) and the likely emotional and cognitive state of other team members and what they might feel needs to be done (what is outside). If, as in the example cited, there is no self-awareness and subsequent self-control, but simply an insistence of their own views, the manager will almost certainly set up negative consequences. As previously, we return to the essential need for a high degree of self-awareness that will enable the manager to work across the boundary between what is inside and what is outside.

Leadership, creativity and power

That is not to say that the manager or leader should not exercise leadership. Creativity, innovation, and change occur when the creative manager exercises leadership. It is therefore important, that when exercising their undoubted power and authority, and their desires to be creative, the manager works to get the followers for their new creation, be that a new way of playing, a new way of training or a new way of obtaining fitness. Without followers any creation is stillborn. However, we need also to see leadership from another perspective. Creativity—the creation of something new—may generally speaking result in the satisfaction of the leader's desires, but this may, at the same time, deprive other people of their satisfaction. They may suffer the anxiety or pain of deprivation, because of the leader's actions. Satisfaction of the leader's desires may be destructive to theirs, and vice versa. By self-awareness, self-control, and awareness of others, the manager or leader can exercise authority in a different way, one which encourages leadership in other team members. In doing so, they will help to provide the conditions where all team members can also be creative, to much mutual advantage.

Leadership inevitably involves the use of power, which can be viewed in many ways. The view taken here, is that advanced by Gregory Bateson who believed that power 'is not a zero sum equation where the less I gain the more there is for others. Rather, it should be seen as an equal equation where the more I gain the more there is for them, and vice versa' (see Skynner, 1989, p. 113). Thus, it is not about the all-powerful leader who continues to seek more and more power with the aim of becoming *the* omnipotent great leader. This sort of manager or leader can only manage by the use of coercion, which must eventually result in failure. Rather, it is about the powerful leader who is made more powerful because other team members also have power. Here, the other team members are committed to the cause and through their creativity and leadership will contribute to the great team and through this process the manager or leader will also become a great leader.

Many managers and leaders will doubtless be shaking their heads and saying something like, 'but I am the leader and leadership is expected of me, my team want me to make decisions'. What if they do manage in this way and impose their decisions on the other team members? Even if a leader insists that their view of a given issue is to prevail and their rules are to be obeyed, this does not guarantee that other team members will accept any of it in their hearts. As far as inner experience (the unique life experience of each individual) is concerned, both team members and leader each follow their own rules. Thus, depending on their previous experience, and for many football players the rules mean that you don't trust people in authority or that there's no point in putting a point of view—it will only be ignored. Whatever they are, these rules have usually never been made explicit to themselves or to the other. Furthermore, not only do most leaders and other team members follow their own rules, they can and do change rules easily in the process of interacting without warning one another, usually without any conscious awareness that they have changed them, or how. There is no clearly understood and freely accepted agreement on what forms or decides the desirable outcome in leader–team member relationships.

Taking the football analogy again, the manager can provide instructions, directions, requests, or agreed approaches to the other team members before any particular game. But, once the players are on the field, he has very limited control over what they do. The individual players are faced with decisions all the time. Decisions about whether to pass to one player or another, whether to head a ball or kick it, whether to make a tackle or stand off the opponent. The manager may not be entirely happy with the decisions made, but like it or not, when performing their task, the leadership is almost entirely in the hands of the eleven players on the field. They cannot stop in the middle of the action to ask the manager to make a decision. The best the manager can do is to ensure that the other team members are as well prepared as possible for every eventuality and do everything they can to encourage leadership in other team members. It seems almost unnecessary to state that in the reverse situation, where, for one reason or another, players are not confident about making decisions and providing leadership, this will almost inevitably result in failure.

Reflection and empathy

Good football players can contemplate in advance a number of possible moves and likely counter-moves, but only because they have learned to reconsider and re-evaluate (or reflect) the overall situation after each step. Managers and leaders who can already reflect in this manner on their relations to other team members hardly need advice; they will know what to do and at every action and reaction of other team members will constantly re-evaluate the situation. If managers and leaders can learn how to project themselves into other team members minds, to gain an understanding of what they are experiencing and most importantly, what they are feeling, while simultaneously trying to understand what motivates themselves, then they will instinctively choose the best course of action.

Reflecting on the above paragraph I can't help thinking how easy it all seems. Yet, having myself been a manager and experienced working with the football manager in the circumstances described, I know that it is far from easy. And, I feel sure that many readers who have been leaders or managers of a team will share those sentiments. But, as stated earlier, they will not gain by simply reading this book as a 'how-to-do it' exercise. It is only if, while reading this book, you are able to reflect on situations that you have experienced and then to get in touch with the feelings that you were then experiencing, that you will develop a true understanding of what it's really like and why you need to follow some of the advice.

Essential though this approach may be, it may be easier said than done, because in projecting ourselves into others minds, we also need to be aware that things are not always as they appear on the surface. If psychoanalytic theories of human development are correct, it is clear that early childhood experience not only influences the development of self-esteem and the perception of oneself in relation to others, but also determines our interpretation of later experiences and leads us to arrange our life's events to conform to our preconceived notions. Thus, we develop the unique rules referred to above.

Reflection and unconscious processes

Since here, and throughout the book I shall refer to the concepts of the unconscious and the preconscious, it may be helpful to discuss their difference. A person is normally unaware of what goes on in either their unconscious or their preconscious. However, through a careful examination of their thoughts, feelings, and motives the content of the preconscious will usually be accessible to them. The process may be a difficult one, but it is possible for them to bring into awareness what goes on in their preconscious. By contrast, there is a nearly impenetrable barrier between their conscious and unconscious mind. This is because what goes on in their unconscious is what is unacceptable to their conscious mind and has therefore been severely repressed. Full awareness of what goes on in the unconscious can be achieved, if achieved at all, only against the greatest resistance. For example, for many years deeply repressed racist views meant that black players were not given the opportunity to play for Football League clubs. At the present time, this appears to be the case regarding players from an Asian background. To penetrate this barrier separating conscious and unconscious, takes concentrated effort and determination and very hard intellectual work and in many cases this may be possible only to a limited degree, or even quite impossible.

Psychoanalytic theory stresses both the intractability of much of our evolutionary inheritance and the importance of our early experiences. Though we are able to alter any of this inheritance, early experiences have a major impact on an individual's personality. Psychoanalytic doctrine is deeply committed to the conviction that how these inherited characteristics will be shaped depends on a person's life experience. Thus it subscribes to a historical view, according to which later events are to a considerable degree conditioned by what has happened before; therefore, the earliest history of the individual is of the greatest importance in respect to what they will be like in their later life, not only because it is the basis for all that follows, but also because early history largely determines how later life will be experienced. While genetic and evolutionary history creates an individual's potentialities, their early personal history, more than anything that follows, accounts for the forms these potentialities will take in the actuality of their life.

Therefore, respect for each team member's unique personality is of paramount importance in all dealings with them. Rather than 'forcing' or 'conditioning' the team member toward whatever the leader thinks best, the aware and concerned leader will respond sensitively to what best suits a particular team member at any given moment. This is perhaps best explained by the following example. Where a manager or leader tries to 'force' compliance from a team member who as a child had the experience of a parent who deserted the family thus causing the child to see all authority figures as 'bad' and 'not to be trusted', the approach is most unlikely to work. On the surface, the team member may appear to comply, but they will at the same time be putting into being their tried and tested plans for dealing with untrustworthy authority figures, which might involve espousing agreement but doing the reverse. When things are still not happening as required, the sort of manager or leader who only has force in their tool kit will then have to use more force. The likely result is that sooner or later they will either dispense with the team member's services or they will leave at their own request.

In any manager–team member relationship there are likely to be difficulties. Everyone gradually develops, through years of experience, characteristic ways of relating to people. However, it is helpful to distinguish relationships that are based on unconscious displacements from early life and those that are primarily reactions to the real attitudes and behaviour of the present day person. A relationship of the latter type, as occurs between manager and team member, is based on the team member's conscious appreciation of the manager as they really are, and may be called a *reality relationship*. It differs from what has come to be known as *'transference'*—the unconscious projection onto the manager of the team member's attitudes toward a potent figure of their early childhood. In these circumstances, the team member is not in a *'reality'* relationship with the manager or leader, but is in fact, albeit unconsciously, relating to them as if they were a totally different person, they literally project onto the manager the personality of some other person from the past and treat the manager as that other person.

In cases where the team member is relatively mature, their contacts with the manager, if they have been satisfactory, will tend to develop a rapport between the two; whereas, if they have been irritating, they may lead to an acrimonious relationship. In either case they are apt to be fairly direct results of *'reality factors'* in the immediate situation. In the case of such reality-adjusted behaviour, the manager can respond by giving attention to the reality situation. If the reality factors that have already affected the team member have been favourable, the manager takes advantage of the initial rapport thus created to get on with the work. If the manager encounters antagonism, they will need to first look at the factual nature of the team member's immediately preceding experiences. In such cases they will need to seek in themselves and in the surrounding environment the objective situations, delays, misunderstandings, and so on, that are occasioning this negative reaction, and should try to remove them and replace them with stimuli conducive to satisfaction, liking, and trust.

In most people, reality factors, that is, the real situation and the real attitude of the team member, are the determining ones in establishing the quality of the early manager–team member relationship. The team member's feelings toward the manager are fairly directly caused, are conscious and are subject to relatively easy control. Genuine transference feelings, on the other hand, although they may be currently stimulated, are remotely caused, are largely unconscious and require considerable skill for their control. When a team member's problem is in part a personality one or requires considerable time for its solution, the influences that bring about transference are increased and transference occurs to a correspondingly greater degree.

The authority situation between team member and manager can recreate, to some extent, a dependency situation analogous to one's infancy and thus tends to reactivate the characteristic way of handling problems which was developed at that time. As the child sought help from their parents, a team member seeks help and assistance from their manager. Even a simple request for something, like a favourable agreement on financial terms, places the team member in a subordinate position to the person in authority. When the help requested is more extensive than this, the feeling of dependency is proportionately greater. It is impossible for a team member to place themselves for long in such a dependency situation without a transference to this new situation of their infantile attitudes. Part of this transference will be positive, corresponding to the love felt for the parental figure; part of it will be negative, corresponding to the fear of anyone's possessing such power over one's own destiny.

Often transference feelings are not direct projections of a parent or other childhood figure onto the manager. In the course of the team member's life they may have *'projected'* this momentous early figure onto a number of other people—teachers, acquaintances, employers, and so on. The projection onto the manager may then be from one of these later persons, or derivatives, as they are called. In the successive transfers that have occurred, the original figure may have become modified or even quite distorted. Thus the manager may be the recipient of the feelings the team member has currently toward an aunt, a teacher, or a child, as well as, or instead of, those they had in childhood toward a parent. Hence, the manager, may need to frequently ask, 'Who is my team member identifying me with?'

The conscious mind develops slowly, and in some respects remains always dominated by the unconscious. According to psychoanalytic theory, as long as we live, our unconscious makes us interpret much of what happens to us in the light of our earlier experiences. For example, our unconscious, on the basis of how we interpreted to ourselves our early experiences with our parents, causes us to believe that the world is either basically accepting and approving of us or rejecting and disapproving. This extends to our belief that we are good or bad persons; it gives us the feeling that we are or are not competent to deal with life; that we are or are not loveable; even whether we will be rewarded or disappointed. Such far-reaching attitudes are formed on the basis of extremely vague feelings which we nevertheless experienced most strongly at a time when, because our reasoning abilities were as yet undeveloped, we could not yet comprehend the meaning of what was happening to us. Since these attitudes which continue to dominate our experiences originate in our unconscious, we do not know what caused them and why they are so convincing to us.

It will be appreciated that as a manager or leader this may pose considerable difficulty and will require a high degree of self-awareness and reflection if we are to understand our own dominant behaviours. However, it also presents potential problems in our dealings with other team members. Hopefully, most of them will be well-adjusted individuals who have their own high level of self-awareness and will be operating on a reality basis; but there will undoubtedly be some team members that, because of the behaviour of the manager or leader, will be unconsciously reminded of past experience and treat the relationship on a non-reality basis.

Fortunately, changes can and do occur in our attitudes, behaviour, and personalities throughout life. But as we become older, far-reaching changes become much more difficult to achieve, as each year we become more settled into seeing and doing things in customary ways. In short, we become less flexible. Changes that may occur when we are older are likely to affect only limited areas of our personalities and our lives. The importance of early experiences thus rests on the fact that they set the stage for all that comes later and the earlier the experiences are, the more emphatic their influence. It seems that the important lesson here is that managers and leaders are generally older than team members, especially in football and, consequently, this may be more of a problem for the manager than for other team members.

Managers and leaders who are trying to work 'with' other team members will not only recognize and make allowance for their struggles as they go through certain stages of change, but will also provide the kind of support which permits them to find good solutions. Each team member's mastery of each new stage of development requires understanding and sensitive help from their manager or leader. In many instances there may be a strong desire for the manager or leader to create the team member they would like to have. This desire may be hard to resist but must be, so that the manager can help the team members to develop—in their own good time—to the fullest, into what they wish to be and can be, in line with their natural endowment and as the consequence of their unique life history. Team members cannot and should not be cloned. Diversity is one of the strengths of a successful team and working with each of the team members and helping them develop to their fullest potential is an important feature of successful teams.

In the same way that we reflect on our experiences as members of teams we can also helpfully reflect on the way these matters were dealt with by our managers and leaders when we were team members. Knowing which of their methods we liked or disliked can be helpful in guiding our actions as managers. But, whether or not we approved of what our managers or leaders did in any particular situation, their methods will have made a deep and lasting impression and will continue to carry the aura of authority, irrespective of whether we have incorporated their ways of acting into our own behaviour or continued to resent them. Thus, in the same way that our parents influenced our development so also will other authority figures influence us later in life.

To return to our desire to find a solution to these seemingly intractable situations; we know that there are many ways to handle any one situation, but only a few which will benefit the team. It is, therefore, only natural that we approach recommendations with the tacit hope that these will conform to the course of action which we have already tried, or originally had in mind. Doubtless all of us will have our favourite authors, but if we reflect on our liking for them we shall almost certainly find that the reason we can identify with them is because they express views similar to our own. In any case, our reaction to a book's advice will be flavoured by the residue of our past experiences—the 'prehistory' of our present attitude to the problem in question. The danger is that this locks us in to pre-determined behaviour that does not take account of other people's desires.

Reflection and feelings

The vast majority of managers and leaders have a positive view of other team members most of the time, and would like nothing better than to be able to enjoy a good relationship with them all the time. There is really no need to point out how pleasant it is when we are able to feel free and enjoy the company of other team members. However, there are few situations where our positive views are entirely free of ambivalence. Not only are the manager's positive feelings for other team members sometimes tinged with annoyance, discouragement, and disappointment, but the same is also true for the positive way other team members feel about them.

This helps us to throw light on two of the most important aspects of team management, namely, the need to give team members genuine praise, and the need to exercise a high degree of skill in giving negative feedback. In my work in the football industry I have frequently noticed and worked with the manager and his staff around the issue of why it is so difficult to give team members praise for good individual or team performance. For example, at a time when the side was not experiencing the best of results and was in a lowly league position they were due to play a home match against another of the less successful sides. Before the match, the manager stressed the importance of 'getting a good result' and the players responded by doing just that, dominating most of the game and winning by a couple of clear goals. At the end of the game, when the players had returned to the dressing room, the manager concentrated on issues concerning individual players, albeit in a constructive manner, but did not give the praise which I felt was legitimately warranted and which was badly needed to boost the players self-esteem. It seems clear that the manager's positive feelings for the team members were tinged with annoyance and disappointment about individual performances which prevented him from giving the players his full-blooded praise.

I have little doubt that the manager's feelings of annoyance, discouragement, and disappointment are also part of the reason why, despite knowing and understanding, as a result of reflecting on his own experiences as a player, that negative feedback was de-motivating, he would still persist in doing so, even at crucial times, such as half-time when the players needed to be lifted. I shall comment further on this sort of situation in the next chapter but, at this point, would simply say that as managers or leaders we need to know ourselves sufficiently well to understand that we 'own' these feelings of disappointment or annoyance and that these are connected with a lack of achievement of our desires. We should not be looking to 'blame' our feelings on other team members when we fail to achieve our own desires.

One can well appreciate that when, as a player, you have been giving your all and finding it exceedingly difficult to play against better organized or more skilful opponents only to be told by your manager that they are annoyed with you or disappointed with you, that the effect will be to totally destroy your self-esteem. The manager who 'blames' their feelings onto the players instead of 'owning' them is likely to be totally counter-productive. If, on the other hand, when a manager is able to provide leadership by working with other team members to help them to see some way of overcoming the problems they have been facing, they may be able to recover some of their lost self-esteem and approach the situation with new hope.

Reflection and values

In many situations of conflict, thoughtful managers or leaders will tell themselves that all this is a necessary, although difficult, part of team development and that they want other team members to develop minds and values of their own. Unfortunately such correct insight is of only limited help when managers or leaders feel that not only their values but their very way of life is challenged and questioned by the other team members, around whom they have built much of their lives in the first place. Such a situation arose in the middle of a season when the team were going through a very unsuccessful spell. Several of the non-playing staff were gently floating the idea that the style of playing might not be right and that the team needed to take a more aggressive approach. This was totally contrary to the values of the manager who saw this as an attempt to turn the team into a sort of 'bully boy outfit' that would win games by brute force rather than by skill.

After some discussion it was agreed that I facilitate a meeting of non-playing staff to analyse the current situation. I started by asking them to address the following question: 'What are the words or phrases you *would not* use to describe the team at this moment?' Their responses were recorded on a flip chart as below:

- DESIRE TO WIN
- HIGH SCORING
- BRAVERY
- NOT DISCIPLINED (BOOKINGS)
- THUGS
- EXPERIENCED
- WINNING ATTITUDE—LEADERSHIP
- STYLE
- PROFESSIONALISM
- FUNCTIONAL
- AGGRESSION
- LEADERSHIP
- NOT TACKLING

This process took a relatively short while. I then asked them, 'What are the words and phrases you *would* use to describe the team at this moment?' Again, their responses were recorded on a flip-chart as below:

- FOOTBALLING SIDE (OVERPLAY)

- UNDERPERFORMING
- DEFENSIVELY IMMATURE
- CONFUSION—INTRODUCTION OF NEW PLAYERS
- LOSS OF DIRECTION
- TOO MUCH STYLE
- FRUSTRATION
- LACK OF CONFIDENCE
- UNBALANCED TEAM
- LACK OF COMMITMENT
- A YOUNG SIDE
- UNLIMITED POTENTIAL
- LACK OF LEADERSHIP (ON AND OFF THE PITCH)
- LACK OF CONSISTENCY OF INDIVIDUAL PLAYERS
- LOSS OF FORM OF SENIOR PLAYERS
- LACK OF COMMUNICATION
- NOT AS BAD AS IT LOOKS
- FITNESS
- INDIVIDUAL BLUNDERS
- LACK OF GOALS
- CONFIDENT DESPITE LET DOWNS

In comparison with the first question, these responses took a long time to elicit with staff seemingly anxious about making any judgements about the team. The meeting ended without any decisions being made, but I was not bothered by this because I felt the manager needed time to work through the issues raised. At a later date, I had a further discussion with the manager about the need for change raised by his colleagues at the meeting. In effect, they were giving a very clear message that the *team* required a more 'aggressive' approach. Staff were not talking about individuals, they were talking about *the team*. They were saying that changes in the environment required that changes in the style of play needed to be made. The manager kept saying that this was contrary to all his beliefs and that he would never send a team out on the field to win by kicking, or words to that effect. There was clearly a threat to the values held by the manager and one which was contrary to his very desires to be the successful manager of a stylish and skilful team. The challenge to these values created extreme anxiety—he was blocked and could not move.

Any change requires the giving up of something, be it a way of working or a state of self-perception. In the circumstances described, the thought of challenging his values was clearly just too much. We might describe the state of the leader in these circumstances as omnipotent, being out of touch, being resistant or defended against feedback, consultation and the differing views being put by his colleagues. Almost certainly, for the manager the thought of this painful and potentially disruptive change resulted in flight from acting upon and implementing necessary organizational change.

Reflection and identification

Team members become close to their managers because they see so much of themselves in them; to put it technically, as much as team members identify with the manager, so the manager also identifies with them, usually much more and in more ways than we consciously realize. Managers are happy when they recognize in other team members features they approve of in themselves. But their closeness to other team members comes not only from positive, but also from negative identifications. When they believe they see in a team member aspects of their own personalities of which they disapprove, they may become very upset. Often these are tendencies in themselves that they have worked hard to overcome. In such emotional constellations, the advice to be patient, under-standing, and caring is sometimes of little help. On the other hand, realizing at such moments that they see in a team member something which is upsetting, because they have also had to battle against the same tendency in themselves, can make them comprehend that they are actually less perturbed about the team member, than about themselves. Then they understand that the problem lies first in themselves and only secondarily with the team member. This makes it easier to cope and helps the manager to avoid coming down hard on the team member for something that is their problem more than that of the team member.

If we remain unable to recognize what goes on in our unconscious, then our rationalizations are often merely a thin overlay which nevertheless effectively hides the driving force behind our behaviour—powerful emotions such as selfishness, desire to retain our superiority, even jealousy. A team member's intuitive understanding based on innumerable observations of the manager or leader's actions and reactions in all kinds of situations, gives them a nearly unerring feeling for whether or not the leader is acting in accordance with their usual beliefs, values, and customary ways of doing things. If the team member senses that the manager or leader is acting 'out of character' (as they might, if they follow advice without having first carefully pondered it and adjusted it to their own feelings), they will become confused and regard their manager or leader's unusual behaviour with mistrust.

Comprehension comes from within, as we explore a problem and its ramifications, and from our own struggle to find a solution appropriate to our own and other team members' personalities. We must all struggle to understand ourselves better, not the least because our efforts to achieve greater clarity about ourselves make it possible for us to achieve clarity in our relation to other team members, with a consequent enrichment of our life. Such understanding of ourselves around some issue of team-management cannot be handed to us by someone else, no matter how great their expertise may be; it can be achieved only by ourselves, as we struggle to remove whatever has obscured this understanding from our consciousness. Only our own efforts to achieve such higher comprehension lead to permanent personal growth of both manager or leader and other team members. All that any book can do—including this one—is to address some of the overall problems of team-management: their origin, significance, meaning, and particularly, possible ways of thinking about them.

Being a leader is a creative endeavour, an art rather than a science. Throughout this chapter I have sought to make some introductory suggestions on how to think about this art, and how it may be applied. I cannot tell the reader how to experience this art, nor how to appreciate what is involved in it, because these are far too personal matters to be decided by others. However, what I can say is that the reader who adopts the suggested approach and develops their self-awareness, self-control, and, a deeper awareness and understanding of other team members, will find their actions much more interesting and rewarding, and will find team-management a more exciting, much happier, experience for both themselves and other team members.

It follows that to be a good manager or leader one must be able to feel secure in one's role and relations to other team members. So secure that, while you are careful in what you do in relation to other team members, you are not over-anxious about it and do not feel guilty about not being a good manager or leader. Your security as manager or leader will, eventually, become the source of other team members feeling secure about themselves. Hence my hope is that this book, far from making leaders and managers anxious or guilty about what they do in relation to other team members, will give them the feeling, 'That's right, that's what I am doing' or at least 'That's what I wanted to do!' In short, I hope that the book will make you feel more secure as managers and leaders, and consequently, less worried about what you may possibly do wrong.

In this chapter I have tried to give the reader a glimpse of what it is like to be a manager or leader and something of the more complex problems that this brings. I have also started to explore, in a most general way, the motivation of leaders and other team members. In the next chapter I shall explore, in some depth, issues concerning why the manager and other team members do things, why some have more energy than others—what motivates them.

CHAPTER TWO

Motivation of the leader in the context of the team

W hy do people do difficult things for little reward? Why does a child, once having learned to walk, continue to walk? Why are we motivated to do anything? What is motivation? By human motivation we mean the drive, the energy, or degree of activity that an individual displays. What we are essentially concerned with is why one person works hard at many different tasks and persists in the face of difficulty, while another is rather lazy at work, has few interests and tends to quit in the face of frustration. These are the central issues to questions that I shall seek to address in this chapter, but it may help to set the scene if I first briefly consider the central object of this study; namely, the self. Who are the individuals that call themselves team manager, team leader or team member? What is the basis for them to claim such an identity?

The self

The question 'Who am I?' has probably tormented people since the dawn of civilisation and remains a vexing question today. I shall first try to answer the question by taking a very pragmatic, basic process which occurs when a person asks, and then answers, 'Who am I? What is my real me? What is my fundamental identity?' When someone asks, 'Who are you?' and you proceed to give a reasonable, honest, and more or less detailed answer, what in fact are you doing? What goes on in your head as you do this? In one sense you are describing your self as you have come to know it, including in your description most of the pertinent facts, both good and bad, that you understand as fundamental to your identity. You might, for example, think that you are a unique individual, a person endowed with certain potentials; I am kind but sometimes cruel, loving but sometimes hostile; I am a husband and a consultant, I enjoy music and football. And so your list of feelings and thoughts might proceed.

Yet there is an even more basic process underlying the whole procedure of establishing an identity. Something very simple happens when you answer the question 'Who am I?' When you are explaining or describing or even just inwardly feeling your 'self', what you are actually doing, whether you know it or not, is drawing a mental line or boundary across the whole field of your experience and everything on the inside of that boundary you are feeling or calling your 'self' while everything outside that boundary you feel to be 'not-self'. Your self-identity, in other words, depends entirely where you draw that boundary line.

You are a person and not, say, a computer and you know that because you consciously or unconsciously draw a boundary line between people and computers, and are able to recognize your identity with the former. You may be a very tall person rather than a short one and so you draw a mental line between tallness and shortness and thus identify yourself as 'tall'. You come to feel that 'I am this and not that' by drawing a boundary line between 'this' and 'that' and then recognizing your identity with 'this' and your non-identity with 'that'. For example the manager that I worked with had an identity of one who would recruit players who would play skilfully and within the rules of the game (clean players), whereas other managers had an identity which depicted them as one who would adopt a 'professional' win-at-all-costs approach. The manager's values, then, were about playing well, which to him meant attractive, attacking football. What he was not was the sort of manager who would win at all costs—if needs be by cheating.

So, when you say 'my self', you draw a boundary line between what is you and what is not you. When you answer the question 'Who am I?', you simply describe what's on the inside of that line. The so-called identity crisis occurs when you can't decide how or where to draw the line. In short, 'Who am I?' means 'Where do I draw the boundary?' All answers to the question 'Who am I?' stem precisely from this basic procedure of drawing a boundary line between self and not-self. Once the general boundary lines have been drawn, the answers to that question may become very complex or they may remain most simple and unarticulated. But any possible answer depends on first drawing the boundary line. However, wherever we draw the line, the most interesting thing about this boundary line is that it can and frequently does shift. It can be re-drawn.

The skin boundary

The most common boundary line that individuals draw up or accept as valid is that of the skin-boundary surrounding the total organism (for a full discussion on the notion of 'skin boundary' see Anzieu, 1989). This seems to be a universally accepted boundary line between self and not-self. Everything on the inside of that skin-boundary is in some sense 'me', while everything outside that boundary is 'not-me'. Something outside the skin-boundary may be 'mine', but it's not 'me'. For example, I recognize objects such as 'my' car, 'my' job, 'my' house, 'my' family, but they are definitely not directly 'me' in the same way all the things inside my skin are 'me'. The skin-boundary then, is one of the most fundamentally accepted boundaries between self and not-self.

We might think that this skin-boundary is so obvious, so real, and so common that there wouldn't be any other types of boundaries that related to an individual. But in fact there is another, extremely common, well-established type of boundary line drawn by a vast number of individuals. For most people, while they recognize and accept as a matter of course the skin as a boundary between self and not-self, they draw another and for them, more significant boundary within the total organism itself.

The body–mind boundary

If a boundary line within the organism seems strange to you, then let me ask, 'Do you feel you are a body, or do you feel you have a body?' Most individuals feel they have a body, as if they owned or possessed it much as they would a car, a house, or any other object. Under these circumstances the body seems not so much 'me' as 'mine' and what is 'mine', by definition, lies outside the boundary between self and not-self. The person identifies more basically and intimately with just a facet of their total organism and this facet, which they feel to be their real self, is known variously as the mind, the psyche, the ego, the personality. Biologically there is not the least foundation for this dissociation or radical split between the mind and body but this categorization is in such regular use that I would cause problems if I did otherwise. Indeed, if I were not to use the word 'psychology' for the study of people's overall behaviour I have little doubt that you would find it most strange.

What we have been describing is what goes on in your head. By this we are very loosely referring to the mind. What do we mean by mind? What is the mind? Basically it is a zone of mediation, a place where meaning is made. It is variously called the 'ego', the 'self', the 'mind' or the 'person'. What an organism does is organize; and what the mind of a human organism organizes is meaning. Thus it is not that a person makes meaning, as much as that the activity of being a person is the activity of meaning-making. There is thus no feeling, no experience, no thought, no perception, independent of a meaning-making context in which it becomes a feeling, an experience, a thought, a perception, because we are the meaning-making context.

Personalities are dynamic continuums and although it is important to discover their content, organization and performance at a given point of time, it is still more important to discover the processes by which they develop, grow, and change. At this time the best and only reliable approach to personality development must remain the study and comparison of life histories which can be obtained from the individuals themselves.

Such is our current understanding of 'person' that we have to strain to recover the process in the words 'human being'; we talk about a 'being' and 'beings' as if they were objects. In this book, contrary to normal usage, we are concerned about human being as an activity. It is not about the doing which a human does; it is about the doing which a human is. A central conviction is that personality development occurs in the context of interactions between the organism and the environment, rather than through the internal processes of maturation alone. This is reflected in the psycho–social approach of Erikson (1950); Fairbairn (1952); Winnicott (1965a & b); Guntrip (1971); and Kernberg (1966), and this involves the bringing together of thought and emotion, of past and present and of psychological and social.

Relationships

As was stated in the Foreword, if we wish to develop the insights and attitudes which will further the development of both leader and other team members as persons it is of prime importance to take a psycho–social approach which considers what is involved in the situation for *each* party. It will be recalled that:

- My reality, or reality from my perspective, may be totally different from that of other team members.
- My 'obvious right answer' may not be at all 'obvious' or 'right' to other team members.
- Furthermore, one should not attempt to understand other team members independently from oneself.

If we make a serious effort at understanding ourselves in the context of a given situation, trying to see how we have contributed to it— willingly or unwillingly, consciously or unconsciously—then our view of the matter is nearly always altered, as is our manner of handling it. In other words, if we are able to adopt a reflective approach, using the procedure detailed above, we may have a deeper understanding of the situation.

I now want to add that learning about the dynamics of life is a matter that has to be considered in the context of a relationship between two people. As Gregory Bateson (1979) pointed out, it is correct (and a great improvement) to begin to think of the two people in an interaction as two eyes, *each giving a monocular view of* what goes on and *together giving a binocular view* in depth. This double view is the relationship. Relationship is not internal to the single person. Indeed, it would be nonsense to talk about 'dependency' or 'aggression' or 'pride' and so on, in terms of an individual. All such words have their roots in what happens between persons, not in something-or-other inside a person.

If you want to talk about, for example, 'pride' you must talk about two persons or two groups and what happens between them. Where the manager is admired by a team member; the team member's admiration is conditional and may turn to contempt and so on. You can then define a particular species of pride by reference to a particular pattern of interaction. The same is true of dependency, courage, passivity, aggression, fatalism, and the like. All derive from patterns of interchange, that is, from combinations of double description. Binocular vision gives the possibility of a new order of information.

Motivation as desires

Let me now turn to the central issue of this chapter, that concerned with the question: Why are we motivated to do anything? Basically we can say that we all have desires and it is the drive to reduce tension by fulfilling these desires that pushes us along. Coupled with desire is the concept of mental energy and the ways in which this energy is distributed and used describes why we do things. The apparatus of the mind is the means by which mental energy, constantly generated through desires, is distributed and allocated throughout the total personality. The observable results are seen in the behaviour displayed by each individual, but equally important are the memories and ideas that remain within the personality but that are now charged with energy and are capable of being activated by stimuli. All theories of motivation admit an interaction between the organism and the environment. There is no completely satisfactory explanation of the origin of many of our needs, nor is there any clear cut list of what human needs actually are.

We all start life in a truly dependent state and our early experience of authority figures will have a lasting impression on the way that we take up management and leadership roles. Even though some of us may have had the same parents or were brought up in the same street, or went to the same school or the same work place, each of us will have had a life experience different from anyone else. In all manner of ways, rather like our fingerprints or DNA, there is something quite unique about all of us. That's why we could never write a book about human behaviour that treats all experiences the same. Nevertheless, the very fact that we are all human means that we have many things in common and, that there are modes of behaviour that social scientists and psychoanalysts have recognized and helpfully categorized as a means of trying to understand why we do things. Not least have been the many studies of behaviour that have been categorized as motivation. Many of the theories developed have basic similarities to each other, stressing a particular notion favoured by the writer. Like anyone else, I have my own preferences, which are based on a psycho-analytic explanation of motivation.

The objects of our study, managers and leaders, differ from other team members in an important way in that they have formal authority. For example, authority to hire and fire; to reward and discipline; and, frequently to be the final decision making authority. This puts them in a position where they may assume authority for the way they are going to manage or lead other team members. At the two extremes, this may be in a participative manner with due regard for the individual members of the team or it may be in an autocratic style that involves 'forcing' or 'conditioning' team members toward whatever the manager or leader thinks best. To gain a deeper understanding of the dynamics concerned, I shall attempt to provide an explanation for some of the behaviour that managers and leaders adopt as individuals. In doing so, I shall try to explain why it is that managers and leaders adopt these forms of behaviour, which will inevitably have an effect on other team members—sometimes bringing about results which are quite the reverse of what was intended.

In looking at the vast amount of published literature, which may lead us to an explanation of why managers and leaders do things, we discover all sorts of words and terminology, such as impulse, drive, instinct, need, motive, wish, striving, intentions or plans. To keep matters simple, I shall use the single term 'desire' to represent psychological needs in general. Even if we take more complex terms, such as intentions, plans, attitudes, interests, and values they are still only an expression of compounds of desires, and, one or a few specific desires can usually be recognized as the strongest of their determinants. A desire is something very basic, it is something we want and we possess no desires that have not at one time been full and active experiences and had our conscious support. If this was not the case, they could not have even formed (Toman, 1960).

No matter what the behaviour is, be it playing football, managing a financial office, or a team of technicians, all behaviour has something to do with the satisfaction of desires. More specifically, we can say that there is no form or aspect of behaviour that would not be satisfying to some extent, no matter how small, if it were not for some identifiable desire. Our desires guide and manifest themselves in, our behaviour. Thus, all behaviour is the result of us gaining control over our desires, by which we basically mean learning how to like or to appreciate something. This is how we come to learn all we know about the world. And, of course, it is only through behaviour that we come in contact with the world. We cannot learn about the world unless we behave in it in some fashion. For example, nobody knew anything about football until someone in England had the desire to kick a ball and then, the desire to do so as two teams competing against each other. In looking for an explanation of behaviour, we are, then, primarily concerned with desires.

Thus a young boy living in any of the countries throughout the world where football is played is able to learn about football first by watching others play, or by watching games on television, or by playing with other children in the street or on the beach. They then develop a desire to master the necessary skills to play the game. To say that these kids are 'crazy about football' is to say that they have strong desires to continually develop their footballing skills, probably with the added desire that one day they may be famous. It will be appreciated, however, that many thousands of these kids will experience disappointment because they do not achieve their desires. In the same way, many football players who are coming to the end of their playing career have a desire to stay in the game as a coach or a manager. But, of course, only a few are lucky enough to achieve this desire. The fortunate ones may then develop a further desire to become the manager of a successful club and to lead a team to victory.

Desires leading to knowledge

Knowledge is not the same thing as desire, but we only come to experience that we have knowledge as we satisfy desires and every satisfaction of a desire, no matter how small a satisfaction it is, adds a little more to our knowledge. In fact, we might say that the world, or 'reality', is our knowledge of it. So it is with the street kids who have the initial desire to play football and to master the basic skills. Having done so, they then have further desires to improve their techniques in various ways. Each time they are successful, they add a little more knowledge about the game. Our knowledge is ever increasing and as we progress through life we learn more and more about the conditions under which our desires can be satisfied and we also learn to satisfy them in different ways. We learn all sorts of ways of riding a bicycle, or driving a car, drawing, reading, skiing, playing football and many other desires. In fact there is no desire that would not tend to develop that way.

At an early stage of our infancy we become capable of developing concepts. Conception is simply the natural flow downstream from the unconscious to the conscious. A child learns a wide variety of skills, such as reading, writing, running and arithmetic and in doing so develops a tool kit of practical, problem-solving skills that provides them with a variety of possible solutions to the conflicts that they must deal with. The way that a person comes to perform appropriately in a wide range of situations is usually known as adjustment or adaptation. Thus, our street kids learn that to be a successful footballer it is not enough to have individual skills, it is also necessary to co-operate with other team members, this being the appropriate behaviour that this situation requires. In like manner, managers and leaders learn that it is not sufficient for them to have a good idea, the other team members must also share the same ideas. This adaptation, not only symbolizes continuity because it is the act of accepting the situation created by past generations, but it also contributes to the situation and changes the environment, if only imperceptibly. If this were not the case, football would have become a chess-like contest where the moves were repeated over and over. But, of course, it is not like that because new skills and new structures and ways of playing are created. Just as the child must finally achieve an inner organization of the relationships among the roles of others in order to behave appropriately in any social context, in a general way, so must the manager. This means that they must organize all manner of objects, ideas, events, and values into a coherent system.

The more we satisfy our desires, the more we learn: the more we learn the more conditions we control under which our desires can be satisfied and our desires can be satisfied in an increasing number of ways. An example is the young footballer who has a desire to be able to 'bend' the ball around a wall of defenders. When he has satisfied this desire he has learnt how to do it and can now continue to do this again (to a greater or lesser degree) when there is the need. He now has control over this type of behaviour. So it is with managers who, initially, because of their own uncertainties, find it difficult to act in anything but an autocratic manner. However, with experience they are able to involve others by satisfying their desires for a more participative approach. They now have control over this type of behaviour. Control permits us to comprehend the slightest inkling or anticipation of an event, judgement of a given condition as appropriate, or anticipation of appropriate potential conditions, all the way up to direct and active manipulation of given conditions. Having once had the desire to learn how to anticipate dangerous or threatening situations during a football match a footballer is subsequently able to 'read' the game and anticipate when their intervention is necessary.

The process of learning how to like something may be taken to mean learning in a general sense, or acquisition of knowledge, provided that we assume that we learn what satisfies desires and that knowledge is nothing academic, but something 'dynamic'. Such learning differs from the sort of learning that we get from reading books—what might be called cognitive learning. Here we are talking about learning from our experience, such learning by its very nature cannot be taught, it is a developed awareness that we achieve through reflection. Nevertheless, it still holds true that whatever we know we have learned about, in principle, while satisfying desires.

Unconscious desires

To further complicate matters, of all the desires that we are experiencing at a given time, only some are conscious as was discussed in the last chapter. Others are preconscious, that is, they are potentially conscious. Still others are unconscious, which basically means that they are not even potentially conscious. For most practical purposes, perception and behaviour are conscious and preconscious, although even they can, in principle, become unconscious, at least in some of their aspects. The terms 'conscious', 'preconscious', and 'unconscious' refer, first of all, to desires. We can be conscious of them. We can feel them and comment about them. Yet we need not necessarily be conscious of all those desires that determine what we think or do in a given situation. Consciousness provides us with a picture of something, but not necessarily with all there is to be seen. In fact, the picture it provides may sometimes be rather inadequate. Because of their position of authority managers and leaders are natural repositories for stirring memories of past authority experiences. This may make things very difficult when managers or leaders are trying to understand either their own behaviour or that of another team member.

When, perhaps, we are faced with circumstances similar to those we have experienced in the past, when desires were not achieved, we may unconsciously accept a lesser outcome as we did then. It is all part of our make up, it is what we have come to learn. For example, when in their formative years a football player was hectored by their father for not gaining control of the ball, they may have learnt that rather than try to achieve this desire with all the pain it brought, they would accept a lesser outcome and pass the ball first time. Later in life, when hectored by their manager, they may unconsciously 'transfer' their father's actions to those of the manager who, in effect, they relate to as their father, or put another way, becomes their father. The player then reacts by accepting the same lesser outcome of passing the ball first time. The manager, who is most unlikely to be aware of the previous experience will have great difficulty in understanding why the player is reacting and behaving in this way. The essential point is that such misunderstandings may occur because the player is acting on unconscious desires.

Having started life dependent on various authority figures, starting with our parents, we should not be at all surprised that this has such a continuing impact on our lives. The problem that is likely to arise, however, is that the manager will look for some form of 'logical' solution. If they feel they have not got their message across to a player adequately, they will try repeating it or reframing it in some different way. Still being unsuccessful, they may implore the player to do as they ask, or as a final resort, they may demand or threaten that the player does as they are instructed. Unfortunately, neither approach is likely to be successful because this is not a *reality relationship* between the manager and the other team member. Rather, it is a *phantasy relationship* where the player is unconsciously relating, not to the manager, but to an authority figure from earlier in their life. In this situation, no matter what the manager says or does the player will simply react in the way that they learnt earlier in life. For the time being, I shall leave this issue but will deal with it in greater detail later.

The results of such misunderstanding can be described by a term that is bound to come up in any relationship such as that between leaders and team members: *annoyance*. When things are not going to plan; when team members are seemingly not committed; when things go against us; both managers and other team members are likely to experience annoyance. Indeed, our feelings may go beyond annoyance to related terms, such as anger, hate, revenge, and hostility. We all have experience of such situations but what do we mean by affects, emotions, or feelings? We all experience feelings but we cannot isolate them from other human processes. However, because they have such an impact on our behaviour it is important that we try to gain an understanding of the processes involved. As a starting point let's look at some typical situations. For example, somebody may feel anxious, angry or elated, fond of someone, moved by a person's distress, by another person's greatness, or feel just very lazy. How can we account for these feelings?

Football is an emotional game—anxiety, anger, and elation

There can be little doubt that football is an emotional game. Indeed, one of my first observations when I started working in football was that it was a physically and emotionally painful experience. So, let's return to the question: how can we account for these feelings? First and foremost, when we feel anxious, we must be feeling a condition that we refer to as anxiety. Anxiety is the automatic consequence of excessive deprivation of our desires. That is, a situation where our world seems to have fallen apart, such as when a manager and players start a game of football with a really deep desire to be successful only to find that that they are clearly being beaten. It is an increasingly uncomfortable state of mind which may result in desires to regress to increasingly primitive forms. Team members may react by using verbal violence against the referee or their opponents or even by using physical violence to try to achieve their desires. Anxiety can come about slowly or suddenly, depending upon whether deprivation is anticipated or acute. At worst it can mount to total panic, if the situation of excessive deprivation continues unchanged. Perceived danger or the threat of not achieving our desires is a familiar condition of anxiety. Even committed supporters of football teams will experience this anxiety after their team loses a vital game. Such is the degree of identification with the team that most will react in a depressed manner, but others will react by using verbal or physical violence against rival fans or inanimate objects such as street furniture or shop windows. In a general sense, we can say that anxiety is pain.

When we feel anxious, we are feeling desires, especially those that are in a state of deprivation beyond a certain point. We will feel them even more clearly when we are 'at rest' or, rather, when we can do little to speed up our pursuits. We feel very anxious in a dangerous situation that we can do nothing about but just await, such as an oncoming battle, whereas we feel less anxious, if we do something about it, say, fight or run. Thus, the point just before a football match is a very anxious time. It is at this point that players will go through regular and routine ways of dealing with their anxiety. For example, in the team that I worked with, one player would always evacuate his bowels twice; one would make himself physically sick; others would have massages; others would do stretching exercises; and yet others would take pain-killers.

What about when we are feeling angry? Basically, the same story applies. The difference is that here we feel what we desire to do will be more primitive and destructive than at other times. For example, we may feel like hitting a person for a particular remark they made. During a match an opponent may deliberately make an offensive remark with the sole intention of making a player angry. Should the player hit them they will not feel angry any more. But, of course, that sort of behaviour is not permitted by the laws of conduct laid down for the game. Much more likely the player will displace their anger by conveying the message about how angry they feel to somebody else and here we shall find the player referring to desires automatically. They will probably say something like, 'I could kill that bastard' or: 'I would really like to beat the hell out of him'.

What about feeling elated or happy? Well, every satisfaction of any desire is presumably pleasurable, although to very different degrees. We feel elated and happy to the extent that we are satisfying our desires and will generally be even more so in certain conditions. The greater the satisfaction value of a desire and the greater the intensity of the desire by the time it is being satisfied the more happy we shall be. Thus, there is greater satisfaction and enhanced elation for the team that defeats the favourites; or for a team that wins a contract against the fiercest competition.

These three feelings, anxiety, anger, and elation, have been referred to as primary emotions outside of psychoanalytic theory and they also assume a distinguished position within psycho-analytic theory. They are those feelings that participate to some extent in all the other feelings we can possibly have and, at the same time, they are those that relate most directly to the prototypes of all situations in which we can possibly desire and act: pursuit and satisfaction of desires (elation), and deprivation of desires, whereby one alternative of the latter is renunciation (anxiety) and the other aggression (more primitive and destructive satisfaction). These feelings or emotions have also been known as affects, although 'affect' has taken on different connotations ranging all the way from standing for just one or two of the three emotions, anxiety, anger, or elation, to any kind of feeling in general. I would rather use it as equivalent to emotion, but we do not really have to make a decision on that matter. Feelings, emotions and affects accompany all motivation, but they are not entities in themselves. They derive meaning only from specific conditions of motivation and it is the latter that we have been and shall be, mainly concerned with.

All the time that we satisfy our desires we shall feel content, happy or elated. Every satisfaction of any desire is pleasurable, but to very different degrees. We feel elated and happy to the extent that we are satisfying our desires and the greater the satisfaction value of a desire, the greater will be the intensity of the desire by the time it is satisfied. Any time a football manager has their desires for leading a successful football team satisfied they will be happy and on those occasions when the team win the 'big match' against their closest opponents or nearest rivals they and the other team members will be elated. Whereas, on those occasions when success is achieved playing against poor opposition the satisfaction is not so great for either players or manager.

In circumstances where the opposition is regarded as weak, the biggest problem for the manager or leader is to ensure that the team do not substitute a desire to win with a different desire, such as the desire to win by playing attractive and entertaining football. This in itself may be a more difficult task than it first appears, as the manager or leader may also lose sight of their basic desires. The danger is that the desire to play attractive and entertaining football may pose a threat to the ultimate aim of winning by providing the opposition with the opportunity to confine such play to safe areas of the field. A classic example of this sort of behaviour occurred in the 1999 European Cup final where Bayern Munich were winning by one goal to nil with but a few minutes remaining. At that point, in the words of the Manchester United player, Teddy Sheringham, they started to 'showboat'. In other words, they substituted a desire to win with a further desire to win cockily and flamboyantly. The result was that the Manchester United players, who stuck to the task of winning, duly did so.

This problem of feeling elated is well known to those participating in sports. There is a moment when we are so elated at achieving our desires that we may drop our guard and fail to concentrate on the task we should be performing. We forget that we have only partially fulfilled our desires. At such a moment, it requires a great deal of self-control on the part of all concerned, not least the manager or leader, to ensure that the team do not lose sight of the task at hand. The most impressive example, of this self-control that I have witnessed, was during an FA Cup semi-final match between Fulham and Birmingham in 1965. Fulham scored the all-important opening goal and the scorer (John Mitchell) was cavorting around the pitch with great excitement and elation roared on by a huge crowd. Bobby Moore, that great England player, who was then playing for Fulham, went up to Mitchell, grabbed him by the front of his shirt, shook him, and in no uncertain manner told him to get back to work! A further example is that of Arsene Wenger the Arsenal manager, who, having completed the double of League and Cup, just before the start of the next season, reminded himself and the team that the past was the past and what mattered now was forgetting past elation and concentrating on new desires. Many will be aware that one of the most vulnerable moments for any football team is just after they have scored.

Lack of self-perception

What was happening when Bobby Moore had to intervene so bluntly, or when Wenger had to impress on his team so firmly? It is a phenomenon where we experience what I shall refer to as a lack of self-perception (Pitt-Aitken & Ellis, 1989). In other words, what happens is that we lose self-control and are unable to perceive what is happening around us. It is this lack of self-perception—that is, the inability or lack of attempt by people to be able to reflect, to look at themselves, to see what they themselves are actually doing, that I identify as the key to understanding the need for self-control.

The example given refers to elation, but it is not just feelings of pleasure that cause us problems, there are many factors that can produce a lack of self-perception in individuals and groups. For example:

- fear and anxiety;
- enthusiasm and excitement; or
- over-involvement or alienation.

This lack of self-perception constantly manifests itself, not only in a lack of self-control in teams and individual players, but even more worrying in those who are attempting to understand and help. The capacity of a manager or leader to prevent individual and group pressures and human failing from distorting or limiting self-perception is, therefore, a vital ability.

The example cited above where Bobby Moore remained calm while team mates, who were the clear underdogs on the day and were achieving what can only have been a distant dream at one stage, thus bringing them joys they could never have hoped for, is clearly a situation that presents a danger to our self-perception.

Equally, I could provide many other examples of situations where our desires are not being achieved, that create feelings that just do not bear thinking about. For example, the sort of situation where a Premiership side is being beaten by a non-league side. The fear and anxiety is so great that players simply cannot concentrate, they have a clear lack of self-perception. So what can the manager or leader do about this? First and foremost they must ensure that despite everything they must retain the capacity for self-perception. This gives new meaning to Kipling's wonderful lines; 'If you can keep your head when all around are losing theirs'. If you can do so, you will retain the capacity for self-reflection and even more important will be able to help other team members to adopt a reflective approach which will enable them to get in touch with their desires.

It has been said that the good players are the ones who can make mistakes and not let it effect their performance. They have self-control, while others, who experience anxiety when they fear that because of their mistakes they will not achieve their desires, lose self-control. They may then take their eyes off the ball, become temporarily witless and have no control over their perceptual process. But, as the 'good' players have shown us this need not be the case, it is possible to retain self-control, to retain contact with reality. As long as players (and managers) are able to remain aware of the dangers they can retain a reflective ability. Basically, what we are talking about here is what is sometimes referred to as 'application' or 'attitude'. The Australian cricket team are renowned for their 'attitude', as was clearly displayed in the 1999 World Cricket Cup when they notched up successes against highly rated sides who, when the anxiety level rose, perhaps did not have the same level of self-control. Something else happens in this uncomfortable world where we have lost our self-perception and contact with reality. Here, phantasy can take the place of reality. For example, feelings of omnipotence, of being unbeatable, may dominate even though you are losing badly. Or, we may view opponents with such awe that they are seen as some sort of giants who are unbeatable.

Anxiety

The problems caused by achieving success and meeting our desires are important and should not be forgotten. In the context of the team it can very quickly turn success into defeat. However, it is my experience that the biggest problems occur when desires are not met. For example:

- when we don't get a promotion we so badly desired;
- when the football team don't win a game; or
- when the marketing team don't win an important contract.

In these, and in other similar circumstances, the automatic consequence of excessive deprivation of our desires is anxiety. All desires, reduce in intensity to zero or close to zero immediately after they have been satisfied. However, they then build again and increase intensity and can finally reach an intolerable state of intensity. For the manager or leader to lose their self-control and to pass their feelings on to the other team members can lead to disaster, because no one is now available to provide the necessary support that they may need. Normally, our desires or some form of substitutes can be satisfied long before things are that bad. For example, we usually eat again, long before we are mad with hunger. We take a walk before we are exasperated sitting still at a desk and we go to bed long before we would fall asleep under almost any circumstances. If, however, there is nothing we can do to end this deprivation and the deprivation of a desire lasts too long, we shall get restless, irritable and impatient with everything. As Freud (1926) put it, we are in alarm, we are in a state of anxiety.

If deprivation continues, the state of alarm or anxiety may increase until we are in a state of panic, a wild, violent outcry, a tantrum, something resembling an epileptic fit, during which we may even become insensible and without memory. In simple terms, we lose it. We completely lose our self control and, albeit temporarily, regress to primitive behaviour. Let's try to imagine what it's like to be a manager who is watching helplessly from the touch-line when the team are being soundly beaten by a team which is regarded by all as inferior. All their desires, perhaps to remain unbeaten; to win the championship; to achieve acclaim; are in danger of being thwarted. They just cannot believe it—the form book has been turned on its head. Far from being acclaimed for their success, they are now more likely to be the subject of derision and scorn. What they face is too unbearable to think about—they becomes witless, out of control and resort to a wild and violent outcry. On the receiving end of this outcry may be the referee or other officials, the opponents, or other team members. The latter, being within their control and eventually likely to be the subject of their rage. Individual players or groups of players become scapegoated and abused. What does this achieve? Most certainly, it achieves nothing positive, but almost certainly it will achieve negative consequences. Feeling that they have been treated unfairly, players lose respect for, and trust in, their manager and subsequently take little notice of what they say. Rather, they do their own thing no matter what they may say in the presence of the manager or leader.

For most of us this has to be an extreme situation, because as we develop and grow and as we gain control over our desires and the conditions of their satisfaction, these extreme states of affairs become more and more unlikely. Most of us can retain our reflective capacity and catch alarm or anxiety when it is just beginning to mount and do something about it. Thus, we learn that anxiety signals that there are problems about and that we need to change the course of our actions. Generally speaking, we are better at this if we have more control over desires and have learned ways of coping. This does not mean, though, that conditions of deprivation cannot become tougher than ever before and work up an individual, who usually can do better, to a full-fledged panic after all. Indeed, although they are usually controlled and play within the rules of the game, it is not unusual for football players to become so frustrated that they reach a point where they will deliberately foul an opponent or swear at the referee.

Panic can cause yet another reaction and that is resignation. Take the footballer who has set his heart on appearing in a cup final and now finds that they are losing 3–0 with 10 minutes left to play. They now realize that all chances of achieving their desire have vanished and they give up—they are resigned to their fate. At an earlier point they experienced panic, which has now resulted in resignation. Panic, whether fully fledged or subdued, tends to bring about resignation with a mature adult, unless the manager is able to provide the sort of environment that presents the deprived player with the required support and containment that will enable them to retain a reflective capacity. This may not result in the winning of the game, but it will permit all team members to start to work on the problems leading to the defeat.

We have said that deprivation of a desire beyond a certain point—of time or intensity—triggers off alarm or anxiety which may grow to full-fledged panic if nothing changes. We have also indicated that through continued reflection we can use alarm or anxiety as a signal of danger, the danger being our own panic. We therefore need to talk about objective danger and to try to understand how we form such a concept. Let us begin by remembering that children are oblivious to many forms of danger. For example, they will put their hand into the fire. Even a child of three is not afraid of traffic and may walk into a busy street. And as adults when we go to the zoo we may be afraid of a lion even though it is behind bars. This, then, teaches us that danger is always perceived danger and threat, is always perceived threat. We may therefore hypothesize that it is related to what we have done and experienced. But, more precisely, perceived danger and threat always relate to desires. Danger is thus any situation in which our desires are impossible to satisfy.

For most football managers and a growing number of managers in other industries, the experience is that losing managers get fired. This insecurity of tenure is therefore perceived as a continual threat to their position. In the circumstances, the majority of football managers live with the threat of failure placing a near impossible demand on them to be successful. As there are only three or four major competitions to be won, there can only be a few successful teams. In such circumstances it takes a great deal of self-awareness and self-control for this threat not to incapacitate them.

Deprivation of desires covers a wide range of situations. For example: a player who is dropped from the team. There is only one desire here: the desire to be part of the team. Yet its deprivation beyond a certain point is a danger or threat. If this goes on for several weeks, it could entail anxiety or alarm that may amount to panic or something close to it. Or, the football manager whose team continually lose and are facing relegation. The desire is to be a successful manager. Yet deprivation of this desire, doubtless reinforced by the perceived threat of dismissal, may result in panic where the manager becomes insensible. In such circumstances, he is likely to temporarily lose his usual good judgement and react in a primitive manner towards other team members, or, as we have seen on many occasions, act in a bizarre way, such as making an unsound player purchase.

Achievement of desires through other people

Certain desires cannot be satisfied without other people's help. For example, think of a professional footballer who is injured and not able to play football again; this may have drastic effects on relations with other people, namely, team mates In this respect, let us not forget that a manager's desires to run a successful football team—or any other sort of team—cannot be satisfied without the help of other team members. Ultimately, the manager or leader depends upon other team members to achieve the task. In football, this means going out on the pitch and winning games. None of the manager's desires can be achieved without them also achieving their desires. It is, therefore, vital that both the manager and team members share the same desires. At first sight, this may not appear too much of a problem—surely, our team want to win! All we can say, with certainty, is that they may do so, but that things may not be quite so clear cut. Of the eleven players that comprise the team each may have different and perhaps conflicting desires. One may have the desire to simply get through the game without injury; one may have the desire to ensure that he does not have to play with a certain team member again; and, this desire may be mutually shared by another team member; one may have the desire to 'get his own back' on an opposing player. These are but a few examples but the list of desires that individual members of the team take into games is endless. The effect of these sort of desires may be to create conflict with their other desire to win.

The degree of danger that a person perceives themselves to be in will be a function of what they might lose. A person who thinks they have less to lose will be less alarmed in a given situation. Thus the football manager who has sound finances, or has achieved success in the past, is likely to be less concerned about dismissal than another who has a large mortgage or has not previously been successful. For the manager who fears their job is on the line: every booking of one of the other team members; every injury to one of the other team members; every goal scored against the team; every loss of points; may feel like nails in their coffin. The perceived danger arising from the fact that it has become impossible to fulfil their desires is likely to be perceived as a massive danger.

Learning how to avoid

The point of the matter is that so-called objective danger is a situation in which our desires have become impossible to satisfy. That is, unless we succeed in doing something about it. Objective danger is not principally different from deprivation of desires beyond a certain point of time or intensity. In either case alarm or anxiety is triggered off and will increase to panic unless the situation changes after all, or substitute desires can be satisfied instead. Here, what I shall refer to as *defence mechanisms* come into use. In simple terms this is achieved by learning how to appreciate substitute conditions or by satisfaction of substitute desires, or both. It is that function by which a person learns not to try situations that have led to excessive deprivation and anxiety.

Thus, in the same way, that through the experience of satisfaction of our desires we learn 'how to like or to appreciate', we also correspondingly 'learn how to avoid or to how to fear' from our experience of non-satisfaction of desires. At the root of this process is a desire that has become impossible to satisfy for one reason or another. Where a manager wants to win the League and now realizes that it is beyond the team's capability the team will continue to play matches, but it will not satisfy the manager's original desire. However, they may have learned that in such circumstances a substitute desire, such as finishing in the top three, will be satisfying.

Where, however, the manager has previously only experienced success, the desire will grow in intensity, like all desires that have been satisfied recurrently until that day and reach a point at which it was usually satisfied before. Now, however, nothing happens. There are other things around. But the manager is looking for something else, and time does not stop. Consequently, the intensity of their desire increases further. From a certain point on the manager get anxious. What is worse, anxiety will continue to mount until it reaches the volume of panic. Under such a prospect and, so to speak, pressed from every corner of the system, the manager will take to reason and accept the achievement of finishing second. Something second rate, if it is available, is better than nothing at all. They can at least achieve a respectable position in the League.

In like manner, the manager of a team which is losing heavily at half-time may set out not to be humiliated and to ensure that it is not a total slaughter; the manager will try to make it a game where they can at least take something from it by, perhaps, making it a respectable score, or by trying something new. Satisfaction of a substitute desire can do something for the original desire. In fact, a desire that can do something for another desire is a substitute desire. It can reduce the other's intensity to a certain extent, although not by as much as satisfaction of the original desire would. In the circumstances described, the manager would get something out of the game, even if it was not what was originally desired.

At this stage, I need to add a further complication, that concerning conflicting desires. Earlier in the chapter I referred to team members having different individual desires and the problems that these conflicting desires could have for the success of the team. In looking for an explanation of our behaviour, let us for a moment return to childhood. In their development, the child achieves an inner organization of objects, ideas, events and values into a coherent system—usually using categories determined by the parents. Here the mind becomes a relatively orderly place and only a limited amount of chaos can be tolerated. In some cases ideas become unacceptable to consciousness if they conflict too much with other ideas. We deal with ideas that are incompatible by repression and other defence mechanisms which are described in Chapter 4. However, in the following chapter, I am going to explore another way of dealing with deprivation of desires, which is a frequent problem for managers and leaders, namely, aggression.

CHAPTER THREE

Managing aggression in the leader and other team members

A t the start of the last chapter I referred to the way that we all form boundaries concerning, 'what is mine', things which constitute our individual personality. I shall proceed from the notion that the boundary line between mind and body is not present at birth. Indeed, I shall suggest that there are no boundaries present at birth. At the start of life there is nothing—no knowledge at all. You might reasonably ask, 'who can tell?' This is a fair question and so far no one has been able, with any certainty, to tell what is in the mind of a new born baby, but it may also be fair to say that we can get a pretty good idea by looking at the experience of later life. As has been said, each of us is a unique individual. All of us are different. True we have similarities, but we also have many differences. Therefore, it may not be much of a leap of faith to fairly conclude that we all start with nothing. This is exceedingly valuable because it provides us with an idea of how we become what we are. It is by developing an awareness of how we became what we are, especially through our early development, that we gain a deeper understanding of some of the events in our adult life. Thus, we may helpfully start at the beginning.

Throughout this book I shall continue to take a developmental approach which investigates how the past affects the present—how the child is father to the man. Basic to the (psychoanalytic) approach taken here is the premise that we develop from infancy onwards. We never completely forget the ways of functioning which we have learnt earlier and, particularly, the ways which we learnt first of all, as infants. Thus, although we may not be aware of it as mature adults, we carry with us ways of functioning and relating to people which are essentially infantile. To understand these ways we must return to the world of the infant.

What the human mind organizes is meaning. At the start of life there is no meaning, no organization, no categorization of material—it starts then. The child's mind is a relatively dissociated one; they experience a series of incompatible thoughts, emotions, feelings, and desires that successively invade their seat of consciousness and this sometimes leads to inappropriate reactions by the infant which are but little modified or checked by one another. At this stage, during the earliest part of its life, the child has not developed a conscience and is an a-moral being. Morality implies the possibility of two or more courses of thought or action— a better and a worse—and at this stage the lack of integration in the child's mind only permits this to a very limited extent.

Primitive mental activity

This is what we might refer to as primitive mental activity. Here, when a child is suffering from frustration and anxiety they respond in very primitive ways. This is a 'black' and 'white' world where grey does not exist and this is the most natural way of dealing with matters at the earliest stages of emotional development. When other persons interfere with the child's desires things are simply experienced by the child as 'good' or 'bad' depending on the perceived experience. Where they are experienced as providing satisfaction of desires they are experienced as 'good'; and, no matter that it is the same person, who at another moment is perceived as thwarting the satisfaction of desires they will be experienced as 'bad'. These views of black and white may be arrayed in the primitive manifestations of love and hate (Bettleheim, 1988).

The processes of the mind originate in the instincts, drives, or desires seeking satisfaction in objects—frequently in other people. We may thus think of the mind as the apparatus that links desires to their objects, or which mediates between the internal reality of the child and the external reality of objects. So, what happens when the desire, say for hunger, is not fulfilled? In this primitive world the infant responds by using primitive defence mechanisms which I shall refer to as 'splitting', 'introjection' and 'projection'. Although these are psychoanalytic terms they may also be described in quite an ordinary way as precisely what the words denote. 'Splitting' means precisely that; splitting of an 'object' be that a person, a car, or a concept into two different parts 'good' and 'bad', as described above. 'Introjection' is simply the taking in of an object, again, be that 'object' another person, such as a team member, a quality of another person, such as empathy, or a concept, such as trust. And, 'Projection' is the projecting out, the pushing out from the self of an 'object', such as your perception of another person, or part of a person or of a concept. Thus, the child may push out their feelings of frustration, anger or inadequacy that they do not want to own.

These more primitive desires, or more primitive forms of satisfying given desires, are also more aggressive or destructive. Melanie Klein (see, for example, 1975) and others have shown that when the child seeks to bring about the permanent removal of a competitor or rival, the ideas of death or murder are, at this stage of life, uncomplicated by the thoughts, feelings, and sentiments that later come to be associated with them. The infliction of death, be that real or imaginary is simply the most natural way of proceeding. Anxiety is the way that the mind reacts to the threat of loss, either of objects (including human objects), or of satisfaction, or of integrity. In common with other behaviour, aggression is an aspect of desire and is the twin brother of anxiety. Anxiety is a state of mind in which more primitive, hence aggressive, desires than usual may prevail. If we act on these primitive desires we may speak of aggression. If they are not acted upon, some form of defence mechanism may become necessary (as will be discussed in the next chapter). Fortunately, as a result of the overall amount of learning that we accumulate through life, aggressiveness of desires decreases with development. Feelings of aggression are feelings of aggressive desires. And, as was explained earlier, all feelings are feelings of desires, satisfactions, and/or fears.

Leader aggression

Aggression manifests itself in aggressive desires and only in those. To try to understand the processes involved let us first recall the process that leads to anxiety. Here you will recall that deprivation of a desire beyond a certain point of intensity or time triggers off anxiety. As anxiety mounts so deprived desires 'become' more primitive and aggressive. But it goes beyond that because if deprivation continues unchanged and anxiety keeps mounting, it will reach panic. At this point, desires have become so primitive and so aggressive that they cannot be satisfied in any other way than by uncontrolled aggressive behaviour. Thus it is that a football manager, suffering the experience of the team sliding nearer and nearer to defeat and with a concomitant non-satisfaction of their desires, becomes more primitive and more aggressive—sometimes reaching uncontrolled aggression. In the case of the manager I worked with it would be confined to uncontrolled verbal aggression, but in many televised incidents managers have been seen to use physical violence, such as assault or throwing cups at other team members.

In most cases, one way or another, something has been done about the situation long before the worst happens. Substitute desires take over and the anxiety level drops accordingly. For example, the manager and perhaps other team members accept that they will not win and will settle for a draw. But there are times when previous experience, such as a defeat followed by the rival manager gloating over the victory, may lead to primitive feelings and aggressive desires for revenge. For example, the manager of one particular opposing team was quite despised by the manager because of his perceived lack of football values. When this fixture came up the manager would be driven by primitive aggressive desires to win. When he did so, he had satisfied a more primitive and aggressive desire and had, thereby, also satisfied the desire that had been deprived in the first place.

In general terms, we can say that satisfaction of a more primitive desire means more to an individual than satisfaction of a more controlled desire. Its capacity to reduce desire intensity, or put another way its satisfaction value, is greater. Anxiety is at a high level in these cases. In fact, anxiety itself may be seen as an attempt to satisfy the deprived desire in more primitive forms, albeit that this is a temporary and unstable one. It is more at the mercy of given opportunities than established regression would be. Remember, to really understand what is being said you need to relate to your own experiences. You need to reflect on an occasion when you satisfied a primitive desire and then ask yourself: What happened? How did you feel about it?

The course of action that we take will depend greatly on the given situation as we have learned to perceive it. Adopting a more or less primitive approach will depend upon our experiences of previous situations and more specifically, all of our previous experiences of conditions under which given desires could and could not be satisfied. By the process of perception we impose some structure on new input, compare it with a pool of old information and then either add to it or eliminate it. We can only make judgements about whether we like or dislike something if it is something that we know. Our sensations must be completed by some form of appraisal before we can decide whether it is good or bad for us. Thus in the example given above, the manager was influenced by his past dislike of the opposing manager.

The basis for our perceptive process is our pool of internalized information, which in turn provides the basis for our self-concepts, which are the individual's views of themselves. As I have explained, they begin in childhood with the bodily self-concept and expand rapidly through object relations: first with the mother and then with other significant family members. The object relations with the parents provide a continual psycho–social basis for learning what is pleasurable and what is distressing. The memory bank grows throughout life to produce that rich mosaic which is the individual personality (Stapley, 1996). Depending on our personality—the result of our experience—we will adopt a more or less primitive approach. In the example cited above, the manager's personality led to a more primitive approach to his opponent. His pool of internalized information informed him that this other man stood for everything that he was opposed to. Others with different values may not have reacted in this way.

Team member aggression

No matter what we, as managers or leaders, may or may not do or what our values are, we do not live in isolation. There are other team members, with other experiences, and different personalities and values, in our world. In the end it is the 'objective' world and above all 'objective' people who will let us get by in some instances and not in others. Exactly when team members will let their manager or leader by and when they will not will depend upon their desires. They, of course, are no different from the manager or leader and they also have desires and if they can help it, they would also rather give up the satisfaction of none. Finally other team members tend not to give up their desires merely because of the manager or leader and the manager or leader tends not to give up theirs merely because of the rest of the team. Yet the 'objective' world and 'objective' people are such that we must all give in somewhere. As I have shown from birth on, and even before, we are hopelessly dependent on other people even for our mere survival. More specifically, the satisfactions of all our desires depend on other people's desires and wherever that is so, there is room for conflict.

Participation and consultation

In the foreword I listed some of the things that others had suggested were necessary for a successful team. Among these was the need for participation. When you consider the last few paragraphs you will now understand why it is so important. And, you will be in no doubt that participation by all team members is essential. The leader or manager may take a variety of approaches: imploring, bullying, manipulating, encouraging, directing, haranguing, threatening, whatever. But, if they do not have an awareness of other team members, and in particular, an awareness that (a) they all have desires, and, (b) what their desires are, they may not get by.

To achieve an awareness of other team members' desires requires their 'participation'. One of the important means that the manager or leader goes about this is by 'consultation'. Many managers and leaders that I have worked with have felt uncomfortable with the notion of consultation because they feel that it means giving up their authority to manage. This is normally because they do not understand what is meant by the term. In order that there is no confusion, let me define what I mean by the term 'consultation'. It is simply, 'seeking the views of others and taking them into consideration before making a decision'. Thus, the manager or leader still has the authority to make the decision.

In many situations a consensus may develop which the manager or leader can rubber stamp. However, in other less clear situations the manager or leader may make the decision after considering all views. These views may include the manager or leader's own views based on knowledge which may not have been previously known to the other team members. This is perfectly legitimate and concerns the manager or leader using their authority in a participative manner. However, what should not happen is that the manager or leader makes a decision and then consults the other team members. This is 'charade consultation' which is the worst of all worlds. It does not truly seek the views of others and it does not satisfy the needs of other team members who will feel that they have wasted their time and been cheated.

It is not difficult to realize that satisfaction of our desires may deprive other people of their own satisfaction. This may result in them suffering anxiety or pain from deprivation because of us. Satisfaction of our desires may be destructive to theirs and vice versa. Moreover, satisfaction of our desires will be more destructive in general, the greater the concomitant deprivation of other people: that is, the greater the number and importance of desires that another person has to give up and the greater the number of people who have to do so. True participation will improve decision making, it will involve the consideration of multiple views rather than the singular view of the manager or leader. And, most importantly, it will enable the manager or leader to become aware of the desires of other team members. A further benefit is that it will allow others to contribute to the achievement of their desires.

Consultation is important and can have a considerable affect on the manager's influence—or lack of it. For example, at half-time during one particular match, without consultation, the manager decided to make a change to the way the team was organized. He clearly felt that this was necessary to achieve his desires to play attractively and win. It seemed clear that other team members were of the view that although they had not achieved tangible results they had, nevertheless, started to gain control of the game and consequently the last thing they wanted to do was change the organization of the team. In these circumstances they were not prepared to let the manager get by, because they felt it would be destructive to the satisfaction of their desires.

There will be occasions when other people, who have desires which would obstruct ours, will let us get by with ours since they will sometimes let us 'scare them' and will give up their own desires. In other instances they will not let us get by. They will, instead, 'scare us' and insist that we renounce. In fact, on every occasion they will let us get by with some things but not with others. The deciding factor will be how aggressive or destructive our desires are compared to theirs. The danger is that in such circumstances we shall experience the worst of all worlds as neither the team manager's desires nor other team members' desires are satisfied. It is thus important that we learn how to control our desires.

We will generally pursue those conditions of satisfaction that are relatively less destructive, and learn to control all those that are more destructive to other people or to the world in general. Although it may make perfect sense to the manager or leader they have to bear in mind that their views may be perceived as destructive by other team members. If we bear in mind the notion that management is about 'getting results through other people'— the team—it may be the case that on many occasions their desires are more important than those of the manager or leader. At crucial times, it may be better for the manager to control his desires and simply encourage other team members to accomplish their desires. At the end of the day, if they do so, the manager will also have achieved his desires. As was stated in Chapter 1, the good manager or leader is one who encourages leadership in other team members. The better that the leader or manager is in fulfilling this aim, the more successful will be the team.

Hurt others—hurt yourself

Destruction or destructiveness is not an absolute, but a relative thing. We cannot do anything at all without being destructive to somebody's desires, no matter how slightly. In any team meeting it will be almost impossible to achieve total agreement. What is more, we cannot even do anything destructive at all without being destructive to ourselves in some respects, no matter how minor that may be. For example, if a manager is jealous or envious of one of the other team members because of their skill and they destroy the other team member by dropping them from the team, not only do they satisfy their desires to control or overpower the other team member, but they also deprive themselves of having the skilful services of that team member thereafter. In other cases of aggressive or destructive satisfactions this may not be so apparent. However, one can generally find some form of self-destructive consequences, no matter how minor, of desires that are destructive to others, or to objects in general.

Where a team member, having resorted to aggressive behaviour, is sent off for foul play one would think that they ought to learn from this experience that this is unacceptable behaviour. But, it is open to question whether these consequences are apparent and evident enough to guarantee that desires become automatically less destructive with development. In general terms, people do learn from their past behaviour and develop less destructive ways of behaving, but there is also evidence from football that some team members, when they are suffering anxiety and their emotions take control of their actions, tend to resort to destructive ways in spite of previous experience. Managers and leaders can be aware of this tendency and can act to reduce the anxiety levels which bring on the destructive behaviour. Helping other team members to come to terms with disappointments arising from failure to achieve desires is an important aspect of the manager or leader's work.

We also need to be aware that destructiveness is not only an aspect of those desires that are related to other people, but of all our desires. Where, for example, the football manager desires to strengthen the playing staff to increase the chances of satisfying a major desire, that of winning the League, they may be destructive to the fellow manager and to the player that they are replacing. Provided we live at all, every one of our desires is related to other people. Here, the new player, the opposing manager, and the old player. Other people are inevitable and indispensable conditions of all satisfactions that we can ever hope to attain. This is particularly evident in teams where the conflicting desires of other team members and the team manager around such issues as team composition, will inevitably lead to a loss of satisfaction for some.

This is true for all associated with football, not least the fans who have their own views as to who should be in or out of the team.

From desires to behaviour

Although we are primarily concerned with desires, we should not forget that desires guide and manifest themselves in behaviour. And, although I have provided examples of behaviour, it has been necessary to concentrate on desires, because behaviour in situations and conditions as complex as we are considering would be impossible to trace in detail. Besides, even if I were aware of all the nuances of any particular interaction between a team manager and other team members it would probably take several pages to describe it in detail. Desires are not unambiguously tied to any one form of behaviour. So, in order not to get lost, we have made desires our element of theorising. But we cannot ignore behaviour, because this is the result of learning and is all we know about the world. As a matter of fact, only through behaviour do we come in contact with the world. We cannot learn about the world unless we behave in it in some fashion. What is more, all behaviour has something to do with the satisfaction of desires. More specifically: there is no form or aspect of behaviour that would not be satisfying to some extent, no matter how small, if it were not for some identifiable desire.

If all behaviour is a manifestation of desires and desires form ever new derivative desires, behaviour should develop ever new forms. Thus the young football manager learns new and more advanced skills as they satisfy their desires to be an accomplished manager. Desires are not satisfied in isolation; if the 'objective' world were such that no desires could be satisfied, without having anything to do with any other, we would go on developing new forms of behaviour indefinitely without ever getting anywhere. Truth is, that the 'objective' world provides conditions that have a degree of constancy at least to some extent as they recur. In fact, that is the very reason why we can say that they recur. Team members may face different opponents in different matches, but those opponents will have learnt some of the ways of other opponents and their behaviour will now be part of the 'objective' world.

In-so-far as we behave, we are a part of the 'objective' world too.

We also learn to adapt to our environment. And in-so-far as we act in a fixed and unchanging manner, to whatever extent, our behaviour must be recurrent in some ways. There is an even stranger thing about us: the fact that through behaviour we can influence the conditions which the objective world outside of ourselves provides. Thus, in football, managers will learn different ways of organizing their teams as a result of the way that other teams are organized. In industry, managers learn to introduce new ways of organizing such as 'total quality management' and 'just-in-time' delivery of supplies. In fact, this is the very reason why we are a part of the objective world. By self-reflection we can even summon the recurrence of the conditions as a whole. Behaviour becomes more efficient with a person's development. Part of a person's knowledge of the world as a whole, which includes himself, is to know in ever so many ways what leads to what. Or, put another way, we become experienced practitioners and our understanding of the management and leadership of teams develops over time.

So, what about aggressive or destructive desires that are activated in response to a sudden insult, to a physical injury, to threats such as that of losing an important game or an important contract. Are these not qualitatively different situations from those referred to so far? In principle they are no different, they are all conditions of deprivation of a person's desires, whether that condition is existent or impending. For example, the loss of an important game may in itself be a frustrated desire, but the effect may be much greater because the loss of this game may mean that the greater desire, for example, win the Cup, may also be frustrated. Anxiety and aggression are twin brothers, we said, or even the same thing looked at from two different angles. It is helpful to view them as conditions of a temporary regression that are ameliorated by learning how to avoid, on the one hand and by more aggressive or destructive satisfactions, on the other. Therefore, the determinants of anxiety, as discussed before, will also be determinants of aggression.

Versions of aggression

Let us now look at a few of the 'versions' of aggression mentioned before, such as anger, annoyance, hate, hostility, and revenge. They too are, or derive their meaning from, specific conditions of motivation. Anger and annoyance refer to a deprivation of desires beyond a certain point, irrespective of whether it came about suddenly or slowly. In football it does not matter at what time the opposition score the goals that lead to your defeat—anger and aggression may follow, whatever. Hate and hostility may also come about slowly or suddenly too. Yet we may say that this aggressive behaviour is more specific. Where opponents mock team members in defeat, hate and hostility may arise whatever the timing. Here the object perceived as the source of deprivation is the goal of the more primitive and destructive desires that make up aggression. On the face of things it may be only another game, but the manager may also be aware that if the team loses this may result in them being sacked. Thus the primitive source of deprivation is survival and this may lead to primitive and destructive desires. Finally, and most importantly in the context of teams, is revenge. The individual tends to satisfy more primitive and destructive desires with that person who, usually, did something similar to that individual.

A classic example of mockery and revenge was reported by Matt Dickinson in The Times on 10th April 1999, under the headline, 'Fowler pays for his "stupid" prank'. Here, it was reported that the Liverpool player Robbie Fowler faced two charges of misconduct when he appeared before a three-man FA disciplinary hearing in Birmingham on 9th April. The first was for taunting Graeme Le Saux, the Chelsea defender, as a homosexual during Liverpool's match against Chelsea at Stamford Bridge in February. Fowler, who was shown on television waving his bottom at his opponent, was suspended for two games for that incident while Le Saux, who subsequently elbowed Fowler in the back of the head, was banned for one match and fined £5000. In this example, the actions of Fowler led to the more primitive and destructive desires of Le Saux.

Learning how to avoid aggressive behaviour

If aggressiveness or destructiveness is an aspect of all our desires and control of desires, derivative formation, learning how to like and learning how to avoid and object formation, all are pervasive aspects of our desires too, there must be a relationship between them and destructiveness. Give team members a chance to develop at all, to learn how to like and to learn how to avoid and the aggressiveness and destructiveness of their desires will diminish automatically. Why should this be so? There are basically two reasons why our desires become less destructive with development. The first concerns the time of development when desires are still primitive. Here, primitive desires could be correspondingly aggressive or destructive desires, if only our ways of implementing them were more advanced. Since they are not, primitive desires, on the one hand, and aggressive or destructive desires, on the other hand, do not seem on brief inspection to be aspects of the same thing. As in the previous example, primitive desires are aggressive and destructive desires by all intentions. They are meant to be, even though they cannot actually destroy.

The second reason why our desires become less destructive with development concerns the behaviour of those we come into contact with. We have already said that the desires of various others come into conflict with ours, and vice versa. We must add now, that we will become increasingly more intolerant of deprivations of desires by a given individual as we develop. Where, for example, the team manager consistently deprives other team members of the opportunity to be creative and to have an impact on their own future plans, other team members will become increasingly intolerant of the manager's autocratic style of management as they develop as a team. This alone is a very good argument for the need for a participative style of management.

A different situation arises when 'primitive' does not refer to the level of development in general, but to particular desires on a given level of development. We have seen that any condition of deprivation beyond a certain point triggers off anxiety, which may be defined as a condition of temporary regression. More primitive desires, that are displacements from the original frustrated desire, are sought to be satisfied. These desires, which are more primitive in relation to the level of development reached, can count on an efficiency of behaviour in general that is appropriate to the level of development. Hence, in any such case they can become aggressive or destructive in reality. The potential destructiveness of behaviour increases with development. Therefore desires of a given primitivity and destructiveness tend to be more dangerous the later in development they occur.

Concluding remarks

If your role as a manager or leader is about 'getting results through other people' it seems clear that one of your important responsibilities is to ensure that 'the other people'—the other team members—are in as good a shape as possible to get results. In football, it goes without saying, that all team members need to be physically fit and if there is any doubt, they are most unlikely to play. This is a common sense approach that would have the universal agreement of all engaged in football, at any level, anywhere in the world.

Why then does this sort of consideration not extend to mental fitness? As I have started to show in this chapter, anxiety can be every bit as crippling to managers and other team members as any physical injury. Here, I'm not talking about mental illness, but simply mental fitness, a state which affects all of us to a greater or lesser degree when the stresses and strains of living become too much to bear. If as a manager or leader you are:

- oblivious to the needs of other team members;
- treat them as extensions of yourself; or
- threaten and bully them.

You will most likely be adding to their anxiety and contribute to triggering its twin brother, aggression. Now the other team member will respond by using primitive defence mechanisms such as 'splitting', where they may view you, the manager, as totally bad and incapable of being good. Or they may 'project' this aggression into you, the manager, leaving them like some sort of gentle creature that could not compete against children.

Ensuring both the mental and physical fitness of all team members are part of the responsibility of the manager or leader. In regard to mental fitness we know that team member's desires will become less destructive with development. One of the key influences of their development will be the behaviour of those they come in contact with, especially those perceived to be in an authority position. If, as a manager or leader, you act as a good role model who is self-aware and acts with a considerable degree of self-control, other team members will seek to emulate you. Conversely, if you are the sort of role model that constantly loses their temper and acts in an aggressive manner, don't be surprised if this is how the other team members act.

In the next chapter, I shall deal with other ways of coping with the anxiety that arises when we fail to achieve our desires.

CHAPTER FOUR

Defence mechanisms — coping with failure

I n the last chapter, I referred to some of the difficulties that can and will arise as we, as individual managers or team members, seek the satisfaction of our desires. There, I sought to explain something of the way we regress to more primitive modes of behaving that result in aggression. Here, I shall be looking at some of the many other devices and approaches that we adopt as a means of coping with the anxiety of failure. Following and adding to the last chapter, I shall provide further explanations for the ways in which we deal with failure to achieve our desires.

Before going too far, this may be an opportune time to remind the reader about application of the material in this book, as much of what follows will provide excellent opportunities for the reader to develop their process of self-reflection. By this, I mean, bringing the material to life by reflecting on your own experiences and your feelings associated with those experiences. Or, as one of my clients put it, having a conversation with yourself. For example, at certain points you might ask yourself:

- what am I feeling?
- if I am feeling (say) angry; why am I feeling angry?

- what is the reason for my anger?

In this chapter you can reflect on the various situations described and link them to past or current experiences, to gain an understanding of the way you have personally coped with the anxiety of failure. By doing so, this will provide you with a valuable opportunity to develop your self-awareness.

You will recall the procedure, first referred to in the Foreword, that will help you as managers and leaders if you wish to gain a deeper understanding of some of the problems associated with your relationships and relatedness to other team members.

- *Self-awareness*, leading to:
- *self-control*, leading to:
- *awareness of others*.

There will be many situations referred to in this Chapter when the way that our emotions and phantasies—our relatedness to others—will come into the equation. To truly understand you need to access and learn from your own experiences.

Anxiety is the way that the mind reacts to the threat of loss, either of objects, or of satisfaction, or of integrity. For football managers there are many opportunities when anxiety may develop. For example:

- when they fear the loss of a key player because of a transfer to another team or through injury;
- when the team lose and fail to satisfy the manager's desire for achievement and success; and
- when their values are challenged.

There are two stages of anxiety that can be differentiated quantitatively. First, a small amount of anxiety, which is the initial signal, the sort of little switch that comes on first. This is called *signal anxiety*. This is the reaction that occurs at the initial perception of danger and is a call to fight or flight. From the very outset the mind has to try to fulfil its task of acting as an intermediary between desires and the external world. We do this in our minds making use of various *coping mechanisms* which enable us to fulfil our task. The whole purpose of this process being, to put it in general terms, to avoid danger, anxiety and unpleasure. In psychoanalytic jargon these devices are called *defence mechanisms*, but even in ordinary usage the meaning is precisely that.

A repertoire of coping techniques

Throughout our lives, we develop a repertoire of coping techniques in difficult situations. This repertoire of techniques, or ways of handling anxiety, be that anxiety arising from external or internal stimuli, is largely built up from the experience of having faced difficulties, having gone through crises, and having overcome them in novel ways. These ways of coping then become part of our normal repertoire and of course, the repertoire is added to throughout life. It may be enriched in a negative way, but in any case it is expanded. The repertoire of coping methods may be added to in a number of ways, for example, by education. We are taught explicitly or implicitly how to deal with problem situations. That is, events in the external environment may provide us with new ways of coping. For example, management models such as the 'Rational Approach to Decision Making' will provide us with a process that if followed will help us to come up with the best option.

Another way we add to our repertoire is that suggested at the start of this chapter: we can learn from our own experience and particularly our own feelings. By the process of self-reflection we can develop self-awareness and gain an understanding of our behaviour. For example, by this process we may become aware that we are 'denying' our true feelings or are 'rationalizing' our behaviour. Thus, a footballer who has just lost a match may rationalize the situation by saying 'it doesn't matter because we are still in the top three'. Another player may deny the implications of defeat by saying 'It's not a problem, we won't be relegated, we're too good a side'.

A further way in which the repertoire is added to is one which, in the context of the manager or leader, they need to know and understand as one of the cornerstones of success. This is the process where team members add to their repertoire of coping through identification with other people who are using certain coping mechanisms: we can learn from role models. In the early days this will be parents and other influential individuals; later in life managers and leaders may fill this role. That is to say, one is on intimate terms with some other person who acts as a model and then, either consciously or unconsciously, team members copy the way the manager or leader sees problems and deals with them. We commonly refer to these highly important and influential individuals as role models. No one should be under any illusions about the impact that role models have on all aspects of team behaviour.

The threat of loss and actual loss

Situations of difficulty that may precipitate a crisis can be broadly divided into two types. One concerns a threat involving the danger of the loss of an 'object', or a source of satisfaction of needs, or a threat to one's integrity. The other kind of difficulty concerns the loss itself, i.e. when you actually lose an object, a person whom you love and admire, a source of gratification; or when you lose your integrity and become damaged or injured. For a football manager such a loss may occur when they are dismissed from their post. In effect they lose the 'object', the team, that they have worked day and night to support and make a success. The significance of this loss can be seen when it is realized that this object was the source of many of their important desires. A variation on this is not an actual loss, but an obstacle which stands in your way, which you have to overcome in order to achieve the object of gratification or your integrity. For example, where a manager is in the sort of situation where they are threatened with dismissal and have pressure applied on them to act contrary to their values, they may be required to sign a player who does not meet the standards of conduct required by the manager. This could be experienced as being worse than getting the sack.

Different situations may produce a crisis in some people and not in others. The character of the person and their repertoire of responses, or ways of dealing with the situation, will determine how they react. Thus, in the example above, some managers would be able to cope with other team members no matter what their perceived quality and morality. Others would experience the same situation as worse than being dismissed. Some managers will perceive difficulty as a challenge and will, for example, thrive on being the underdog and will turn it to their advantage. Others will perceive the same situation as totally hopeless and will simply buckle under the constant struggles to climb mountains. Only you, the reader, can know how you will react and you will only know this if you develop the capacity for self-awareness.

Coping by regression

Most of us faced with a crisis will work out a way of dealing with it. Faced with difficulties we can deal with them by a whole range of actions, from dealing with the problem by reality-based means, to dealing with it by a wide variety of more primitive methods. However, frequently there is no solution in reality. In that case we are thrown back to the use of a more primitive mechanism, namely the mechanism of regression. For instance, the person may deal with the situation by a kind of childlike magic and wishful thinking and this may lead to a condition which we recognize as *'neurosis'*. Many readers may be under the impression that neurosis is a serious situation and a strange way to describe what might be seen as a response to a minor panic. But, neurosis does not only refer to serious conditions it can also refer to lesser conditions and really only refers to a means of dealing with problems by magic, irrational or symbolic means.

It is not unusual for a team that is in difficulty to come up with a means of dealing with the problem by some sort of magic, irrational or symbolic means. One of the most prevalent is the situation where a constantly losing team deals with the anxiety by claiming that they are 'really a very good side' and that they are 'really better than other teams'. Having thus created this illusory symbol of a successful side they are able to 'magic away' the anxiety of continually losing. For any team caught up in this sort of behaviour it may be exceedingly difficult to get out of it.

Phantasy solutions

As has been explained, faced with a crisis we shall most likely experience anxiety. It is anxiety that interferes with and interrupts our way of behaving in pursuit of our desires. To retain our self-awareness in such situations may be very difficult. If it is severe enough, it is likely that it will leave us with a lack of perception—or put another way will leave us witless. However, where we can retain our self-awareness we can develop a reality-based solution, difficult as that may be. It is when we lose our self-awareness that we seek solutions in phantasy. For example, faced with a situation where a manager or leader is experiencing difficulty in obtaining support from the Board they may perhaps phantasize that a key figure in the process may resign thus creating a more co-operative environment; or, they may seek a magical solution such as winning the lottery, when again they will be able to change their environment and everything will be all right.

If the door to neurosis is not open, further regression may lead to more primitive forms of disorganization and alienation from the world of reality. One of the ways that the manager or other team member may deal with difficulties and the tensions associated with them was referred to earlier and that is by splitting them off from the rest of their personality. A problem is that when this happens the individual splits them off together with a bit of their personality. For example, a football manager may split off the disappointment of a loss and the feelings of anger or frustration that accompany the disappointment. The problem then is that the manager may not be in total control of themselves and will be in no position to help others or even to relate to others about anger and frustration, because they have, albeit temporarily, cut this out of their personality. In other words, by losing self-awareness and self-control and in order to avoid facing the tensions that their unified, integrated personality would face if dealing with this unsolved problem, the manager just smashes up their personality, as it were.

In technical parlance we would say that this gives them a 'psychosis' and you will understand more fully what I mean when I say that one of the most typical of these is schizophrenia. Here we are not talking about mental illness which is normally associated with schizophrenia. However, it is serious enough if you are a manager or leader because if your personality is fragmented you cease to exist from a certain point of view, and then cease to feel the tensions of the unsolved problem. It's a bit like a car that has a part missing such as the brakes. However, a car does not have feelings as we humans do and it is this loss of feelings that is serious for the manager or leader. Without feelings they may become uncaring, cold and unresponsive to the needs of other team members. For the manager or leader this is a way of escape, and is a quite primitive way, it is a regression to the way we dealt with anxiety as infants. In this state the manager or leader can be of little assistance to other team members.

Anxiety—again!

Anxiety is the term which covers three levels of alerting responses: apprehension, free anxiety, and panic. All the alerting responses are reactions to stress which can enter through any of the internal or external systems. If the individual does not believe either consciously or unconsciously that they can cope with the stress, they will react with some level of anxiety. Although anxiety is an attempt at functional response, it is an over-reaction and can lead to dysfunction. In most instances this will be a temporary dysfunction, such as the times when we feel we just need a little time to clear our heads and think things through. However, if the threat is not relieved by the effort to relieve it, if the danger continues or increases and we have no means of adaptation or adjustment to enable us to cope we are in trouble. In other words if the reality condition continues and the person does not deal with it—the anxiety increases; at a certain threshold we say it changes from signal anxiety to actual anxiety.

Anxiety now becomes not a call to action, but a burden. Instead of being a stimulus to fight or flight or to adjust in an active way, after it passes a certain threshold it becomes a force that becomes an ever increasingly regressed mental state where we may adopt an increasing use of phantasy and magic and irrational methods, which then eventually results in disintegration and alienation leaving behind neurosis, psychosomatic illness, or psychosis (Toman, 1960). Something of this nature happened with one of the team members that I worked with on a one-to-one basis. When I saw him he said, 'My head's gone'. He was describing very accurately the anxiety that he was experiencing. For various reasons anxiety about playing had been building up and he felt that he could not cope with the stress. Almost certainly this was an unconscious process connected to early life experience. The manager and others not being fully aware of his past experience had, at first, failed to understand the seriousness of the situation, some members of staff even resorting to calling him a badly motivated and non-caring individual who should be 'got rid of'. The manager, realizing that something was wrong, sought my assistance and with some reality-based development and support from the manager the player returned to successful ways.

Previous experience and coping

What I shall refer to as 'worry work' is the work of internal adjustment stimulated by signal anxiety. As with the player referred to above, one of the most important factors that interfere with successful worrying is the revival of old memories, of old phantasies of loss, due to previously unsolved conflicts in similar situations. Your previous experience of threat and how you dealt with it rises as a kind of spectre to haunt you when you are in a state of being stimulated by signal anxiety to do worry work. This is what leads to the effect of childhood experiences in influencing the precipitation in later life of neurosis or psychosis. As in the instance referred to above, the sort of anxiety experienced in early life triggers our memories and triggers the same sort of responses. Psychoanalysis has paid much attention to the tremendous effect of the way in which we originally solved our conflicts as a small child, has on what happens to us in later life, in regard to how we deal with threat situations. If, as a child, you learnt how to cope by, for example, running away, then the chances are that you will, in some shape or form, do the same as an adult.

Mental strength and coping

In addition to the rising of old spectres, the success of worry work is also influenced by a number of factors that are operating in the here-and-now current situation of the threat and the attempts to grapple with it. Among them we must refer to the current strength of team members and manager or leader alike. This current strength is dependent not only on the person's physical health, but also on something that might be called his mental toughness, what has sometimes been referred to as 'attitude', 'application' or 'persistence'. There can be little doubt that some people actually are tougher in dealing with problem situations than others. We might say that some team members are on a 'short fuse' and that they will become aggressive (or passive) at the slightest hint of difficulty. Others will thrive on the challenges posed by difficulties presented.

The example given earlier of Bobby Moore rising above the tension and emotion of the moment to retain his self-awareness and his self-control is a classic example of one who thrived on challenges and was able to cope with the toughest of circumstances as the many readers who saw him play will testify. Others, such as, for example, Stan Collymore and Paul Gascoine are seemingly on a 'short fuse' and as soon as things start to go wrong or as soon as the anxiety level gets too high they will sadly react aggressively, or at times passively, as we have seen with Gascoine's tears.

Strength is dependent not only on 'attitude', but also on the repertoire of coping responses and on the ability to withstand frustration, which are dependent upon the way managers and other team members have successfully dealt with past crises. We know that some people, as they go through life, get more and more bowed down, burdened by one failure after another. If a manager or other team member has had many failures in the past, the chances of failing are greater when they are faced with another difficult situation. Conversely, if the manager or other team member has enjoyed many successes in the past the chances of succeeding are greater when faced with another difficult situation.

Actual danger and coping

Another factor that will influence the fate of the current problem-solving is the actual environmental danger from a reality point of view. That is, how dangerous is the situation in actuality; what are the real consequences. For football managers and other team members the loss of a game at the start of a season may not be viewed as dangerous. But, the loss of a game near the end of a season, when relegation threatens, may be perceived as highly dangerous. We also need to consider whether the stress continues and whether it gets worse, or does it start and then finish, or start and get better. Again, in the football world, one defeat may be stressful, but if this is followed by a victory in the next match the stress will soon reduce. Indeed, the football manager would welcome the chance of a mid-week game after a defeat on a Saturday as it would be an early opportunity to reduce the stress. It is when the team experience a string of defeats that stress really builds.

Support and coping

The other factor that is important in determining the outcome is the type and degree of environmental support. When a person is dealing with problems and is in crisis, they are not usually alone. In football, the manager has the coaches and other team members have the manager, other non-playing staff and their team mates around them, all of whom can rally around them at a time of crisis. This active support and offer of help are a potent factor in determining the outcome. But football management, and a growing number of other management and leadership positions, is also notorious for what I refer to as 'insecurity of tenure' which results in most football managers perceiving that they have little, if any, support when in a crisis. It would seem that this is becoming increasingly so in other industries.

Experience of failure and coping

Let's return to the influence of the past, the effect of unfortunate childhood experiences on situations in later life. I think it is important to say a few words about how these influences operate. The way they manifest themselves is by weakening the mental strength in the present, because during past situations there was experience of failure. This experience of failure becomes embedded in the manager or other team member, so that now when they are faced with a difficulty, they have a phantasy (a sort of flashback) of the inevitability of failure. In other words, they are not able to relate to things in a reality based manner because they automatically by-pass reality to connect with a previous failure. It is not difficult to envisage how this phantasy of the inevitability of failure can weaken the individual be they the manager or other team member. When the team manager or leader is certain that they are going to fail, they become weaker. It is usually only when the individual team manager or team member feels that they have a chance that they can stand up and fight.

Leader support and coping

One of the aspects of effective leadership is that the leader, at the moment of danger, increases the mental strength of other team members by painting a picture of the possibility of success. An excellent example of this sort of activity is to be found in the many war time speeches of Winston Churchill such as the famous and inspiring 'we will fight them on the beaches' speech. Here Churchill painted a hopeful picture that, even if they were to lose, they would do so by going down fighting. But, more than that, they were going to achieve something even in defeat. In other words, they were not going to just lie down and say the situation was hopeless. I feel I hardly need say this, but, of course, where the leader paints or implies a gloomy picture to other team members it will have the effect of weakening their mental strength.

Active support and the offer of help are a potent factor in determining the mental strength of team members. Yet, there are many football managers who constantly engage in unprofessional management practices. This includes the practice of giving players negative feedback, which, as all research and experience has shown, does not have the desired affect of motivating players, but, on the contrary, it demotivates. We have all seen and experienced the football manager from hell, as seen on television: the manager who treats the players like dirt. The manager who doesn't think the players have had an original thought in their entire life. The manager who is indifferent to their players, has a superior attitude, and considers players as something to use and abuse. The manager who has poor listening and feedback skills. The manager who can't delegate, develop their players, conduct performance appraisals, or establish priorities. The manager who has a short fuse and little patience with players. The manager who criticizes players personally for the work they do. The manager who has created a work environment full of fear and paranoia. All that this achieves is to weaken the mental strength of team members

Towards repression as coping

At this stage, I need to add a further complication, that concerning conflicting desires. In the last chapter I referred to the possibility that managers and other team members could have different individual desires and that these conflicting desires might create problems for the success of the team. In looking for an explanation of our behaviour, let's return for a moment to childhood. In their development, within the boundary of the self, the child achieves an inner organization of 'objects', ideas, events and values into a coherent system—usually using categories determined by the parents. Here the mind becomes a relatively orderly place and only a limited amount of chaos can be tolerated. In some cases ideas become unacceptable to consciousness if they conflict too much with other ideas. We deal with ideas that are incompatible by repression and other defence mechanisms.

To avoid the conflict between both loving and hating the mother that sometimes feeds them and sometimes is absent, the infant splits the 'object' which is mother into two parts: a good mother whom they love and a bad mother whom they hate. In adult life we employ precisely the same device. A graphic example concerns the leaders of the political parties that you support, who are seen as good and admired, while those of the other party are seen as bad and denigrated. Popular literature also relies heavily on the device of the good hero and the bad villain. The essence of splitting is that a good impulse and object cannot be split off without leaving a bad and vice versa. Thus idealization of one object (the Prime Minister or Republicans) necessarily entails the denigration of another (the Leader of the Opposition or Democrats)—and the greater the idealization the greater the denigration.

In football, managers frequently 'split' their team members into idealized team members who are regarded as 'good objects' who can do no wrong; and others who are denigrated and regarded as 'bad objects', who, in the eyes of the manager can do no right. And, of course, football supporters regularly use this device when splitting their own team, which they see as wonderful and without fault, and opposing teams (especially those in the same City), which they see as evil and subject of much venom and denigration. Thus, we see how passionate the 'local Derby's' between say, Newcastle and Sunderland, Arsenal and Tottenham, or Liverpool and Everton, can become. The greater the idealization of one team the greater the denigration of the other.

By means of the primitive processes of *splitting, projection* and particularly of *introjection*, a rich world of inner objects, or representations in the mind of external objects; be these 'objects' significant people, values, feelings or concepts, is built up. In this way the manager may hold, as an internal object, a representation of a past manager from which they may obtain support in the absence of the external manager. Thus, the football manager would frequently refer to what Ron Greenwood did or what Bill Shankly did. In essence what was happening when he was experiencing a problem was that he was recalling a mental image of these people and looking to them for support by relating to what they might have done in the current situation. The same thing may apply to circumstances where the manager or leader has a perceived enemy to deal with. Here a manager may obtain support in some sense from an internal enemy; they will recall the mental image of a past enemy and the manner of dealing with them and repeat that behaviour.

Early introjections (taking in of external objects), since they are virtually all the infant has, are particularly potent and the inner 'objects' (the mental images) they create are never forgotten. These early introjections, which of necessity are of parents or parental figures, create an inner object commonly referred to as the conscience or in technical terms the superego. The introjection of the 'good' parent creates what I shall refer to as the ideal conscience, that is, a sense of ideals and positive morality—a pattern of what to do. And introjection of the 'bad' parent creates what I shall refer to as the persecutory conscience, a sense of guilt and negative morality —of what not to do. Conscience, then, is built up by identifying with, that is forming and taking in and retaining mental images of, parental figures. It will be realized that these images may not be built on the reality of parents' behaviour, but on the way that the infant perceives reality, which of course may be total phantasy. Thus the reality may have been that the parent was very caring, but that their behaviour was perceived as uncaring by the infant. As will be further explained, this same sort of process may occur later in life in exchanges between managers and other team members.

Conflict resolution begins as soon as the infant has some control or restraint imposed by the parent upon its behaviour. In other words, as soon as some semblance of conscience has developed. In later life, conflicts may be between needs in any system or regarding any purpose. Each of us has only a certain amount of mental energy and the total amount of mental energy available at any one time is finite and therefore the investment of energy in one particular mental process means that less is available for any other. For instance, a particular memory or association may be energized but, if it is considered dangerous or painful, it may be repressed into the unconscious. As an equal amount of energy must be used to keep it repressed, less is available for other mental work. We can therefore say that the manager or leader who has a high degree of self-awareness will be more able to use their mental energy in the service of the task.

Although no longer conscious in adult life, the imaginings and memories of infantile experience, particularly when associated with anxiety, have a profound influence on subsequent mental development and help to determine the character of personal and social relationships, cultural interests and way of living—they become part of the boundaried self. The growth of an infant in a human environment creates a transactional field in which most affect—or feeling—becomes oriented to human objects. Thus even if the object is not human, for example a construct such as a football club or other organization, it is associated with human activity and the feelings about the club or organization will be those associated with humans.

Conflict, which simply means that two or more desires are opposed in a living situation, is present and vital throughout human life. The nature and outcome of the conflict that takes place within the mind between the two sets of antagonistic tendencies results in anxiety. Resolution of conflict is more often a compromise than a solution. It is often positive and may lead to adjustment and adaptation and the learning of new skills. For example, a football manager may find that they are faced with a conflict concerning their desire to win a game and a desire to be fair to a player. The player may have been in the team recently and given their all, but to enable the manager to play their favoured formation they may now need to drop the player. The anxiety may be so great that the manager finds a way of resolving the conflict by adapting or adjusting the formation to accommodate the team member. In doing so, they learn new approaches to the game.

Faced with anxiety there are several courses of action we can take. At one extreme we have repression—the exclusion of any direct influence on consciousness or on behaviour; the individual then normally becoming quite unaware of the existence of any such tendency within their mind. Such an outcome of conflict, in which one tendency is driven down to the unconscious and confined there by the other, is usually designated by the technical term 'repression'.

Unconscious processes

It may help, at this stage, if I further briefly explain what has previously been referred to as the unconscious. William James, one of America's most famous psychologists, repeatedly stressed that 'our normal waking consciousness is but one special type of consciousness, while all about it parted from it by the filmiest of screens there lie potential forms of consciousness entirely different'. It is as if our everyday awareness is but an insignificant island, surrounded by a vast ocean of unsuspected and uncharted consciousness, whose waves beat continuously upon the shores of our normal awareness, until, quite spontaneously, they may break through, flooding our island awareness with knowledge of a vast, largely unexplored, but intensely real domain.

Of all desires that are active and effective in a person at a given time only some are conscious. Others are preconscious, by which we mean that they are potentially conscious. Still others are unconscious, by which we literally mean that they are not even potentially conscious. Perception and behaviour are conscious and preconscious for most practical purposes, although even they can, in principle, become unconscious, at least in some of their aspects. In the context of this book, the terms 'conscious', 'preconscious', and '*unconscious*' refer, first of all, to desires. We can be conscious of them and we can feel them and comment about them. Yet we need not necessarily be conscious of all of those that determine what we think or do in a given situation. Consciousness provides us with a picture of something, but not necessarily with all there is to be seen. In fact, the picture it provides may sometimes be rather inadequate.

Repression

To understand in a very simple way how psychoanalytic theory can explain human motivation, we need to understand not only the unconscious mind but also repression. As has been explained above, the former implies mental tendencies and traces of past experiences which once acted in full consciousness. These affect our behaviour without entering consciousness; they may also come back into consciousness again, given the appropriate stimulus. But as was first discovered by Freud, the unconscious mind consists mainly of repressed sentiments which have their foundations in infancy. The term repression means the exclusion of painful and unpleasant material from consciousness. An example might concern a child who experiences the break up of their parents marriage, with the father leaving the family home and setting up home with another woman. The child may feel distraught, angry and let down but will repress or blot out these painful and unpleasant feelings from their conscious.

It is not difficult to understand, then, that repression is a defence mechanism. However, it must also be apparent that it is also an unconscious one, for the subject—like the child referred to above— does not realize that they are repressing certain sentiments. As the infant grows up they soon realize that certain of their actions and most importantly their feelings evoke disapproval in adults and these forbidden impulses tend to be pushed out of consciousness by this mechanism. From time to time, footballers will experience feelings of fear, as we all do. However, in the macho world of football any team member that admitted to such feelings would be regarded as 'having no bottle'. In such circumstances, footballers tend to repress or put this feeling out of their conscious mind. Although repressed and unconscious this does not mean, however, that these feelings are not present, they are simply blotted out. Still being part of us they affect our behaviour in ways of which we are not aware. There is considerable agreement that our behaviour is frequently influenced by motives and attitudes of which we are quite unaware.

We can say, then, that the essence of repression lies in the function of rejecting and keeping something out of consciousness. When we experience extreme anxiety the object of the desire involved tends to crumble a little. If deprivation of the desire persists, extreme anxiety or panic will recur and if that happens often enough the object of the desire will eventually 'collapse' altogether. It will be blotted out from the person's psychological world. For example a team member may have a desperate desire to win the League, to be successful and to be a champion. After one or two defeats they may experience anxiety when they see the satisfaction of their desires slipping away. After several defeats they may experience extreme anxiety when the desire will be 'collapsed' and forgotten. Repression has been achieved and the object is annulled, psychologically speaking.

In its most primitive form, repression would take care of a desire that has become unobtainable and does not yet have any substitute or derivative desires. As in the example above, the more difficult it gets, the more it will take on the character of 'mourning'. Once all repressions have been completed, mourning is over. For a manager who is trying to understand why other team members are not performing in a motivated fashion, they might consider that what is happening can be explained by repression. This may be expressed in behaviour such as laziness, social withdrawal, secretiveness and indecision, all of which are of value to the individual in reducing anxiety. For the manager the challenge is to help team members by doing all they can to help reduce anxiety so that reality-based solutions can be found. Repression of this kind is the most primitive of all the defence mechanisms. We shall see that all other forms of defence mechanisms use, among other things, substitution of another object or of a derivative desire. Repression in its most primitive form does not.

Defence mechanisms

Defence mechanisms are specific types of learning not to like. In the following paragraphs I shall try to explain some of those that we more frequently use. Several are referred to in everyday conversation and will be familiar to the reader. All of these unconscious psychological techniques of thinking and feeling, have the objective of reducing anxiety from stress and conflict among different needs. As with much of our behaviour defence mechanisms are not to be regarded as good or bad. Above all, they serve a useful and necessary purpose of reducing anxiety.

Displacement

A frequently used defence mechanism is that known as 'displacement'. As its name implies this is the substitution of one desire by another or of one object of satisfaction by another. For example, during a football match a team member may become angry because the team are losing and develop a desire to hit the referee, but, fortunately for all concerned, when leaving the field of play they kick the changing room door instead. What they are doing is displacing or substituting their desire to hit the referee onto an inanimate object. You will note here that although it is a door, the same feelings are associated with this object as with the referee. Displacement refers to some acute impossibility to satisfy one desire and its ready substitution by another. Thus, in the example above, the original desire of the team member would possibly have concerned success and achievement, but being unsuccessful in satisfying that desire they substitute a desire to hit the referee. There is no reference as to what will become of the desire in the long run. However, there is a reference to the degree of control involved. It is a more primitive desire that gets satisfied, be it for no other reason than that the object (the door) matters less than were the team member to satisfy the original desire.

Displacement is, then, a shifting of one aspect of a conflict from the original object to a substitute object. In this way the conflict no longer exists in the original focus. Perhaps the most common form of displacement is, as in the example given above, with the affect of hostile aggression that arises from frustration. The team manager may be frustrated in a situation over which they have no control, such as other team members seemingly forgetting the basics as practised and agreed in training, and now being badly organized with the result that they are being beaten. The increase of the manager's undischarged hostile aggression may then be directed toward a particular team member who is seen as a 'bad' object. This is the familiar and widely used technique that we refer to as scapegoating.

Sublimation

Like displacement, the defence mechanism that we call 'sublimation' also concerns the substitution of one desire by another. The difference here, however, is that the substitute desire is socially acceptable and much more controlled than in displacement. It also differs in the fact that it does not refer so much to an instant relief but rather to a long-range solution for desires that have become impossible to satisfy. An example might be a football player who has a desire to be successful on the pitch, who, finding themselves released from their club, takes up football video games. In like manner, a football manager may find a long-range solution to their failed desire to lead a successful team by becoming a television or radio pundit. Sublimation is the redirection of unacceptable aspects of the self into areas which are acceptable to others. The term sublimation is used to cover all conflict resolution which leads to satisfactory results for the individual and perhaps his surrounding society and culture. It is the most desirable mechanism, as it is most constructive. It makes the unacceptable acceptable and useful.

In reading about the lives of many great people, it is often possible to assess the effects of sublimation on their careers. It cannot be coincidence that most have achieved success in spite of obstacles, as much as because of positive goals, support, and encouragement. Indeed, it appears that a combination of strong frustration and positive encouragement is a part of every great person's biography. There are several examples of footballers whose careers have been shortened by injury which has, in turn, resulted in the impossibility of them achieving their desires to be great players, who have then sublimated their desires by substituting a desire to be a great manager. It seems that sublimated desires can sometimes be stronger than the original. A classic example may be that of Brian Clough. After a successful playing career was cut short by a serious injury he then embarked upon a successful career as a football manager.

Rationalization

Perhaps the most familiar type of defence mechanism is that which we refer to as 'rationalization'. I feel sure that every reader will be aware of this form of coping and will be able to reflect on the many occasions that they have used this defence mechanism when faced with anxiety. Basically, what we refer to as 'rationalization' is the unconscious manipulation of our opinions to evade the recognition of the unpleasant or forbidden. Thus a footballer who had difficulty coping during a game might claim that they did not know what they were supposed to do. Or, the football manager who had just seen their dreams and desires frustrated following another defeat may rationalize their position by saying something like, 'It's only a game'. Rationalization could be called a denial of internal psychological 'facts'.

Regression

Another of the well known and frequently used defence mechanisms is that called 'regression'. I have already referred to this type of activity, when regression was described as a reversion to a less mature level of behaviour. The basis of regression is that the individual mentally returns to an earlier period of life which was more gratifying or less stressful than their present period. Doubtless many readers will recall occasions when they have been accused, or have accused others, of 'behaving like children'—a sure sign of regression. In its mildest form it is the result of a drop-out of a desire without any replacement by new substitute desires. It's a bit like 'sulking' or 'having a tantrum'. In all other defence mechanisms new substitute desires are likely to be recruited in order to make up for the loss of a given one. In regression, no new substitute desires have been found. It is rather like a manager or team member giving up on their desires for success and treating a match, not as a serious business, but simply as play. It is the last alternative. Here the manager or other team members regain their balance on a lower level.

Denial

Another of those defence mechanisms we will all be familiar with is that which we refer to as 'denial'. As the name suggests, denial is the unconscious process of disowning some aspect(s) of a conflict, with the result that the conflict no longer appears to exist. It is to be distinguished from conscious denial, which is a wilful act. Denial refers to aspects of a situation that the person does not want to perceive. The manager who has lost the Cup Final may pretend that it is not really a loss; that they did well to get to the final anyway. Or, as the manager I worked with would say when the team had been winning but only for the opposition to equalize late in the game—'We'd have settled for a draw before the game'. In both of these instances there is a denial that there was a loss, which is what many of us who have suffered a loss may find ourselves doing. A denial is a more or less futile attempt to deny the obvious reality.

Projection

I have already referred to the primitive defence mechanism known as 'projection', in some detail above. Projection is the process of attributing one's own unacceptable behaviour to others. A mechanical comparison is that of the film projector: an image inside the object is thrown out onto a screen, where it then appears to have its primary existence. It is the thrusting forth onto the external world, or perhaps more accurately into another person or group, of an individual's unconscious wishes and ideas, which would be painful if accepted as part of the self. This may sound complicated but the following example will help to explain what I mean. A team member may be offered an improved contract with another club. In one sense they may feel excited and pleased by this seemingly great opportunity. In another sense they may experience a great deal of guilt and unhappiness about being disloyal to their current manager who has done so much to develop their career. The way the team member deals with this situation is to split off the painful and unacceptable feelings and project them into the manager who they then treat as if they had been the disloyal party.

Some projection occurs in all persons, although usually not with any major dysfunctional consequences. Some common examples of projection are these: the promiscuous housewife who sees all other women as sexually evil and promiscuous; the nefarious business-man who believes that rivals are making every effort to undercut them; the ageing player who believes that younger players are jealous of them; the neglecting manager who accuses the coaches of neglecting and ignoring team members; the Rovers fan who knows that all United fans are barbarians. In all these examples we can see how painful and unacceptable desires and feelings are transferred to the 'outside world', usually to other people.

Projection, almost like displacement, refers to a more or less transitional condition. Repressions are already operating by the time projection becomes necessary. Projection, like all defence mechanisms, is automatic and involuntary. We are not aware that this is what we are doing, as is explained in the following example. During a game of football the anxiety level may be rising for a number of reasons. As a result, a team member may see the referee as threatening and have the painful and unacceptable desire to hit them. At a surface level, the team member really does see the referee as threatening but, at another level, through the process of projection they may perceive the referee as being an angry individual who wishes to do the very same thing to themselves. In this case, a desire within the player is perceived in the outside world or, more specifically, in another person (the referee). Like all defence mechanisms there is a benefit in that this projected desire helps to check the desire within the team member. More precisely speaking: that substitute satisfaction, which is sought in the disguise of another person, here the referee, seems not only to reduce the intensity of the desire within the team member to some extent, but also to make it more dangerous to satisfy the desire directly.

Introjection

I have also referred to the defence mechanism known as 'introjection' at some length above. Introjection is simply the taking in of an object be that object another person, a quality of another person, or a concept. Put another way, it is the substitution of a desire by an 'existent' external desire, or the adoption of a desire of the 'outside world', preferably of other people, to replace one's own. This sort of defence mechanism would be particularly obvious after a defeat when the team would trudge off the field back to the dressing room full of anxiety. Here the manager would set the tone be that anger, sound reason, despair or whatever and within a short while other team members would take in the quality of the manager and respond in like manner. It seems clear that if the manager is able to maintain self-control and adopt a reality-based approach to the situation it will encourage the other team members to do like-wise.

Reaction-formation

A defence mechanism, not commonly well known by its technical name, but which may nevertheless be recognized by its description is that known as 'reaction-formation', which is prevalent in everyday life. This is the mechanism whereby one tendency is hidden from awareness by its opposite. For example, a footballer, because of infantile experience, is inclined to behave in an overly aggressive manner, may unconsciously respond by doing the opposite and playing like a big softie. Reaction-formation is the substitution of a desire by an 'opposite' one; whereby 'opposite' means greater than usual difference in satisfaction value. Instead of modifying their desires, so that they become a moderately aggressive player, the team member hides their aggressive desires by playing in a gentle manner. The essence of this defence mechanism is that an unconsciously desired behaviour or attitude that has been con-sciously disowned is replaced by the reverse behaviour. This may lead to the sort of situation where a team member who resents being dependent on their manager loudly asserts their independence.

Phobia

Another defence mechanism which is commonly referred to, possibly in other contexts, is that which we call 'phobia'. Phobia is a fear which, on first sight, does not make sense. A person may have all sorts of fears, for example, that of appearing in front of a large crowd. More precisely, we can say that an individual faces a situation, similar to previous experiences, which they simply could not handle. Staying away from such a situation altogether, or running away when they find that such a situation has sneaked up on them, may be their only solution. That means of dealing with the anxiety of such a solution, however, is the phobia. There are milder and more sensible forms too, such as the driver who has had an accident and does not dare to drive for a while thereafter. Or, the footballer who has broken a leg and is concerned about going into a tackle again. In fact, all situations where we are learning to avoid could be called phobic. An example, is the extremely mild form of behaviour adopted by some managers, who continue to wear the same tie or the same suit fearing that any change will result in defeat.

Identification

A defence mechanism which is similar to introjection is that which we refer to as 'identification'. As in introjection, identification will also involve the substitution of one's desires by 'existent' external desires. What the person adopts will come closer to what they mean to adopt. Identification by a team member with a star player such as Pele or Ronaldo is a defence to a desire that cannot be or is not being, satisfied, namely, to earn all the glamour and fame and be admired by many.

Identification with the aggressor

A particular form of identification is that referred to as 'identification with the aggressor'. To conquer our misery we can identify with the person who appears as a source of danger to our desires. Thus we can take the word identification as meaning our desire to behave and be like the aggressor who is thus internalized in our mind. This is the same sort of process as the mechanism of introjection referred to before. In this process the manager or leader is seen as a source of danger, because they are perceived as being all powerful and demand submission by bullying and humiliating the other team members. To conquer their misery team members identify with the manager or leader and seek for self-realization in 'being like the aggressor'.

Identification means that we want to be like the aggressor. Thus the aggressor that is introjected in the mind, is the aggressor with all their severity, their authority, their absolute law, their omnipotence. This introjection now occupies a special place in the mind, constituting what Freud called the super-ego. One of the results of this sort of defence mechanism is that those identifying with the aggressor take on the characteristics of the aggressor. This is why we see the phenomenon whereby a child who is often and severely punished by their parents will frequently become such a punisher themselves, whether with respect to others, or by turning against the self. Thus, abused children become abusing parents. In the same way, abused team members become abusing team managers and leaders when they take on those roles.

This is the core of the problem in industries such as the football industry where they train and develop their own personnel. Here, the most common way that managers learn is from their own experience of the managers that they play for. This frequently results in the perpetuation of outdated management practices. Players are at times bullied, humiliated and sometimes berated for their failings in public. This inadequate style of management, when coupled with the tremendous demands that professional footballers currently face, leads to great anxiety. One of the results is that players turn to drink or drugs as a means of coping. A further sad consequence is, that if their manager or leader was abusing, then they will most likely perpetuate this way of managing when they take up the role. As was said above, I cannot stress the importance of role models enough. This has implications for the way that the leader or manager approaches the notion of discipline and punishment, which are topics for later chapters.

CHAPTER FIVE

Authority — who does what?

T his chapter is about a concept that has become much discredited during the last century; namely, that which we refer to as 'authority'. That this should be so is, to say the least, unfortunate as authority is one of, if not perhaps the most important concept for any manager to understand. At the heart of many organizational difficulties lies a lack of clarity regarding issues of authority. To appreciate just how important the notion of authority is we only have to reflect on the fact that we all start our lives dependent on authority figures. We can, therefore, begin to have an appreciation of the likely effect that authority will have on all of us throughout our lives.

Whether we like it or not we cannot escape the notion of authority. Any cursory reflection on our history will show us that natural social groups have developed in the form of families, clans, tribes, states, and nations. Within these groups, superior–subordinate relationships have developed in the form of status and role systems. Based on any number of characteristics, power structures evolve naturally and they, in turn, are perpetuated by tradition. Indeed, it may be hard to imagine that the human community could proceed in its endeavours without an institutionalized power structure, which we call authority. However, as in so many similar conceptual frameworks, what is required is a workable compromise. On the one hand, we need enough authority to ensure co-operative action and progress towards group goals. But on the other hand, we also want to encourage individuality, creativity, and innovation. At one extreme, anarchy is inconceivable; but so is the other extreme, authoritarianism.

'Authority' may be seen as a neutral term, but such is the emotion surrounding the exercise of authority that there are many misconceptions. A common error is for authority to be confused with both influence and authoritarianism. In effect, 'authority' means that the person (or persons) with authority has the sole right to do anything within their terms of authority. This is in contrast to influence, which may be affected over any area, but the influencer may have to make reference to someone or something else for the necessary approvals. In other words, influence may not be co-existent with authority. Moving now to authoritarianism, this is simply a particular kind of authority that exists at the expense of freedom. On the one hand, authoritarianism results from an obsession with hierarchical relationships to the degree that superiors eschew consultation with subordinates; and on the other hand, subordinates are disposed toward zealous obedience to hierarchic superiors. Thus, we may end up with a collusive dynamic leading to authoritarianism.

It is easy to take a puritanical approach to management and leadership and to condemn those who adopt an authoritarian manner, but we need to see the manager or leader's role in the context of the task. As previously said being a manager in any organization is a difficult job. Being a football manager is a very difficult job. Quite often the difficulty of the work results in the manager becoming angry, frustrated, worried, and even being in a position where they do not know where to turn to next; what on earth can they do to move things forward. Sometimes even the whole world seems against them. The Chairman or other Board members are being difficult for any one of a number of reasons, lack of money, lack of success, or personal preferences about players or team selection. The coaching staff don't want to listen, they want to adopt their own ways of working regardless of what you want. The physiotherapist doesn't seem to understand that you want players back in the team—yesterday. The players are all walking around and looking at you as if you are an alien and while they do as you tell them, they appear to be grudging and sullen. Not least is the insecurity of tenure that goes with the job—football managers frequently get the sack!

Little wonder then, that managers may become totally engrossed in themselves. Totally absorbed with what they can do to get themselves out of this ghastly situation and make life better for themselves. Therefore, they think long and hard and come up with a solution that they are confident will solve the problems. Having come up with a decision they then tell others what they have decided and demand their support. By now they are beginning to feel a bit better because they have worked out some of their own problems and seemingly found a way forward. However, all that they have been concerned with is satisfaction of:

- their *own* needs;
- their *own* desires; and
- their *own* gratification.

This has been at the expense of other team members:

- needs;
- desires; and
- gratification.

And this is the struggle. It is about managers having to struggle with the process of managing the boundary between what is inside themselves and what is outside, by developing sufficient self-awareness and self-control while still carrying out their primary task of managing a successful football team.

Abuse of authority

Authority does not mean that the person (or persons) with authority has the sole right to do anything that they wish; it is solely confined to that which is within their terms of authority. It does not mean that the manager or leader can:

- treat other team members as they wish;

- make all the decisions;
- ignore the desires of other team members;
- assume that other team members are mindless and treat them accordingly;
- act as if they are better than other team members;
- grab all the head lines, grab the full credit and act as if the team results were as a result of a solo performance; and
- ignore the feelings of other team members.

In many situations, perhaps as a result of the above sort of dynamics, the concept of 'authority' is considered as distasteful. In view of the fact that we have experienced the tyranny and injustice of world wars and of communism it may not be surprising that there should exist a certain resentment and fear of all forms of authority. Under Hitler and Stalin, and subsequent Soviet and Chinese Communist administrations, as they overturned the old order, children were encouraged to betray their parents in the name of the 'cause' and the concept of authority became meaningless, morally and spiritually destitute, a deformed and monstrous rootless growth. The aforesaid pair, who can be regarded as the ultimate in authoritarianism, can perhaps be held responsible for, among other things, the widespread distaste for authority current today in the West. Anybody giving a peremptory order, no matter how valid or necessary, is liable to be called 'Hitler' or told to 'go back to Russia'.

But, we should not be fooled into thinking that this sort of behaviour only happens in other places. We only have to look at our own recent work history to see that much of our management in the industrial era was based on an old military model (probably the only one available at the time), which involved highly autocratic practices whereby non-managers were treated as an extension of the machinery that they operated. What they were most certainly not treated as, was human beings with brains that could contribute to the success and creativity of the organization. Although we have seemingly come a long way in recent times, it was only a short while ago that Jack Walsh was writing about his experience as Chief Executive of GE when he said, 'We hired them for their backs, arms and legs and forgot that they had a brain'.

As we shall see, old habits die hard, mainly because of the values that we internalize from our various experiences. When we are spending at least a third of every working day in the actual or virtual presence of an authority figure (or figures) it will not be surprising that successive managers have identified with their managers or leaders and taken on much of the old military style of leadership. This is so in many organizations I have worked and consulted in, not least, the football industry. In the next few paragraphs I will give some examples of what I mean by this style of management and leadership. However, I should like to stress that an autocratic approach is not the only way to manage; and, furthermore, that if we want a highly disciplined, committed team, it is far from the most successful way to manage.

Many of those reading this book will have seen and experienced the football manager from hell, as seen on television:

- managers who treat 'their' players like dirt;
- managers who don't think 'their' players have had an original thought in their entire life;
- managers who are indifferent to 'their' players, have a superior attitude, and consider players as something to use and abuse;
- managers who have poor listening and feedback skills;
- managers who can't delegate, develop 'their' players, conduct performance appraisals, or establish priorities;
- managers who have a short fuse and little patience with players;
- managers who criticize players personally for the work they do; and
- managers who have created a work environment full of fear and paranoia.

I wish this were an exaggeration, but many of us will have seen and know managers who, if anything, are worse than described, the sort that will even resort to physical coercion. This style of management and leadership is destructive and damaging. Team members who are treated in this manner are likely to have such a poor view of their worth or such a low self-esteem, that they can have little pride in their behaviour. Here the manager's role is paramount. How can any manager expect their players to behave in a professional manner when they are led in such a non-professional way. By following outmoded styles of management that were originally designed to run an efficient army in the last century, managers and leaders are continuing to use non-professional management practices. This includes practices such as giving players negative feedback, which, as all research and experience has shown, does not have the desired affect of motivating players, but precisely the opposite effect—it demotivates.

The most common way that football managers learn is not from books or training courses, but from their own experience of the managers that they work for. Doubtless, those in other organizations where personnel do attend training events are also strongly influenced by their managers and leaders. This frequently results in the perpetuation of outdated management practices. For example, football team members are frequently bullied, humiliated, and sometimes berated for their failings, in public. This inadequate style of management, when coupled with the tremendous demands that professional footballers and other work team members currently face, leads to great anxiety. One of the results of not having good enough management is that they turn to drink or drugs as an escape from this anxiety. In football this is a rapidly growing problem.

One is tempted to ask why it is that managers and leaders who constantly abuse their authority, only to achieve negative results, continue to adopt this unsuccessful approach. At the time of writing, no one can be under any illusions that the state of British football, compared with that in other parts of the world, is parlous. It lacks creativity, discipline, freedom, and skill. Many identify problems associated with the induction and development of youth, blaming a lack of playing fields and school attitudes. These may be associated factors, but, when it comes to identifying the real causes of unsatisfactory performance in the football industry, there is one simple theme, managerial incompetence, leading to player incompetence. Without referring to specific incidents, I feel sure that many would agree that in nearly all instances, we can identify managerial malpractice as encouraging and supporting practices that produce unprofessional, unproductive, and incompetent players. So, to return to the question why don't they change, I would answer it with the following analogy; if you are brought up in a butcher's shop it is exceedingly difficult to appreciate vegetarianism. In other words, because of their exclusive experience of working in an authoritarian world those in football (and other industries) are unable to even appreciate a different approach. In effect, it is all too threatening. It would mean giving up so much of their previous knowledge and understanding that it is just not thinkable. However, the introduction of managers and leaders, not to mention other team members, from overseas gives reason for hope, and may begin to cause those in authority to think again.

Sources of authority

To gain a deeper understanding of authority, it will help to explore something of its sources and foundations. In practice, authority— the right to carry out task leadership—stems from various sources. The most obvious, and most often related to, is the notion of authority as institutionalized power, which is established legally to achieve the objectives of a formal organization. It is based on legal foundations (e.g., legislation, articles of incorporation, partnership agreements, bylaws) that define an organization's mission and empower its members to carry out its activities. The fountainhead of all authority in a private enterprise such as a Football Club is the owner(s), and in a corporation, it is the shareholders. It is they who delegate the authority to managers and leaders and, most importantly, set the boundaries of that authority. What we are referring to here is 'managerial authority' which refers to that part of the leader's authority that has been delegated to them by the institution they work in.

In many organizations the extent and details of this sort of authority is contained in a Job Description and perhaps a Job Specification. These documents, taken together, formally set out the boundaries of the authority that is being delegated to the individual manager. This sort of formality may not occur in the football setting, but some form of verbal agreement on the boundaries of the football manager's authority will almost certainly take place at the time when they are appointed. It may be in general terms, such as the manager being delegated authority for all matters concerning the team. Or, there may be limitations on the general theme. Whatever the 'job description' may be, it is important to understand that it concerns authority for matters which have been delegated by someone who, in turn, has the right to delegate that degree of authority.

'Leadership authority' is very different and refers to that aspect of the manager or leader's authority that is derived from the recognition of other team members that they have the capacity to carry out the task. Here, following Tannanbaum et al. (1961), I am defining 'leadership' as 'always involving attempts on the part of the leader (influencer) to affect (influence) the behaviour of a follower'. However, I have to confess to a degree of discomfort with the term 'follower'. My discomfort is with the connotation of a set and determined hierarchical relationship between *the* leader and their followers. I have in mind a picture of the manager being *the* leader, the one with all the knowledge, the one with all the ideas, and the followers being expected to thank the leader profusely and blindly follow whatever they say. I much prefer to think of leaders and 'joiners': of any member of the team leading on a particular issue and others (including the manager) joining them to further consider and build on the idea that the team member seeks to influence them about.

There are, of course, some aspects of the manager or leader's role that are their personal responsibility. For example, the manager or leader must take personal responsibility for ensuring that the organization is aligned and that all the component parts are pointing in the same direction or are working to the same ends. In a football club this means ensuring that those responsible for the care and maintenance of the pitch, the laundry people, the dressing room attendant, the physiotherapist, the coaches, scouts, and various others are all aligned and heading in the desired direction. The leader or manager must also personally set and encourage the values and create a long-term vision for the club. However, while these are personal responsibilities of the manager or leader, it is also highly desirable that others are consulted and their views taken into consideration *before* a decision is made by the manager. In this way, the manager or leader will ensure that all are working together to achieve not only the same objectives but *shared objectives*. To achieve this position, the starting point for any manager or leader is an ability to have an awareness of others and to value them and their contribution—to see them as prized assets rather than someone to be kicked around.

The way other team members are viewed can affect their performance. It is a well known fact that if you treat team members like fools they are likely to act like fools—it is what we call self-fulfilling prophecies. Fortunately, the reverse is also true, if we treat team members as bright and clever they are likely to act in a bright and clever way. This is important, because, unlike those situations referred to above where the manager or leader must personally take responsibility, there are many others where all team members can play a leadership role. Indeed, when it comes to determining how the team will carry out the task of playing and winning football matches, I would suggest that all team members will need to be committed at multiple levels if they are to be successful.

It is in this context that I stated in Chapter 1, that, among other things, the good manager or leader is one who encourages leadership in other team members. The better that the leader or manager is in fulfilling this aim—the more successful will be the team. It is my contention that this is what makes the difference, this is what makes a great team and consequently, a great leader. For the leader or manager who feels the demands to succeed lying heavily on their shoulders there will be many times when the temptation to 'take control' and to impose a solution will be exceedingly strong. It is the great manager or leader who has the self-awareness and the self-control to withstand these many pressures, to be aware of and understand the needs, emotions, and desires of other team members and thus, to be able to encourage them to provide leadership.

Managerial and leadership authority reinforce each other; both are, in turn, dependent upon other sources of authority, such as the leader's technical knowledge, their personality, their human skills, and the social tasks and responsibilities they assume outside the organization. The manager or leader is responsible not only to the football club, but also to the other staff, to their professional and ethical values, to the community, and to society at large; responsibility and accountability represent the reciprocal obligation of the manager to the sources of their authority. The management structure can be considered functional when the distribution and delegation of authority, task performance, and task monitoring are matched by appropriate—that is, sufficient and stable but not excessive—investment of authority in managerial leaders at all levels.

Clarity in authority relations

Difficulties may arise when an individual has responsibility for some work but lacks the concomitant authority. For example, a foreman may be held responsible for the punctuality of other workers, but is not given the authority to discipline them for lateness. A football example may be where the manager or leader is responsible for the team performance, but is not allowed to drop a player, or is pressured into keeping a player in the team. The converse of this situation, which may also cause difficulties, is when a person is empowered to take decisions, but is not held responsible for what results. For example, personnel specialists may have the authority for recruitment decisions in some companies, but they are not held responsible for staff performance which is a matter for line managers. In football, the same sort of situation may occur when Directors take authority for recruitment of players, but the manager has responsibility for their subsequent performance.

Let's return for a moment to the issue of 'managerial authority', those things that are delegated to you as manager or leader and which set the boundaries of your role. What are these things you are responsible for? What is the position you are being promoted to? What is your authority? What is not your authority? Before taking up your role you need to know and understand where and what the boundaries are. Some may appear obvious. For example, it may seem common sense that the manager of a football team should and needs to have authority for the following:

- team selection;
- discipline;
- levels of pay and bonuses; and,
- for the results of the team.

However, what may appear to be common sense frequently proves not to be so commonly shared. Difficulties start to arise when we ask the question whose common sense are we referring to? For the football manager, common sense may mean that all matters pertaining to team performance and development should be part of their authority. However, for the club owner(s), common sense may mean that some matters pertaining to team performance and development should be part of their authority. Thus, some owners may feel they have the authority to hire and fire players. Some may feel they have the authority, on occasion, to reward individual players intrinsically or extrinsically. Some may feel they have the authority to make public comments about individual players or team performance. As has been stated above, in many football clubs, the practice now is for the owners to have the authority to recruit new players.

This conflict of understanding regarding authority is not confined to matters concerning delegation of authority to the appropriate level. There are also situations where managers feel they have authority for matters beyond an appropriate level. The classic example has to be that of Bryan Clough who, throughout his career, is reported to have demanded near total autonomy in the clubs where he worked. An example of this is demonstrated in the following extracts taken from 'Clough a Biography' (Francis, 1987). The perspective of the Derby County Chairman, Sam Longson, is clearly demonstrated in the following: 'He (Clough) thought he was God—thought he could twist me round his little finger like he has everyone else. How wrong he was. When I imposed my will he couldn't take it. He could never accept that there was another authority at the club and it's been his problem everywhere'. Clough's perspective is demonstrated as follows: 'What brought on the bust-up at Derby was a bloke called Longson who wanted success as an old man. He got a partnership which brought him success, then he wanted a bigger say'. Shortly after this highly toxic conflict Clough resigned.

Whenever and wherever there are differences regarding the understanding of authority by the various personnel concerned, the result must inevitably be conflict. Not a healthy conflict but a toxic and highly damaging conflict that can result in stress and dysfunctionality throughout the organization. An example concerns a football manager appointed to a Football League side, who, when he took on the role knew that by reputation the club chairman was a strong-willed individual who liked to become involved in team matters. However, from his previous experience, he clearly felt that this was not a problem, because he would have authority for all matters concerning the performance and development of the team. Not long after he took up his role, the manager wanted to drop a player whom he considered was not good enough. When the chairman heard of this, through his contacts with the players, he approached the manager and persuaded him that this particular player was such a favourite of the fans that it would be bad business to leave him out and left the manager in little doubt that he should continue to play him.

The effect of this conflict was that some team members lost respect for the team manager, while some lost respect for the chairman. Some felt they were being handicapped by the presence of this player in the team, others felt they were being handicapped by a manager who didn't know what he was doing. I am also sure that there were other less obvious conflicts occurring. Whatever, the result was a great degree of confusion, frustration and even stress arising from the conflict not least because the other team members did not know which authority to follow. Whichever way they went, be it with the manager or the chairman they would be wrong with the other. A situation which can be compared with a child who has one parent saying 'go to bed' and the other saying 'no, you can stay up'.

The moral of all this is that it is in everyone's interest, essential even, if the team is going to perform to its best ability, that these matters are explored and mutually agreed before managers takes up their post. No team can perform while team members are suffering from confusion, conflict, and stress. A result of this dysfunction is that all of the attention may become focused on the manager and chairman rather than on the needs of the team. Thus, it becomes almost impossible for the manager or leader to provide the sort of containment and support that is necessary to encourage leadership in other team members. The result of this sort of dysfunction can only be a poorly motivated team who produce equally poor results.

Clarity in the leader's role

For the manager or leader of teams it is important that they adopt the appropriate leadership approach as guided and required by the circumstances. In this respect, the contingency approach to leadership referred to by Lawrence and Lorsch (1967) is a practical and helpful guide for managers. However, it is not simply a matter of selection—if only it were that easy! We are also influenced by our cultural and organizational experiences which may create an inner conflict in the leader or manager, which is just as strong and dysfunctional to the working of the team as that concerning the various parties concerned.

The true nature of authority is that the leader or manager is able to directly affect the behaviour of a team member if they possess authority with respect to that team member. However, the real source of authority possessed by a manager or leader lies in the *acceptance* of its exercise by those who are subject to it. A football manager, or any other team manager, may have the authority to tell other team members how to play or what to do, but it is other team members who determine the authority which the manager or leader may wield. In effect, formal authority is nominal authority. It only becomes real when it is accepted. No matter that the manager may tell them to do, or demand that they do, it may all be in vain. A manager or leader may possess formal authority, but this is meaningless unless that authority can be effectively used. Also, it can be so used only if it is accepted by the other team members. Thus, to be effective, formal authority must coincide with authority determined by its acceptance. The latter defines the useful limits of the former. We may usefully summarize the situation with the slogan: 'leadership is nothing without followership' (or joiners).

In most instances the managers or leaders may, on the face of things, have immense authority. They may have the right to hire and fire; or to reward and punish other team members without referral to anyone else. But, in practice, although they may demand or insist there is no guarantee that other team members will fully comply. The concept 'authority' then, describes an interpersonal relationship in which one individual, the team member, accepts a decision made by another individual, the manager or leader, permitting that decision directly to affect their behaviour. A team member always has an opportunity, with respect to a decision made by the manager or leader which directly affects his behaviour, to accept or reject that decision. It is appreciated, of course, that such a rejection by the team member could result in dismissal, or at the very least, the need for a voluntary leaving.

In the last chapter, reference was made to the circumstances where team members will accept, rather than reject the authority of the manager or leader. Team members will accept an exercise of authority if they perceive that the advantages accruing to them from accepting outweigh the perceived disadvantages accruing to them from not accepting. Put another way, exactly when they will let the manager or leader by and when they will not, will depend upon their desires. If what the manager or leader decides seems likely to result in the satisfaction of the individual team members' desires they will do as the manager or leader wishes. If, on the contrary, they feel that this will result in failure of their desires they will not co-operate. The team members have desires just as do the manager or leader and if they can help it, they would rather not give up the satisfaction of any of theirs; which, of course, is just as the manager or leader would act.

This presents quite a problem for the manager or leader who, from their perspective and experience, is able to see changes that will benefit the performance of the team. At first glance, it seems obvious that the manager should use this superior knowledge by giving instructions to the team to put into being the beneficial changes—or does it? While working with the football manager there were several occasions when, having used his vast knowledge and experience of the game to carefully analyse the performance of the team during the first half, would come up with an innovative approach for dealing with some of the problems arising. In bold and confident terms he would introduce his instructions for change that the team were supposed to embrace and comply with in the second half. To him, this all seemed quite obvious, eminently sensible and the sort of things leaders should do. But, in his solitary world he had been too busy in finding a solution to the problems to consider other team members. He could even be forgiven for thinking that everyone was committed to his instructions, as no one disagreed. However, a look at the non-verbal cues and contact with the feelings of most of the other team members quite clearly demonstrated that they were not going to comply with the instruction. Subsequent events on the field showed this to be correct, they continued as before, and would not let him by.

We are back to the matter of the struggle referred to above. It is about the manager having to struggle with the process of managing the boundary between what is inside and what is outside by developing sufficient self-awareness and self-control while still carrying out his primary task of managing a successful football team. It is about working across the boundary of 'self' with other team members, others who also have a 'self'. Before the manager could work across that boundary he would need to develop a relationship with the other team members. That requires an understanding of the emotional state of those team members. Where there is limited time available, there must always be a consideration of what and how much can be achieved. In the above circumstances, it was clearly asking too much to communicate a complicated change that all team members could share.

How do you get results?

How do you get results? Management is about getting results through other people. Ultimately, it's what they do that matters— not what you do. As a manager or leader you may be quite brilliant in building your professional and even your administrative, knowledge. In football terms you may be up to date with all the latest playing, training, and fitness techniques. You might even be considered to be one of the best brains in the game. So what? I might ask. If you cannot also do what is necessary to 'get results through other people' you will undoubtedly be a failure. As we have frequently seen, the best brains in the game may also be the least successful managers. Over the years there has been a never ending list of highly accomplished professional footballers such as Billy Wright, Bobby Charlton, Bobby Moore and more recently John Barnes, who have all failed to make their mark as managers.

In the last chapter I referred to the fact that it cannot be coincidence that many highly successful people have achieved success in spite of obstacles, as much as because of positive goals, support, and encouragement. It would appear that a combination of strong frustration and positive encouragement is a part of every great person's biography. By way of example, I referred to the many footballers, whose careers have been shortened by injury thus making it impossible for them to achieve their desires to be great players, who have then sublimated their desires by substituting a desire to be a great manager. I concluded that it seems that sublimated desires can sometimes be stronger than the original.

Success as a professional, the fulfilment of desires to play at the highest levels of skill and achievement, may act to prevent the desire to encourage leadership in others: the desire to be a good manager. This may at least partly explain why so many successful footballers fail miserably when they turn to management. This may not only be the case with football but also in other occupations where people move from professional to managerial roles. I have in mind many of our public services such as the National Health Service, the Police Service, Social Services, and, I also have in mind those in the private sector such as those employed in sales.

If the team consists of, say, 15 or 16 members it seems reasonable to suggest that using all those brains is likely to result in an improved and more successful team performance. The logicality of this statement is so overwhelmingly obvious; yet, how many managers or leaders live this sort of approach. Doubtless much is to do with their own concerns, their own anxieties about themselves. Frequently, when football managers are interviewed they will be asked about their personal role and about their success and failure in that role. They will also be asked to carry the hopes and desires of the owners or Board members and the fans to bring the team success. Perhaps not surprisingly, one result is that managers and leaders become consumed with their own performance. When things are going well they take full credit for the results, as if they personally have worked some sort of magic; and, when things go wrong they suffer all sorts of anxiety and worries. In both instances, the danger is that they are so consumed with their own feelings that they are unable to provide the support and containment required by other team members. Left with their own self as the centre of their worries (or successes) they feel that the world starts and stops there—no one else exists and no one else's ideas exist. Thus, they become more and more alienated from other team members—those that they get results through.

Even if your brain was the best; even if all your ideas were better than anyone else; an unlikely scenario! It is still only in your head. The question remains how do you get your ideas into the heads of the rest of the team? How do you transfer your knowledge, understanding, and skills to others? How do you get the totality of your knowledge into their heads? It seems that the answer must necessarily be 'with great difficulty'. They do not have your unique history and therefore cannot 'plug in' to your experience in the way you can. To get your ideas across may take a considerable amount of leadership—attempts to influence others to take up your ideas. In the process, other team members may experience all sorts of emotions such as envy arising out of the fact that you've got an idea while they haven't (see Stein, 2000 for a most interesting discussion about envy). You may also experience conflict arising from the fact that others may have different ideas about achieving their desires from those you are proposing, or, others may have totally different desires from those in your head. There is also likely to be some degree of anxiety and defensiveness arising from the need to change. So, what may appear to some managers and leaders as a simple process of telling other team members what to do, is in fact a highly complicated interaction. Ignorance is not bliss!

Relating at an emotional level

Much will depend on the emotional state of other team members at the time the manager is trying to engage with them. For example, on frequent occasions the players coming off the pitch at half-time were either elated or depressed to such a degree that they had lost their capacity for self-perception. In these circumstances, it was utterly pointless for the manager to try to get across a new way of playing, they simply could not take it in even if they wished to. What was really needed at this time, was support, encouragement, and containment to enable team members to recover their self-aware-ness and self-control. Without achieving this the team members were not going to be capable of performing in any manner.

Any manager or leader worth their salt will first and foremost try to ensure that they know the current emotional state of their players, especially when they have been in an anxiety provoking environment. Secondly, if the team members are emotionally capable of expressing views, the manager will consult and obtain the views of other team members before they make a decision. They may, as hopefully will other team members, have a strong desire to win a game. But there is not just one way that they can achieve this desire, there are, in fact, many possible ways to go about it. Knowing the views of other team members will help them to make a decision that as many of the team members as possible will be committed to.

Emotional development is needed if the feelings of others are to be recognized and respected. Most stereotypes are based on ignorance or the wish to scapegoat others who are different in some way. Familiarity with those different from ourselves is necessary if these labels are to be overcome, with opportunity to explore mutual feelings in some depth. Many unexpected situations can give rise to anxiety and worry, particularly if we feel isolated and insecure. If these feelings are recognized early on they can, in theory, be managed by applying logical problem solving techniques. But this is easier said than done, particularly without someone to talk it through with. Success is dependent on personal confidence and previous experience of success.

Before you can relate at an emotional level with others, understand what they are feeling and identify with those feelings (that is, empathize) you need to be self-aware, in touch with and understanding your own feelings. You also need to be sensitive to the non-verbal cues that indicate how others are feeling. This includes tone and volume of voice, eye contact, facial expression, posture, and gestures. It is recognized that it is not what is said but how it is said that really matters. If a large percentage of an emotional message is communicated non-verbally then skill in interpreting these signals is essential if misunderstandings are to be avoided. Too often the manager or leader will jump in to tell others what to do, interrogate them or talk about themselves, showing that they did not hear what was really said at all. Empathy is demonstrating understanding and acceptance of the other person at the emotional level, feeling with them. When responding to a statement of feelings, perhaps by summarizing it to show understanding, this summary has to communicate recognition of the emotions behind the message and the response, not just the words. Listening skills are essential, and are reflected in the sensitivity of the response.

If we are to truly participate with other team members we need to communicate understanding and acceptance of the other team members at the emotional level, feeling with them. In effect, we need to communicate at three levels as below:

● what we hear (what the other team members say);

- what we see (the non-verbal cues that the other team members give us); and,
- what we feel (the expressed feelings of other team members).

If, as is frequently the case, we solely rely on communication at the level of what people say, we shall miss a vast amount of what is being communicated.

There is a well known psychological response to anxiety which is, that when we get in trouble we tend to do more and more of the same thing. When we are in a hole we tend to dig deeper. What seems right to us, what we may have seen some other authority figure—perhaps one of our previous managers—do, in the past, is the only way we can see to take us forward and thus we get locked in. Unless, of course, we can adopt the process of reflection outlined in the Foreword:

- *self-reflection*, leading to;
- *self-awareness*, leading to;
- *self-control*, leading to;
- *awareness of others*.

It seems clear that the more participation there is by team members before decision making takes place the more chance there is of a greater number of team members being committed to the same desires. In other words, we move from a single person's desires to shared desires by a majority of team members. In football this might include involving the team members in decisions concerning, for example, the way the team play. As stated above, there may be occasions when others will let you through with your desires but on other occasions they may not let you through, because it conflicts so much with their own desires. It seems that if you try to impose your ideas, or more accurately, your decisions, on others they are much more likely to not let you through. True, they may not make it obvious that they disagree, but their performance will show it in no uncertain manner.

Another way of viewing the situation is through the slogan 'don't work harder work smarter'. In the industrial era the saying, 'many hands make light work' was highly appropriate. Today, it seems that a more appropriate version might be 'many brains make 'bright' work'. As I suggested earlier, leadership is about encouraging leadership in other team members. This is the way that, for a team, 'many brains can make bright work'.

Vision

Sadly, many leadership books promote the 'visionary' role of leaders. The sort of leadership that looks just like Moses descending from the mountaintop and unveiling the new order. For their part in this scenario, dependent followers are supposed to dutifully applaud, thank the leader profusely, and line up behind the leader's vision and stop wandering around aimlessly. For reasons previously stated I do not agree with this view. However, the manager or leader does have a vital role to play in regard to vision which I briefly want to explore.

The leader of an organization requires the skill to develop a vision of the future, a long-term desire. Sometimes this may involve looking several years ahead, to determine where they are going, how they will get there, and the type of organization they should be. At all times, short-term goals and actions need to be clearly related to the long-term. In practice, this can be a difficult task, as is well demonstrated in football. Many will be familiar with the saying, 'We need to take one game at a time'. In other words, for team purposes, there needs to be a concentration of effort on achieving immediate, short-term desires—to attempt to win individual matches. The danger is, if team members start to think about longer term desires for success these are likely to over-ride short-term desires, with the result that team members may not be fully motivated at that point. In football parlance, they may not be 'up for it'.

In this respect, it is important that the manager or leader is able to hold the long-term vision in mind while providing the environment for other team members to concentrate on short-term desires. Vision is no good without determined leaders or managers who, in the tough times will have the responsibility to watch for the long-term goal. In terms of motivation as desires, vision requires that the manager or leader acquires a different skill, that of deferring gratification, recognizing, and preferring long-term goals. The inter-relationship of these different skills is clear. Deferring gratification requires high self-esteem. If the manager or leader gets anxious after every set-back and does not have sufficient self-esteem they are likely to abandon their previously agreed long-term vision and replace it with another short- to medium-term solution. We have all seen managers and leaders who constantly perform in this manner to the confusion and disgust of other team members who gradually lose respect and support for the manager.

Too many managers and leaders are under the misapprehension that team members follow a leader's vision or charisma. In reality, there are some team members who look for a manager or leader that they can follow in the hope of success. However, many others are motivated by their own personal vision that they want to bring to life. They prefer a manager or leader who is a partner who will help to facilitate their achievement of a goal. In most circumstances team members generally know where they are going. If not, they want to be part of the process that determines the end goal. This might be called 'leadership by informed consent', or, leaders and joiners. As partners, team members want to forge the vision together to increase the probability of success. This, in turn, requires the efforts and talents of more than one person. It may be helpful to see the manager or leader as a partner of the other team members who from time to time does different things than other team members.

Bonding

There are moments in the life of team members when being part of a team shapes your desires and behaviour. Your reason for wanting to be part of the team may have nothing to do with getting ahead, personal growth, or intellectual development. Instead, it may be about the intimacy and social support that develop when people bond together. In these environments there is a feeling of mutual trust and sharing that goes beyond the individual. The psychology behind this 'bonding' is one of intimacy that comes from belonging. We all have very basic desires for attachment—to be part of something. Once you feel part of something you transcend your feelings of isolation and even your feelings of self. This explains why team members will join with others rather than seek personal glory and why they give their all so that their team mates can succeed.

People also bond together as a way of coping with stress. In these situations you follow for mutually reinforcing reasons: your feeling of goodwill toward the group and the belief that survival is more likely if you collectively share and watch out for each other. This is the added something that is present when a 'minnow' takes on a 'giant'; when a lowly placed team face the champions and match them on the day, sometimes even beat them. Such is the fusion of individuals into a collective unit all ready to share and watch out for each other that the team takes on a different level of desires and commitment against this 'common enemy'.

Delegation

In many organizations the foreman or supervisor is not regarded as part of management. In football, this is often the case regarding the captain; and, in other sports the team leader, or whatever their designation. Yet, no matter what the attitudes of the top leadership may be, it is the people in the middle of the organization, the foreman, the supervisor, or the captain who make things happen. Top managers can pontificate and inspire all they want but unless they get the foreman, supervisor or captain on their side they will fail. It is the foreman, supervisor or captain who delivers top management's policies in the workplace or on the field. Like the foreman or supervisor in other organizations, the football captain can make more difference to the long-term success of the team than anyone other than the manager or leader.

I was not always of this view. When I first started working with the manager I did not appreciate just how important the role of captain was. At that time, the very competent and distinguished captain was so good at his job that I just did not notice. It was only when this particular player retired that I came to fully value what he had brought to the role. Above all, there was an empathy with the manager which meant that they were communicating with each other at multiple levels. On most occasions, they each knew what the other was thinking and feeling. A result was that the captain was an extension of the manager on the field.

While the team is playing, it is helpful to have someone 'within the team boundary' who is delegated with the authority to make changes and to act as a conduit to and from the manager or leader so that their wishes are carried out effectively. Above all, this person needs to have a high degree of self-awareness and self-control to be able to help others who may be less emotionally mature. The sort of skills required by the captain are those that were displayed by that great and successful England captain, Bobby Moore, an exemplar of self-control. The captain needs to be the professional at managing the processes and the people. While the captain is expected to lead the team, they cannot lead unless they are accepted as part of it. It is the process of gaining the commitment of other team members and control of the processes which is necessary to secure long-term success.

Concluding remarks

Every organization faces the task of somehow reducing the variability, instability, and unpredictability of individual human acts. Authority, coupled with status and role systems, supplies this necessary element. These key ingredients result in reasonably well-defined roles to be performed by organizational participants so that behaviour is not entirely, 'spontaneous and unrehearsed'. In many cases behaviour of organizational members is identical—starting at nine and ending at five, for example. They may wear certain styles of attire (uniform) that distinguish them from other organizations, or they may develop special behaviour patterns that are essential to the work of the organization.

So that's it then! We've solved most of our problems by sorting out the authority issues be they internal conflicts that the manager or leader is suffering; or, conflicts between the other team members and the manager; or, conflicts between the manager and others in authority positions. Sorry, but that's not all. There is still the important issue about ensuring that decisions when agreed are carried out in a disciplined way. And that, is the topic of the next chapter.

CHAPTER SIX

Leaders and discipline

For many managers and leaders the issue of discipline is a key question. How do they ensure that other team members do what has been agreed will be done? Many managers and leaders will have concerns about the best way to ensure that they can instil discipline in other team members. How they can act to ensure that other team members adopt a sense of responsibility and self-discipline in their actions and reactions. As is the case with 'authority' there is also widespread distaste for the notion of 'discipline' throughout society today. Yet, this is such an important issue that it cannot be ignored. Football teams—and other work teams—have to ensure that there is a degree of discipline if they are to succeed in the highly competitive environment in which they operate.

It is right, then, that managers and leaders should be concerned about how discipline is achieved throughout the team. Of course, some will simply not care about the way they obtain discipline, which for them, is usually through submission and sometimes through humiliation. Frequently, we can see that at the heart of this type of management is a high degree of insecurity on the part of the manager or leader. They are scared to death of rejection or failure and respond in a truly autocratic way. Hopefully, however, other managers are concerned about other team members and will see discipline not in an authoritarian way but rather, as a means of setting boundaries for creative activities by all team members.

A reference to the dictionary definition of 'discipline' shows that like 'authority', the concept has been much misunderstood and has now become wrongly associated with and understood as *punishment* only. It is true that while the word can be used in the sense of punishment, this is not the most important meaning. Only one small part of the many definitions of this term suggest that 'discipline' can also be used in the sense of punishment and since even this meaning is given only a special subdivision of a larger one concerning correction, it is very questionable whether 'punishment', or a 'beating', or the 'like' are good ways to correct anybody. Rather, the idea that is paramount in the definition is that of *instruction*. Thus, the major problem for managers and leaders in ensuring that team members act in a disciplined way, is the matter of how to instruct other team members so that they will develop a healthy measure of self-control.

The Oxford definition tells us that the original meaning of the word 'discipline' suggests that it is an instruction to be imparted to 'disciples'—which has its derivation in two words that stem from the same Latin root, '*discipulus*', a learner. For most of us, the term Disciple will be associated with the followers of Christ. Given this meaning of the word 'discipline', it is difficult to see how we could possibly believe that it can be imposed or forced on another person. Any discipline worth acquiring cannot be beaten into or forced upon anyone; indeed, such effort is contrary to the very idea of discipleship. As was pointed out in the last chapter, the manager or leader may consider they have the right to impose and demand their decisions be carried out but team members will be the ones who make the ultimate decision about whether or not they will accept that authority. The fact is, that the best and probably only way one can turn oneself into a disciplined person is by emulating someone whose example one admires—not by being instructed verbally, which at best can be only part of it, and certainly not by threats.

Role models

For all team members, personality is never a finished product but an ever-changing or transitive process. Part of this process may involve the emulation of a role model that one admires and might equally be related to as a process of identification with the role model. In this process the admired values and behaviour of this role model become internalized by the team members and these become part of their personality. Other factors will also play their part, for example, if we believe ourselves to be the manager or leader's favourite, or at least one of their favourites, we are further motivated to develop ourselves in the manager or leader's image, or in short, to identify with them.

Any emotion that has us in its power will shape us—such as a child's love and admiration for their parents—and thus has the potential for both good or evil. When working with the manager (and others), it was so easy for him to get in touch with his feelings regarding his son's development. Young children cannot distinguish between the morally good and the morally bad. They know only what feels good and what doesn't, what they like and dislike. Thus love will induce them to emulate their parents, whatever the nature of their parents' morals—they will identify with good as well as bad traits. Identification with the parent takes place very early in life and becomes so securely anchored in the deepest layers of the developing personality that it can be eradicated only with great difficulty by later experiences.

We are all familiar with the old saying, 'do as I say, not as I do', but we are still loathe to agree that this simply does not hold water when working with other team members. Whether or not they obey our orders, deep down they are responding less to our commands than to their perception of our character and conduct. We should not underestimate the degree to which other team members model themselves on our behaviour. The more they care for us, the more they emulate us, and the more they internalize, not only our consciously held values, but also those of which we ourselves are not conscious but which also influence our actions. Conversely, the less they like and admire us, the more negatively they respond to us in modelling their personalities. What seems to make the difference is how closely and well the managers and leaders live by their stated values and by the values they try to teach other team members: how consistent was the behaviour of the authority figure; how consistent they are as role models rather than as critics.

Many managers and leaders are preoccupied with the need to

gain control and to obtain unswerving loyalty, by which they frequently mean unquestioning loyalty, of other team members. There will, of course, be times when this sort of leadership is both necessary and appropriate in the interests of everyone's welfare, such as during an emergency. However, we would do well to remember that 'many brains make bright work', which requires that the team is comprised of people who have minds of their own, who are able to think and question and not be replicas of the manager; regardless of how wonderful managers may feel about themselves. It does not take too much imagination to see the huge benefits to be gained from a diversity of views that may provide us with a competitive advantage over our rivals. For example, in football, there are many ways a corner or a free kick can be taken. Teams that follow a rigid pattern for taking these set pieces are relatively easy to defend against—the opposition know what's coming. Where, however, team members are permitted to be creative and to try new approaches, the opposition will find it infinitely more difficult to predict and defend accordingly.

Given the likely conflicts in attitudes and values, let alone difficulties in communication, frequent opportunities for misunderstanding will develop. If team members are to willingly carry out the wishes of the manager or leader, team members must learn to trust them. Trust develops out of experience; it is difficult to obtain and easy to lose. With trust, other team members can gradually come to learn that although they may not always understand why they are told to do this, or not to do that, there is, nevertheless, likely to be some rationale behind the manager or leader's instructions. Later on, they may want to argue about the reason and sometimes they may well be right. The prize of a justifiably trusted self comes from the model of justifiably trusted others.

Developing trust

How is trust established? In our search for some answers it may help to consider our first authority relationship—that between mother and child. For the infant to develop there is a need for what has been referred to by Winnicott (1965b) as, a 'basic trust'. This basic trust is developed as a result of the infant's perceived experience of their holding environment (for a fuller description of holding environments see Stapley, 1996). From holding in the mother's womb this extends to holding in the mother's arms. However, what we are referring to is much more than just physical holding. It is about the mother providing boundaries, agreeing rules, which help the infant to make sense of its world. A fortunate child eventually learns to trust the outside world only where trust is warranted. For example, if the mother is able to help the child make sense of the world by helping them to understand that there is danger in putting a hand in the fire or in going into the roadway.

As time goes by (and the trusted people and concepts outside begin to retreat), the now adult person has to learn to trust the internalized images of these people and concepts—'himself', all over again. Applying this to the team situation, a team member's trust will be built up in imperceptible, unconscious, non-dramatic ways; these ways need to be understood by the concerned manager or leader. Thus, in football, it is not sufficient to lay down a dictum that players will not drink alcohol on Friday nights. Rather, it is essential that the manager helps the other team members to make sense of the world by helping them to understand and value why they should not drink alcohol on a Friday night.

Being there

One of the most important ways a manager or leader can help other team members is by simply 'being there'. The concept of 'being there' is not easy to appreciate, until we realize that team members may have previously experienced situations where authority figures had 'been there' very little (if at all), or inconsistently. The team member's experience may have been based on a perception that an authority figure, such as a parent, school teacher or a previous manager, was not there for them. Such a problem existed for one of the players whose father had left the family home to set up house with another woman when he was 13 years of age. To the team member the father was perceived to be uncaring and untrustworthy; and, based on this experience he thus treated all subsequent authority figures as also being uncaring. There is no question of a manager or leader replacing a 'not there' parent, but there is every reason to expect a manager or leader to understand that they have to work at developing the necessary trust and that this may not be readily forthcoming, particularly in situations where the team member has not previously experienced a trusting relationship. In this instant, the manager had a very clear understanding of his team member and quickly developed his trust in a way which was rewarding for both parties. In effect, when we talk about 'being there' we are not just talking about a physical presence but more about a psychological presence.

At one level, we understand the need to be there for all our team members. However, at another level all managers and leaders will doubtless have their favourites, especially those that remind them of themselves; and their pet hates, especially those that remind them of some of their not so attractive features. This was certainly the case with regard to the football manager who not infrequently forgave his pets and scapegoated those he disliked, all the while rationalizing his actions. This leads us to an important element in that the building of trust of others concerns the realization by the other team members that the manager or leader's acceptance of them is metaphorically grey, not black or white, not totally good nor totally bad. An over conditioning, such as scapegoating, or an over idealizing, seeing only goodness, leads to blindness by managers or leaders which is perceived by team members as neglect. In effect, the message that the manager or leader is giving is that the team members concerned are either so good or so bad that they don't need to worry about them. It is the realization that the manager or leader sees other team members as grey which is a confirmation of his interest in them and of their sense of reality. The opportunity for other team members to perceive their manager or leader's realistic perception of them provides the model that will enable them to eventually perceive themselves realistically.

Where managers or leaders are over-protective or over-controlling in assuming authority over other team members they encourage and create a dependency relationship. Team members look to the manager or leader for a solution to all their problems, they stop thinking: there's no point in thinking because the manager or leader is going to do it anyway. Yet, come Saturday, when the team members go out on the pitch, they are expected to take their own authority. The problem is, they are now on their own but because of the manager's activities, they don't know how to handle it. Having made them dependent, the team members are now lacking in original thought and creativity. As has been stated, for the leader or manager who feels the demands to succeed lying heavily on their shoulders there will be many times when the temptation to 'take control' and to impose a solution will be exceedingly strong. It is the great manager or leader who has the self-awareness, and the self-control to withstand these many pressures, to be aware of and understand the needs, emotions, and desires of other team members and thus, to be able to encourage them to provide leadership.

Sometimes we do things with the best of intentions. For example, a common reaction for many managers is to 'reward' team members who have been viewed as difficult or undisciplined by giving them more and more trust. As their training and development progresses and is perceived as being effective they are given more freedom. The problem is that for many team members this is misunderstood, being trusted is experienced by them as being neglected and therefore such an approach is unhelpful and will often engender unexpected reactions. Far from the intended reaction of the team member to become more disciplined they may in fact revert to indiscipline. It is the same old story, a perception of being neglected, of no one caring, of not 'being there'. It is possible that the team member has simply learned how to work the system, how to please and how to stay out of trouble, without any fundamental change of attitude at all. Many team members will espouse their allegiance to the manager on being rewarded, but will treat him as a fool.

The fortunate team members are the ones whose manager or leader does not trust them to be left alone, but who anticipates that left to their own devices they will slacken off, play hooky, or get into some sort of bother and decides to keep a careful eye on them and to continue to set boundaries for their development. Poorly disciplined team members often have a manager or leader who has, rejectingly, 'trusted' them and whom in their turn the team members do not trust. All of us have a strong need or desire for attachment. Because we are born very helpless and throughout childhood remain primarily dependent on our parenting figures to protect, feed, and care for us, the attention of our parents was our only weapon of defence. Hence a child's most crucial task, for its own survival, was to make its attachment relationships secure. Since attachment is so overwhelmingly important to us, above all in the early years, it underlies all our understanding of how to survive and to manage the world we inhabit (Stapley, 1996).

It is perhaps interesting to note that the derivation of the term delinquency refers to dereliction of duty. Managers and leaders will be guilty of a dereliction of duty where they are not providing for the attachment needs of other team members. If they are perceived as uncaring or neglecting they may be deemed to be delinquent. Team members need a manager or leader, who is absolutely trustworthy, whom eventually even the team member with the worst sort of experiences can trust. This is all part of the manager or leader's role: they earn their living partly by performing distasteful tasks, refraining from natural tendencies such as the wish to physically punish or swear at other team members and having to work efficiently with their colleagues whom they may dislike.

To be effective in such circumstances requires constant:

- *self-reflection*;
- *self-awareness*; and
- *self-control*, which can lead to:
- *awareness of others*.

There will doubtless be frequent occasions when other team members will disagree with managers or leaders or have their own strongly held views about the way that things should be done. Managers or leaders may have their own firm views which they feel are important to both the team and the individual concerned. However, if managers do not take account of other team members' views, they are likely to force them into being over-conformers (who may break out violently some day when they have gathered up the strength) or unduly obstinate and not to be relied upon when it really is important that they should do as they are told. For example, if the football team is working to a system of man-to-man marking and one of the team members, no matter how brilliant, decides to mark on a zonal basis, the resulting disorganization is likely to lead to defeat.

Participation and consultation

Doubtless encouraged by the Moses syndrome, there seems to be a commonly held misconception that leadership means that the manager or leader is the one who must come up with all the initiatives. Or that the manager or leader must be the one who decides where the team will go next. The nonsense of this conception was discussed in the last chapter. But there is another aspect to this which is equally important. Because of the concentration on the leader, other facets of leadership seem to be overlooked and not regarded as leadership. For example, a vital leadership role for any manager or leader is to ensure that the sort of environment exists which will encourage others to consider and come up with solutions for problems facing the team or that will give the team a competitive advantage. Leadership also involves providing opportunities for team members to develop their self-confidence and autonomy.

A further misconception concerns the matter of consulting team members and seeking to involve them in a participative manner in decision making. Many leaders and managers are of the view that this involves them making the decision and then seeking the views of other team members so as to get their commitment to the decision. This sort of charade consultation can only result in team members regarding the manager or leader with a large dose of cynicism and a resultant lack of trust. They will not only regard it as a waste of time, but will also feel they are being duped. True consultation involves seeking the views of team members and taking them into consideration before making a decision. In this way, team members will know that they are genuinely participating in matters which have a considerable effect on their lives and will be more likely to be committed to the final decision.

Where managers and leaders can and should, always be prepared to take the lead is by setting an example. By being an admired role model, managers and leaders will gain the trust of other team members who will seek to emulate them. This is a constant requirement and is leadership of the highest order. It is not easy, because it requires the manager to be constantly exercising self-control and to have a high level of self-awareness. As has been stated, trust is hard to develop and very easy to lose. Doubtless team members will forgive the odd 'out-of-character' blow up by their manager or leader, but when it comes at frequent intervals team members will start to lose their trust and with it their desire to emulate.

There are many things that the leader or manager must convey to other team members about what they should and should not do for their necessary instruction. However, we must be careful that we aren't adding to them unnecessarily, that we do not come over as a long-playing record of ourselves and one therefore that tends not to be heeded. It is only effective to give a small amount of feedback at any given time. Furthermore, if we want to communicate effectively with other team members we can only give two or three pieces of information to a team at any given time. Consequently, any briefing, such as that given before a football match, needs to be limited by this knowledge. Of course, there may be a million things the leader or manager might want to say, but to do so would be of negative value. The skill lies in the identification of the two or three essential things and ensuring that the team understand these.

Setting boundaries

Some form of instruction or guidance, some setting of ground rules for all concerned is essential. If the leader or manager is to expect that other team members will have the necessary self-discipline to perform their task, they, in turn, must know what is expected of them. This all seems fairly obvious, but I am not certain that team members are always provided with this knowledge. I can remember one player, who, on being berated for being out of position during a set-piece play, responded by saying that he didn't know where he should be. This could have been a form of denial on his behalf, simply covering his error. Indeed, the manager's view when we discussed it, was precisely that. That may or may not have been so in this specific case, but in general, I do think there is a danger that managers or leaders who are constantly preoccupied with issues concerning the way the team play, will make assumptions that the team members have the same level of knowledge as they do. Some, particularly those who admire them, will be attuned to their thinking in a way that ensures they are highly compatible with the manager or leader. Others and I suspect that the team member referred to above is among them, who are not admirers of the manager, who do not have trust in them, and view them with suspicion, will not be attuned to their thinking and will not be having compatible thoughts. In truth, they will not know what is expected of them.

This is an issue that was referred to in the last chapter when I discussed how the manager or leader needed to work across the boundaries of each of the other team members in a way which ensures that the knowledge in his mind was transferred to that of the other team members. The notion of working across boundaries is perhaps a helpful way of viewing this difficulty. It will also be helpful, at this point, to reflect back on the discussion in Chapter 2 where we referred to the self and not-self. Thus, we can see both the manager or leader and each of the other team members as discreet entities with their own boundaries, inside which are unique individuals, the self; and, outside that boundary the other team members, the not-self.

It will also be recalled that we identify more basically and intimately with just a facet of our total organism and this facet, which we feel is our real self, is known variously as the mind, the psyche, the ego, the personality. What do we mean by mind? What is the mind? Basically it is a zone of mediation, a place where meaning is made. What an organism does is organize; and what the mind of a human organism organizes is meaning. Thus, it is not that a person makes meaning, as much as that the activity of being a person is the activity of meaning-making. There is no feeling, no experience, no thought, no perception, independent of a meaning-making context in which it becomes a feeling, an experience, a thought, a perception, because we are the meaning-making context. However, each of us being a separate self is likely to make a different meaning.

So, now we need to think about matters in the context of a relationship between two people: to begin to think of the two people to the interaction as two eyes, *each giving a monocular view* of what goes on and *together giving a binocular view* in depth. This double view is the relationship. Relationship is not internal to the single person, a relationship is what happens between persons, not in something-or-other inside a person. Developing a relationship means moving from the singular monocular views of the manager or leader and other team members, by working across the boundaries to a situation where both parties are able to see things from both perspectives, taking a binocular view.

This was an issue that I helped the manager to explore. We started from the notion that all team members need to know the basic rules. Rather like an army which learns its basic drills and then puts them into practice while carrying out their task of fighting a battle; so it is with any team. In regard to the football team there were basic drills which needed to be learnt which would then be carried out by the team members while they were carrying out the task of playing a competitive match.

If we see discipline as a means of setting the boundaries for creative activities by other team members what do we mean by this? What are the boundaries that we need to set? Basically, it means setting and agreeing the ground rules so that individually and collectively, team members are clear about what is expected of them and are thus able to adopt them and maintain them in a self-disciplined way. It means moving from the individual monocular views of each team member to a shared and collective binocular view. The following were the methods adopted by the manager for clarifying boundary settings at four different levels.

Individual level

This first level, as the title suggests, is purely concerned with the individual and the conduct and responsibilities we want that individual to adopt as second nature. For example, in a football team, a centre half has a specific role which has attached to it various responsibilities; a payroll clerk also has specific role responsibilities in a finance team. It is important at this level that the individual knows, understands and agrees what the requirements of that role are.

Unit level

In addition to their specific individual role each player or clerk will have a shared responsibility. For example, the centre half in the football team will have the shared responsibility for ensuring that the defence (unit) is organized as a unit, and that the defenders in the team are able to cover each other's role, if necessary. Much the same applies to the finance clerk who will have a shared responsibility for carrying out the particular work of the unit, and be able to cover other clerk's roles, if necessary. Here it is not only important that the individuals in the unit know, understand, and agree what is expected, but that this is a shared knowledge, understanding, and agreement.

Team level

Over-riding individual and unit roles, the whole team have a collective role. For example, in a football setting, while defenders, mid-fielders, and attackers need to be organized to perform as units, they also need to link together as a total team: even to the extent that sometimes an attacker may need to temporarily cover a defender's role or vice versa. At this level, it is important that the whole team have a shared and agreed understanding of their responsibility.

Organizational level

Finally, there are requirements affecting all. For example, in a football setting this would include team members, reserves, juniors, non-playing staff, such as coaches, trainers, and managers. Here, we are referring to what we might call organizational or professional standards. Many of these will be comprised of codes, for example, those for standards of dress, fitness, and behaviour. At this time these codes are usually imposed from above. However, if we are to achieve self-discipline it is important that there is a shared and agreed understanding of these codes.

No team can be truly successful if it does not learn to organize as a team; that is, to get away from being a group of individuals acting alone, to being a group of individuals acting in concert. A group of talented individuals, who go out and do their own thing may be successful, until they come up against a highly organized team that knows and understands its individual, unit and team roles and defends and attacks in an organized, self-disciplined manner. To reach this point will almost certainly require a whole lot of practice and perseverance, working at the individual, unit, and team levels until there is an agreed understanding and willingness on the part of all to adopt the necessary roles. Once the roles are agreed and understood all that should be required is a gentle nudge on the tiller to ensure that team discipline is maintained. It will, of course, be appreciated that such nudges relate to individual or team behaviour and not to the characteristics of the individual. This last point is most important. When anyone calls us a fool the chances are we won't like it. We will become annoyed and challenge the person who is making this seemingly unfair judgement. Assertiveness training teaches us to provide feedback about the behaviour and not the individual.

Who's discipline are we concerned with?

When we are prohibiting another team member or berating them, it is often useful to stop and think, or perhaps more accurately to reflect, whether they are really doing something wrong either individually or to the team as a whole. Everybody makes mistakes, everybody does things in different ways. If we reflect carefully we may discover that what we are concerned with is something which is irritating ourselves as managers or leaders, but is not really a matter of deep concern. What in fact we are doing, if we try to stop them, is trying to stop them from worrying us. It is not what the team member is doing or not doing, but rather it is our desires which are not being satisfied and it is our frustration or anger that is accompanying this non-satisfaction of our desires. We may not actually say to the team member, 'don't do that because it worries me', or 'if you keep on doing that I'll get angry', but the meaning can get across to them as an insidious threat or blackmail. In such situations it is important that we 'own' our anger or frustration and do not 'blame' it on other team members.

It may be aiming for a standard of unattainable perfection to imagine that we can manage never to behave in this way. By virtue of being very close to the other team members, (this is especially so in football), managers and leaders are bound to have their own childhood emotions strongly reactivated. Frequently, it is much easier for someone who is outside the circle to see the irrationality of a manager's responses. Not that such observations would be accepted by the manager even if they were made. We don't want to hear people tell us things about ourselves that we are not aware of. However, that is not to say that someone cannot help a manager or leader to reflect. Indeed, much of the work I have done with the football manager has been to help him in a process of self-reflection. It is rather in the nature of holding up a mirror so that he can see a wider picture which then allows him to make decisions based on greater knowledge. That is not to say that we must have someone from outside to help us. If we are not too hard on ourselves as managers, recognizing our unfairness, hastiness, and irrationality, sometimes even after the event, we may learn to do a little better next time. Sharing concerns with someone such as the assistant manager can be quite a solace and support in many instances. Above all, though, there is a need for self-reflection.

It is often when we are plagued too strongly with our own demands for an unattainable perfection that we tend to pass these on to other team members. We expect them to behave in the way that we feel we ought to, but cannot. This may be particularly so in the professions where managers and leaders have had previous experience of doing the job. For example, most football managers have come to their position from the ranks of professional footballers. In many ways this is valuable, even essential, but the down side is that they expect other team members to have the same levels of skill, commitment, and energy as they had when they were playing. Clearly, each player is an individual and each brings their own diverse contribution. To try to clone them would amount to coercion. That is not to say the manager or leader will not suffer frustration and anger when they realize that their desires are not being met, but the message has got to be 'own it, don't blame'.

Diversity is desirable for all the benefits that it can bring, but it can also create problems within a team because perceptions and unconscious prejudices come into play. I have referred to self-fulfilling prophecies whereby a person treated as useless all too easily conforms to this image and thus becomes useless. If we tell a team member that they are stupid, or constantly treat them as a fun figure, the chances are that they will conform to this image. Sadly, these images are frequently misconceptions based on a team member being 'different' in some way from their team mates. For example, they may be a Northerner playing for a Southern club where their accent is 'different'; or they may be black or Asian. Whatever the 'difference' team members and managers tend to attribute 'labels' to these team members. These are not always negative, sometimes they can be positive, rather like assuming that all Brazilians are superb football players. Where the manager or leader is guilty of this sort of behaviour, other team members can scarcely be expected to maintain self-respect and self-esteem in the face of such non-recognition by important others.

Good discipline is a necessary feature in any team, but, it's not what you do but the way that you do it that is vital. Aristotle said that 'Anyone can become angry—that is easy. But to be angry with the right person, to the right degree, at the right time, for the right purpose, and in the right way, is not easy'. If there is seemingly poor discipline the leader or manager is likely to experience anxiety, in particular, anxieties about whether they as managers and leaders have carried out their role effectively and whether they will be 'blamed' in some way for this lack of discipline by the team. As has been described, this can become a near intolerable state for the manager or leader who will be under immense pressure to act. If they are not sufficiently self-aware, they are likely to adopt a response which seeks to force the other team members into submission.

When this happens, it can become a battle of wills. In the short-term, the manager or leader may demand and gain the sought after compliance; but, in the longer-term, other team members will withdraw their support and perhaps in subtle ways reject and defy the manager's injunctions. They just simply will not want to conform because they feel their freedom to act, as they want to, has been too limited. The result will be non-compliance, albeit not a full frontal non-compliance, more likely it will be a secret one. Team members need to feel that they have some control over what they do, if they do not, they will not conform, they will not play in a disciplined way, and will thus lose. At every stage all team members need to have some control over the processes and plans, they should be able to feel that these are *their* plans and that they have achieved *their* desired results, albeit with the manager's co-operation.

Breakdowns in discipline

Even in the best ordered teams there will, from time to time, be breakdowns in discipline—it is almost inevitable. All manner of things may cause this to happen, especially where there is a high degree of anxiety, in which case team members may adopt a different form of behaviour that they think is appropriate in the circumstances. This will be very, very irritating for the manager who may see all their plans threatened by the perceived indiscipline of one or other of the team members. Should a manager or leader succumb to their feelings and come down on the other team member with harsh strictures which may, or may not, force them into conformity, then almost certainly the manager or leader is going to underline their grudge against being deprived of their own control. They will weaken the other team member's self-esteem and may cause them to regress further to a state of indiscipline. It may be more difficult and will undoubtedly take longer, but it will be less trouble in the end, if the manager or leader appeals to their more adult nature by asking for their co-operation.

What is most important in these circumstances is that you do not ignore the behaviour. Doubtless, many managers and leaders will want to convince themselves that this was just a minor aberration, something that occurred in the heat of the moment, and, that it is best forgotten. This sort of rationalization may solve the immediate problem of the leader or manager but it will certainly be no help to the other team member if they feel that you are not interested in whether they learn to perform in a disciplined way or not. In this, as in other things, team members need a little firmness and encouragement at the right time. By way of example, I am reminded of the following incidents in football matches, the first being an attempt to force a player into conformity and the second an appeal to maturity. In the first instant, a player made several errors in the first half of a football match. At half-time the manager berated him and demanded that he get his act together in the next ten minutes or he would be substituted. Shortly after the restart, the player was cautioned by the referee for dangerous play, he then ran around aimlessly until he was substituted. In the second instant, contrary to the agreed system, an attacking player took a quick throw-in which resulted in the opposition gaining possession of the ball and subsequently scoring a goal from this weakened position. Here, the player was firmly reminded of the agreed system and encouraged to get it right next time. He responded by showing that he understood what he had done was to the detriment of the team and carried on playing with self-control.

As managers and leaders we may need a little extra patience when it comes to the need to bear with other team member's desires and struggles to do things for themselves. When managers or leaders are themselves busy and preoccupied with matters it may be difficult not to provide a ready made solution in the interests of time and energy. However, this achieves very little for other team member for whom it is most important that they should be given the chance to try. Dependence leads to a lack of creativity which means that when other team members are let loose on the field of play they are not capable of independent thought. If we can manage to do so, it's important not to get involved in a clash of wills. This can tend to happen over almost anything. It is important that we encourage the independent explorations of other team members. If they can discover it by themselves the team members will believe in it.

Given the manager or leader's desires for success and their undoubted knowledge and experience of the game it would hardly be surprising if they did not have a good idea of how to improve things when the team was not doing well. A frequent problem for all managers and leaders is concerning the questions, 'to what extent can we ask and expect other team members to cope with frustration and anxiety themselves', and, 'when do we need to step in, to help them and to take over responsibility?' Getting this difficult balance right is an important yet complicated affair. If the manager or leader is too helpful it will simply encourage dependence, but equally, if we provide other team members with the space to explore for themselves when they are truly suffering anxiety, without providing sufficient containment, we may send the message that we don't care which then results in feelings of neglect and a lack of trust in managers and leaders.

An example of the sort of behaviour I am referring to is attributed to a current Premiership manager. Sensing that there was a problem regarding the way the team were organizing in defence he set the other team members the task of going out onto the practice pitch to find out what was wrong and to develop a solution for the future. From the manager's perspective there is little doubt that he was aware of what needed doing. However, the important thing was that other team members knew what needed doing. If the manager had told them they may never have truly discovered what was required; by working out a solution themselves they not only knew why, but were committed to the solution that was their idea. The leadership provided was to set other team members a clear task and to keep them to that task providing containment for the anxiety and frustration they might experience while seeking a solution.

There will, of course, be times when it is appropriate for the manager or leader to provide help to other team members—even to the extent of making a decision on their behalf. However, it is my experience that this is not the main problem; the real problem for managers and leaders is to stop providing help to other team members. If we are to be successful, we need to give other team members a chance to test their resources and their capacities. Trying these out alone, within a secure framework of a caring manager or leader to help when really necessary, gives them the chance to feel that they are learning and growing in their roles. The leadership in this sort of circumstance lies in providing support and containment while other team members struggle for a solution.

We do not always have the time to let them try out their experiments, and often we do not have the patience to let them make mistakes, when it would be much quicker for us to do things for them. It may be quicker, for instance, to feed the football players with all sorts of solutions to set piece play on the pitch, even though they may want to think about doing it for themselves. No doubt there are times when a quick response is necessary, when you have to make these decisions for them, even when they want to do it. For example, a decision may be needed regarding who will take a penalty kick when the regular penalty taker is off the field. By making the decision the manager may prevent a reluctant penalty taker from taking a responsibility that is being projected onto them by their peers.

Nevertheless, one does need to avoid hurrying other team members along more than is necessary. Each team member has a pace beyond which you can't hurry them without causing undue anxiety. And what is undue anxiety? As described in Chapter 4, it is when we perceive that our desires are not being satisfied, alarm bells are ringing and panic is setting in. When anxiety reaches this level, it is so strong that team members seek to avoid it by turning away from tackling the obstacles and frustrations causing it. It is not difficult to detect as the team members seem to be going through the motions rather than playing with creativity and flair. It is anxiety that makes them limit their vision and split off from their mental experience, impulses, and areas of themselves that cause them pain.

Under too much pressure some team members will tend to resort to the use of defence mechanisms which tend to restrict and break up contact with people, with objects, and with life in general. They are methods that fail to integrate or that actively disintegrate their capacity to perceive and to feel. These methods can, if employed excessively, result in a team member who appears to be unintelligent, or dull and apathetic, or lost in daydreams that never lead anywhere. This was precisely the case with one particular team member, who, experiencing the manager as a wholly bad object appeared a big softie. Because others did not understand him and because he was seen as different, other team members and staff members referred to him as being 'thick'. We all use such methods to some degree or other, if only momentarily, when we wish to escape from the life we find too much to cope with. They become serious only when they are impairing development. From the manager or leader's perspective it is important to adjust their standards and expectations to their perception of the stage at which any particular team member is, at any given time, and to refrain from putting too much pressure on them to do more than they are able to manage without getting too worried. And, of course, we need to be aware that managers and leaders also resort to using defence mechanisms.

Giving feedback

As is frequently the case when we are talking about relationships, it is not what you do but the way that you do it. Where team members are not behaving in the agreed manner it is the manager or leader's job to bring this to their notice, but how they do this will have a direct affect on performance. There are a multitude of pitfalls awaiting the manager or leader as they seek to give feedback that will result in improved behaviour by other team members. For example, too much instruction and they will become dependent; while making it personal will make them angry and resentful. How you do it, then, is a skill well worth developing. The starting point as ever, is self-awareness, so that you are aware of the other.

Feedback and how it is given is a vitally important skill requirement for all managers and leaders. Correcting team members—not to mention ordering them what to do—has the effect of lowering their self-respect and self-esteem, by bringing their short-comings to their attention. Even if they obey, they will not profit from the correction; the formation of a truly autonomous individual with an independent personality will not be encouraged. The principles, or underlying assumptions, of their behaviour will alter only if and when they themselves realize that a change will gain for them what they most deeply desire: self-respect.

Some simple guidelines for giving feedback are detailed below, following these guidelines can help decrease the potential for interpersonal conflict.

Don't blow your cool

The manager or leader should remain relatively calm and use only a moderate level of emotion. Keep the emotional level only high enough to get the person's attention, make it obvious that a problem exists, but don't get carried away. Remember self-control follows self-reflection and self-awareness.

Don't attack personalities

Don't attack the person's worth as a human being. Separate the individual as a person from their behaviour. The individual is OK, but their behaviour is not. Zero in on that behaviour and not on the person.

Be specific

It is not very helpful to an individual to say, 'I don't like the way you've been performing lately'. That kind of feedback is too general. For development to occur effectively, we must tell the individual specifically what they have done wrong, for example, 'You did not look across the back line and played the opposing striker on side'.

Be timely

Unless feedback occurs as close to the behaviour or poor performance as possible, it won't be helpful in influencing future behaviour. Some managers want to store up feedback until they are armed with all sorts of things to chuck at players. When they've done so they then charge in and dump them all on the table. Frequently this results in manager and player arguing about the 'facts' and the player doesn't really hear what they have done wrong. If managers would only intervene early, they could calmly deal with one behaviour at a time, and the player could hear the feedback.

Be consistent

Managers should avoid inconsistency in giving feedback to their players. The same behaviour should always be met by the same response. Players will become confused if they are reprimanded for poor performance one week and ignored when they engage in the same poor performance the next week. We must also be careful to treat one staff member the same as another. Be careful not to have favourites. Positive reinforcement should be given for performance, not because of who a person is.

Don't threaten

So many managers announce in ominous tones that they are going to do such and such if a person continues to behave or perform in a certain way, and then never follow through. If players realize we are bluffing, they won't pay any attention to threats. Then, when we finally do follow through on a threat, we are usually so out of control that we come down excessively hard. So, very simply, we must say what we mean and mean what we say.

Be fair

Managers should be careful not to make feedback greater than the problem and *vice versa*. Many managers come down harder on people for little things than for more major performance problems. If individuals know what is expected of them and they don't do it, they will readily accept feedback (in fact, sometimes they are confused when they don't get it). But if the feedback is punishing and way out of proportion to the performance, they will justifiably resent their manager.

Be careful that feedback does not reinforce poor behaviour

Sometimes the only way that players can get a manager's attention is by playing badly or by misbehaving. If that is true and attention from their manager is important to them, they may behave inappropriately just to be recognized, even if they get punished and have to pay a price in the bargain. Remember given a choice between no attention and negative attention, players may take the negative option. Attachment needs are important to us all.

The foregoing are helpful as a guide to giving feedback, but I would strongly recommend that the reader reflects on the occasions when they have been given feedback and get in touch with the feelings they experienced at the time. Those occasions where the behaviour of those giving feedback was experienced as a pleasurable outcome which resulted in high self-esteem, may be worthy of replication with others. However, those occasions where the experience of the feedback given was experienced as unpleasant, with a subsequent lowering of self-esteem, may be avoided at all costs. Remember, you can't learn these things from a book; you can't learn it from other people telling you about their experience; you *can* learn about them by self-reflection.

Lack of self-control and self-perception

You will have gathered from much of what has been said so far that self-control is a vital aspect of all management and leadership. In Chapter 4, I introduced a concept that I referred to as a lack of self-perception—that is, the inability or lack of attempt by people to look at themselves, to see what they themselves were actually doing—that resulted in poor management and leadership. As discussed, there are many factors that can produce this lack of self-perception in individuals and groups: fear and anxiety, enthusiasm and excitement, over-involvement or alienation; and this lack may constantly manifest itself, not only in the other team members but also in managers and leaders. The successful managers and leaders are those that have the capacity to prevent group and organizational pressures and human failings from distorting or limiting self-perception. To achieve this requires continual self-reflection.

There are particular circumstances when our human failings may result in a lack of self-control and even lack of self-perception. Not least, are the occasions when activities by other team members remind us of aspects of ourselves we cannot tolerate, which we have not considered enough and have not learned to modify and integrate within our own personalities. In these circumstances we have a tendency to be over-severe with other team members and to stamp on these aspects, either with overt severity or more implicitly. We may assume for example, a 'we don't do that kind of thing' attitude, which can be even more difficult for a team member to withstand.

For example, a manager or leader, when a player, may not have suffered fools gladly and consequently challenged and confronted coaches that they did not respect. This may have brought about negative results which were to the detriment of the player. On these many occasions they may have reflected and regretted not being able to take a different stance. Now, they are the manager or leader and being confronted with a player who does not suffer fools gladly, it awakens all these old feelings, with the result that the player gets slapped down most firmly. The player, for their part, will find this difficult to understand and may well lose respect for the manager and for anything they say in the future. The only real way that this situation could have been avoided was if the manager or leader had sufficient self-awareness.

Team members cannot learn to control their undesirable, aggressive emotions unless they have had a chance to experience them, to know them at first hand. Like the manager or leader, they cannot learn about them from a book or from someone else telling them, the only way they can gain understanding and, the only way they can find resources within themselves to harness their efforts and, if possible to utilize them to good purpose, is to experience their emotions. This requires time and patience on their part. But equally important in developing self-discipline is the patience with which a manager or leader waits for other team members to make up their own minds. The manager or leader's patience sets an important example and also implies the conviction that, given enough time, other team members will arrive at the right decision all by themselves —a conviction which additionally greatly enhances their self-respect.

Because of our ability as human beings to perceive the subjective experience of another person, be that pleasure or pain, this creates a temptation, which at times may be immense, for the manager or leader to provide leadership. The usual typically unrecognized quality of this good, residing in our own common sense, has to struggle against over-involvement. There are several ways that this can be done, for example, in some circumstances it can be done by sleeping on it or at least by taking sufficient time to reflect on the events before raising it with the other team members concerned. The wish to be worrying, re-worrying, doing, meddling, fixing, mending, replacing, and trying to change oneself or somebody else can often contribute only to an increasing and spreading anxiety. Frequently, the most valuable leadership role that can be provided is to encourage leadership in others.

There are occasions, however, when team member's unchecked impulses get the better of them and lead them to do things that end up with them feeling frightened or overwhelmingly guilty. On such occasions, it is important that the manager or leader is around to firmly take control and to put a stop to it, or if things have gone too far, to take steps to prevent this arising next time. The onus is on the manager to stop the team member if he sees that it is too much for them to control. This may be the case with a footballer who during a game is suffering a torrid time at the expense of a highly capable opponent. As the match develops frustration and anger may grow until the player is ready to resort to more primitive desires such as the desire to physically injure their opponent. Where the manager entreats a team member to 'get stuck in' to their opponent they are simply stoking the fires and adding to their primitive desires. The good manager or leader will be able to prevent this by firmly taking control, by providing the player with support and encouragement and generally helping to promote the player's self-esteem.

Emotional distance

Of the many factors that can produce a lack of self-control or even a lack of self-perception in managers or leaders, the single most important is what I shall call over-emotional involvement. This may be either fear and anxiety, enthusiasm and excitement, over-involvement or alienation. Whatever the cause, the effect is a temporary incapacitation of the manager or leader's self-control leading to a loss of their ability to carry out the control function of management or leadership. In other words, given the above circumstances, where a team member has lost control, if the manager or leader had also lost control they would not be able to provide the firm support necessary. They would not be in a position to provide the leadership that the other team member so desperately needed. They would have let the player down.

But, I hear the reader saying, football is an emotional game, we need managers and leaders who are enthusiastic. Whatever sort of business we are in we need to encourage other team members to develop and to move on to greater and better things. It is hardly surprising, therefore, that managers or leaders should become emotional. This may be so and who, I also hear the reader saying, would not expect the manager or leader to react with great pleasure when their team won the Cup Final. It would indeed be a strange world if those in managerial and leadership roles did not experience both high and low emotions from time to time. However, the important point is that managers and leaders are aware of the incapacitating effects that over-emotional involvement can have. In the cases cited in Chapter 4, Arsene Wenger and Bobby Moore were both aware of this problem and dealt with it. Despite the difficulties, it is perfectly possible that good managers and leaders can develop the capacity to prevent group and organizational pressures and human failing from distorting or limiting self-perception.

If the manager or leader is also emotionally involved in the sort of activity that is causing dysfunctional team behaviour they will not be able to help. And this brings us to another important concept; that of 'distance'. This was a concept referred to by Fiedler (1967) many years ago, but it seems to have disappeared from more recent management thinking. The 'distance' a manager or leader keeps may help them in their struggles to maintain self-awareness and self-control and thus make themselves beneficial to other team members who are in need of firm support. To explain what is meant by 'distance' let's look at the examples provided in the next two paragraphs which were used to help the manager to begin to come to terms with his over-emotional involvement during games.

In this first example, imagine that you are standing about half a mile outside a forest. From this position you can see the extent of the forest and you can locate where you are in relation to other places. Now let's take a walk into the forest and keep walking for about a mile. The deeper we go, the less able are we to get our bearings and we literally cannot see the wood from the trees. All we are able to see is the immediate surroundings and we cannot take a wider perspective of things. When we were outside the forest, when we were at a 'distance' we were able to see things in a wider perspective but when we lost this 'distance' we became partially blind.

Now, let's imagine that we are standing in the street when we see a fight taking place about a hundred yards away. We can see what appears to be several men physically fighting each other. Exactly what it is about and whether or not it is deadly serious or simply over-exuberance we don't know. We then start to walk towards the fight and as we get nearer and nearer we realize that the combatants are fighting in earnest and at some stage we can feel that all are extremely angry. At a certain moment we reach a point 'at the boundary' of the fight where we are able to see and hear precisely what is going on and to gain a real sense of the anger and other emotions of the participants. Being good citizens we keep going in an attempt to separate the fighters. Now, we are 'inside the boundary' and are likely to become embroiled in the fight. When this happens there is a grave danger that we also will become part of the fight and also, in turn, like those involved become angry and emotional. Eventually, we may reach a point where our self-perception is affected so that, our inability or lack of attempt to look at ourselves, to see what we ourselves are actually doing, is so limited that we can no longer make objective judgements.

Let's reflect on the two examples. In the first situation, we were mainly concerned with 'physical distance'. Here it became difficult to see the wood from the trees but we retained our capacity for thought and self-reflection. However, in the second situation, we were also concerned with 'emotional distance'. Here at a certain stage, the emotion impaired our self-perception and prevented us from thinking straight. It is this latter distance that we are more concerned with when it comes to managing and leading teams. Physical distance may be of assistance in helping us to keep an emotional distance but it is emotional distance which may lead to a lack of self-perception, with all its attendant failings. This occurs when we become overwhelmed by our own emotions or those of the team members.

'Emotional distance' is essential if we are to be able to take a clearer view of past, present and future. It is a definite advantage to have a trusted leader who, for instance, knows that a past chance has been lost, and who insists that everyone should realize that there is no turning the clock back. In all sorts of organizations there will be pressures on managers and leaders to 'get good results', it is important that they are able to deal with these pressures, that they have the capacity to prevent group and organizational pressures and human failing from distorting or limiting their self-perception. While in the middle of a crisis, an overwhelmed team might well appreciate a reminder that difficult times have beginnings, middles, and blessed ends. At the time they may have no concept of ends or beginnings—just of awful, never ending middles.

However, this distance-keeping needs to be understood in order for it to become an appreciated good, rather than devalued. There is a danger that if we do not get the balance right, it may have the effect of making the distance seem like lack of interest, or rejection, even to the manager or leader themselves. To try to understand more about this balance let's return for a moment to the example of the fight. When we are walking towards the fight, up to a certain point, we still have no 'feeling' for what is going on. They are still strangers who could be larking about and this is not causing us any great emotional concern. However, at a certain point, the point I will identify as 'at the boundary' of the fight, we are not only aware of the physical nature of the fight but more importantly we can fully sense the emotion. We can tell just how angry and how emotional the participants are.

This is the point that managers and leaders need to be at with the team, close enough to sense and understand the feelings of the team members but far enough to avoid being swamped by the emotion and in danger of losing their self-perception. Developing an awareness of the prevalent emotions is a necessary part of all managerial and leadership roles. It is only if you are capable of self-control that you can gain an awareness of the emotions of others. It is only when managers and leaders are working at this level of awareness with other team members that they can truly understand where they are at and what they are experiencing—both physically and emotionally. If managers and leaders do not have this level of understanding of other team members they may well be uninterested in their fate and, in any event, may appear remote and uninterested and be experienced as rejecting by other team members. 'Being there' for the other team members means being close enough to reach out and truly understand the emotions they are experiencing without going so far as to be overwhelmed by the emotions and thus becoming incapacitated.

Relatedness

There is another aspect to this issue that needs exploration: that concerning our relatedness to others. By this I mean the way that our phantasies and feelings about one's self or one's group and the other person or other group affects our behaviour. I have already referred to a phantasy relationship as opposed to a reality relationship and the use of phantasy here is used in the same sort of context. For example, from our past experience we may phantasize that an opposing team is going to approach a game in a particular way. The phantasy may range from viewing them as soft or a pushover to being brutal and tough. Whatever the phantasy, should that guide the team's actions, it will affect the way they approach the game and may either cause them to be over-confident or scared before they even take the field.

These phantasies are not developed out of experience, but simply from phantasies formed by the team members about the opposing side. Clearly, if the team members are confident and there is a high degree of self-esteem the danger may be a phantasy that the other side may be a pushover. Where the team is lacking in confidence and there is low self-esteem they may develop a phantasy that the other side are unbeatable. Both phantasies are equally dangerous because they are not based on reality and the resulting behaviour may be totally inappropriate. The manager or leader can also become part of this phantasizing if they are not able to remain at the boundary. By keeping an emotional distance, they will be aware of other team members' phantasies, will be able to challenge them, and create a space for more reality based thinking.

Before leaving this matter there is another angle that I want to pursue. In the circumstances of the team referred to above we have a traditional group that meets together to carry out their work—in this case playing football. However, groups can also exist in the mind. An example concerns a 'group' of personnel managers distributed at geographic locations throughout a large organization. These employees seldom, if ever, meet as an actual group but they most certainly exist as a 'group in the mind'. As such, they are subject to the same sort of dynamics and processes as those concerning the football team. The members of this 'group in the mind' may develop the same sort of phantasies and feelings about other groups in the organization. Where they are a large group the dynamics may be negative as are those frequently associated with the large group.

To take an example from football let us consider referees. They are distributed throughout the country and seldom come together as a group, but almost certainly they exist as 'a group in the mind'. However, this 'group (of referees) in the mind' is not something that exists solely in the mind of referees but also in other groups such as the media, supporters, and players. The phantasies and feelings that these other groups have about referees effects the way they relate to them—frequently in negative ways. In due course, this may also effect the way that referees relate to these other groups. Thus we get into a sort of vortex where phantasy builds on phantasy and affects the behaviour of both footballers and referees.

Empathy

'Empathy' has been described as 'feeling into', that is the ability to perceive the subjective experience of another person. It is posited that empathy is a process where we imitate the distress or elation of another, which then evokes the same feelings in us. In family life we frequently empathize with the pain and suffering or sheer delight of our parents, siblings or children. If we are able to do it in those circumstances we can do it in others. It is really only a matter of application. Emotions accompany almost all behaviour; it is detectable in our verbal communications and even more so in our non-verbal communications. When we walk into our home we can almost instantly tell 'the mood' or emotional state of our family. We can tune in to their emotions; we can communicate with each other at an emotional level.

Developing the skills required for an understanding of emotions is paramount for all leaders and managers. It may seem difficult to achieve, but if it allows you to get in touch with the feelings of other team members prior to an important event it is absolutely invaluable. By attuning oneself to other team member's feelings and then using yourself in a reflective manner to identify your feelings you will almost certainly be identifying those feelings you have picked up from other team members. Before a football match, if you are communicating at an emotional level, it is always possible to tell how the team are approaching the game. Emotional communication may indicate that the mental state of the team members is anywhere on a scale from over-confident to lacking in confidence. At a verbal communication level they may indicate a similar scale. However, you may find that emotional and verbal communication do not indicate the same mental state. For example, the team members may be saying things like 'we're going to murder them' or 'we're really up for it today', but the emotional message may be very different. The emotional message (the authentic message), may show that they are exceedingly anxious and worried about the prospect of going out to play the contest. Armed with this knowledge the manager or leader can work with the team, in these circumstances, to increase their self-esteem; in other circumstances they may have to bring them down to earth.

Providing containment

Sometimes value-judgements are neither here nor there. What is important is the decision: that it should be made, who makes it, and whether the maker is the proper authority. There are times when team members are greatly relieved when a decision is made in a difficult matter. The relief stems from the knowledge that the appropriate authority has decided what to do and is strong enough to accept the consequences, even should the decision prove to be wrong. The responsibility lies with the manager or leader. This is important because an organization or institution that knows it has an authority that can be trusted, no matter what, may certainly experience anxiety, but the anxiety is likely to be more tolerable. Life can still proceed in a productive and creative fashion, which would be impossible if there were unspoken doubts as to who holds ultimate responsibility.

We are all members of a group from the moment we are born and we are all 'group animals' (Bion, 1961). Our experiences in this first group, the family, has a lasting effect on us throughout life. I therefore want to return to that stage for a short while. The younger the child, the more they admire their parents. In fact, they cannot do otherwise; they need to believe in their perfection in order to feel safe. In what image can they form themselves but that of the persons who act as parents to them? Who else is so close and so important to them? And if things are as they should be, nobody loves them so well, takes such good care of them as their parents do. Every child wishes to believe that they are their parent's favourite; and the fear that they might not be is the root of sibling rivalry, the intensity of which is a measure of this anxiety.

As the child grows older their wish to emulate their parents will grow weaker. However, their wish to be favourite will continue in full force, although it may be extended to include teachers and some friends, for their earlier need to admire their parents unconditionally was so strong and deeply rooted that it will be powerfully at work in their unconscious for a long time. Thus, in most teams we are indeed fortunate that there is a solid basis for the other team members childhood wish to be their parent's disciple, to love and admire them, and to emulate them, if not totally, then in some important respects. It exists, if not in their conscious, then certainly in their unconscious mind. Team members need a leader that they can feel proud of, one they can look up to, one they can love and admire. It is part of the role of managers and leaders to build on other team member's childhood needs for attachment so as to promote self-control around particular issues and, even more important, an inner commitment to be a disciplined team member. The team members who neither admire their manager or leader nor wish to emulate them may very well find some other person to look up to and in whose image to form themselves. In those instances, the team member concerned will soon be banging on the manager's door asking for a transfer.

There is yet another hangover from childhood, the tendency of team members to respond more readily—both positively and negatively—if they feel the strength of the manager or leader's emotional involvement. Throughout the book I have referred to the need for self-control and self-awareness and nothing which follows is intended to contradict this advice. However, as has also been said, but perhaps with not quite the same strength of emphasis, managers and leaders need to be emotional. They should not attempt to hide their feelings, but to work with other team members in a way which clearly shows their feelings, be that pleasure and elation or anger and frustration. Disciplined behaviour can preclude a display of feelings, even when we feel strongly about what is involved. It is when managers or leaders express their feelings that team members are most impressed, for then they are receiving powerful signals. The paradox is that the teaching of self-control requires great patience on the part of the manager or leader; but patience is a quiet virtue and almost certainly will not make as deep and immediate impression as an expression of feelings. It takes what seems to be an infinite number of examples of self-control and patience on the part of the manager or leader to model the values of this kind of behaviour and to influence other team members to internalize these values.

Authenticity is about communicating at all levels, especially at an emotional level. Recognizing and managing feelings are important aspects of emotional development. Everyone always has feelings, whether or not they recognize or talk about them. Some of us find it difficult to talk about our feelings. In certain parts of our society it is an almost 'no go' area. Sadly, in many football clubs where there is a highly macho culture it may not be appropriate to relate to feelings. Yet, this does not mean that emotional difficulties do not exist and any one can see the results. For example, team members, especially young players, may withdraw from their family and friends, be lethargic and unhappy or depressed. At the Club they may be unable to concentrate, underachieve or be aggressive and attention seeking. All are indicators of emotional difficulties which, if not recognized and dealt with, may seriously hinder the playing performance of those concerned.

Personal behaviour is frequently influenced by feelings. Compulsive behaviour (repeated patterns of behaviour, cannot help oneself) and impulsive behaviour (instant response, without thought for the consequences) are extreme forms. We need to identify and explore examples. What triggers them? What are the feelings experienced at the time? How might these feelings be managed differently? Handling impulsive behaviour can be linked to problem solving, by recognizing the need to calm down, describe the problem, with a conscious identification of possible solutions and their consequences, selecting the best solution and implementing it.

When responding to a statement of feelings, perhaps by summarizing it to show understanding, this summary has to communicate recognition of the emotions behind the message and the response, not just the words. Listening skills are essential, and are reflected in the sensitivity of the response. Too often people will jump in to tell others what to do, interrogate them or talk about themselves, showing that they did not hear what was really said at all. Empathy is demonstrating understanding and acceptance of the other person at the emotional level, feeling with them.

I have frequently seen the football manager with his team either at half-time or at full-time berating a particular player or the team in general for some perceived failure. None of the other team members could possibly be in any doubt about the power and level of feelings that the manager is experiencing at this time. As such, it serves to 'hook' the individual player or the team into a response. However, that response is more often than not a response to the manager's anger rather than the perceived failure. Thus it tends to develop into a slanging match about who is most angry, which is of no value to any of those concerned. Conversely, I have seen the manager retain his self-control to such an extent that his feelings have not come across. Here, the team meeting has been something of a damp squib. It is as though the players have not felt able to trust the manager and are fearful that the more primitive aspects will soon raise their head again.

Feelings are often at their most intense and least managed, during conflict. Exploring real conflict situations is a starting point—what happened and why? What else might you have done? Some situations may have arisen through misinterpreting the other person's actions, a failure in communication. Reading non-verbal signals is an acquired skill which many people lack. By exploring these situations and recognizing alternative causes and possible responses, and their consequences, can give a measure of control based on understanding of one's own behaviour and new, learnt, reactions. Before you can relate at an emotional level with others, understand what they are feeling and identify with those feelings (that is, empathize) you have to be self-aware, in touch with and understanding your own feelings so that you can distinguish your own feelings from those of other team members.

The difficult and slow process of change

In many ways, changing one's behaviour is a difficult and thankless task. It frequently involves attempts by other team members to get you to revert to your old ways of behaving. They don't trust this 'new' behaviour and would rather have the devil they knew than this unpredictable person they now have to deal with. There is a need to be aware that for both the manager or leader and for other team members the acquisition of self-discipline is a continuous but slow process of many small steps and many backslides, a process so protracted that in retrospect it may seem to have been unremarkable, as if 'natural', and fairly painless. Having forgotten what this process was really like, managers and leaders tend to be impatient when other team members have a hard time of it. Moreover, they may forget how powerful a motivator the fear of hellfire and damnation once was, and expect other team members to acquire self-discipline even without this kind of spur.

For the football manager there were occasions when it was somehow easier and from his point of view relieving to shout and yell. For the team members, though, this sort of impatience was hardly likely to provide them with containment or a role model that they might emulate. If we are able to reflect and get in touch with our own feelings and try to remember our own struggles in this area—how undisciplined we ourselves often were as team members, and how hard a time we had before we became managers and leaders in disciplining ourselves, how we felt put upon, if not actually abused, when our managers and leaders forced us to behave in a disciplined manner against our will—then we and other team members would be much better off.

Often when working with the manager it would be highly

valuable to get him to reflect on his experience as a player. He also found it highly rewarding to reflect on his experience concerning the development of his son. Almost certainly, the ability to get in touch with his feelings was enhanced by the deep love and affection that he felt for his son. So frequently did we reflect on aspects of his son's development that we had a running joke about 'poor old George being under the microscope again'. In reality it was not the son who was under the microscope but the father.

To be disciplined by others, to accept living by their rules, makes self-control superfluous. When the important aspects of other team members' lives and behaviour are regulated by the manager they will see no need to learn to control themselves, since it will be done for them. By the same token, they cannot learn self-control before they are ready to do so. That is before they are mature enough to understand why it is a necessary and advantageous ability to acquire. Only after other team members have achieved sufficient maturity to be able to make their own decisions can they learn to be self-controlled. With a consistent role model who is prepared to work with team members in a patient and caring manner this can be achieved within a relatively short time scale. In getting to that point other team members will learn to reason on their own, since self-control is based on the wish to act on the basis of one's own decisions, arrived at through one's own deliberations. The manager's patience sets an important example and provides the containment for team members to develop the belief that, given enough time, they will arrive at the right decision all by themselves—a belief which additionally greatly enhances their self-respect.

But, I hear you say, what if all else fails? Shouldn't I punish my team members? Shouldn't I make them understand that their performance was just simply not good enough by imposing some sort of sanction on them? Wouldn't punishment make them obey the orders they are given? The next chapter, which is devoted to the matter of punishment, will seek to answer these and other questions.

CHAPTER SEVEN

Why punishment does not achieve discipline

S o that we have some shared understanding of the notion of 'punishment' I shall define it as 'exacting payment in terms of pain, or frustration, or inconvenience for offences committed, and discipline as measures taken to prevent them from occurring again'. And, let me make it clear right from the start that, in my view, punishment, unlike discipline, has no necessary place in team development. That having been said, I will gladly acknowledge that punishment of some kind or another will inevitably have been meted out by every manager to every team member, at some time or another. It may not be given in cold blood and it may well be rationalized as being for the team member's good. It may even be quite inadvertent. But, while punishment may make us obey the orders we are given, the best it will do is to teach us an obedience to authority, it will never result in self-control which enhances our self-respect.

Whatever the circumstances, there can be few managers or leaders who have not given the odd slap-down to other team members when they have been driven by exasperation, or when sensing that what the team, or one or more of its members, are doing is likely to result in some sort of calamity. In most cases these occasional 'slap-downs' are probably taken correctly by the team members as signifying that they have gone too far and have stepped outside the agreed boundaries. The team member concerned understands that they had maybe better stop and think about their behaviour even though their feelings have been hurt by this 'slap-down'.

A team member will accept the occasional 'slap-down' when they have just made a dreadful error. Footballers will generally readily acknowledge this fact to the manager when they know what they've done has been costly to the side. They may even accept the manager's chastisement on some of the occasions when they have not really been the guilty party, but get the blame instead of someone else who has paved the way by too much provocation. I guess that in their own way they are empathizing with their manager and understanding their feelings of annoyance. It may even be salutary for team members to realize that the manager's patience is getting thin and that managers and leaders also have rights. Salutary that is, provided that these spells of 'slap-downs' occur as exceptions within the context of a relationship on the part of the manager or leader that is predominantly containing, protective, and secure. If team members' are accustomed to being 'slapped-down' for all kinds of thing, they will probably be too bewildered and used to being in trouble to have the heart to wonder and try to puzzle out the reason why (Bettleheim, 1988).

Excessive harshness on the part of the manager or leader can confirm the fears of a team member and may result in great anxiety for them as they will not only feel the need to placate this external aggressor, but may also be suffering from their own crippling and possibly primitive conscience. This is what happened to the player who had suffered a miserable first-half of a particular game, when seemingly nothing had gone right. At half-time, the manager berated him and told him in no uncertain manner that he should get his act together or he'd be off. On his return to the field of play, the player was clearly motivated by primitive aggression and within a short while was booked for foul play. Now, not knowing how to respond, he ran around aimlessly until being substituted.

Where, however, the manager is able to express understanding with firmness it leaves the team member freer to develop a more realistic conscience less prompted by fear and more influenced by care and concern for others. This is precisely what happened on another occasion, when a different player had also suffered a really bad first-half, and came off the pitch full of self-doubt. At half-time the manager took him to one side and in a most empathic manner showed that he understood the situation, offered some help and guidance, and some firm instructions as to how to improve in the second-half. The result was that the player went out for the second-half with an improved mental attitude and stuck at the task, difficult as it was.

Distinguishing between firmness and punishment

A vital distinction, then, and an important good is the ability of managers and leaders to differentiate between firmness and punitiveness. In the minds of some managers and leaders firmness and punitiveness or violence are often confused. Being firm means an insistence on keeping to agreed boundaries. For example, on match days it is important that all players report by a determined and agreed time. All players are aware of this boundary and know that there are few, if any, excuses for non-compliance. Where one or more team members fail to observe this boundary the manager needs to be firm and insist on compliance. Being punitive would involve certain actions by the manager such as fining the player concerned as a means of coercion. Quite apart from the unfairness of such action, punishment will not result in future compliance, it simply means that the player concerned learns to pay a fine. As we shall see, firmness may lead to understanding and self-discipline.

That some managers and leaders often confuse the notion of firmness with that of punitiveness, or even violence is not in doubt. Most certainly this is the case in football where many managers are known to be guilty of violent acts such as cup throwing and physical assaults on players. The widespread adoption of such behaviour and the belief that this is an appropriate approach, or even the only approach and that players will understand and respond, means that we need to look at this in some detail. So, where do we start? Well, as was discussed in the last chapter, the bottom line is that boundaries have to be set for the good of both individuals and teams and this may at time require firmness on the part of those charged with authority for the team. For example, boundaries are set for footballers which require them to refrain from alcohol and late nights immediately before a game. Players are also expected to play within the rules of the game. If these boundaries were not reinforced with a degree of firmness, players would not behave in a manner that was necessary for a successful football team.

However, there is a world of difference between firmness and punishment, which inevitably involves some form of coercion. Coercion as a trait of human behaviour may be said to obtain wherever action or thought by one individual or group is compelled or restrained by another. To coerce is to exercise some form of physical or moral compulsion. There are numerous coercive devices the actual use or fear of which is often effective in obtaining an acquiescence to authority. Some examples of these that one frequently sees in football are as follows.

- *Social disapprobation*: where the manager, usually after a defeat, will individually or collectively publicly berate players, telling them they are a disgrace. Or, if not in public, will do so in front of other team members in the dressing room in no uncertain manner.
- *Expulsion from a group (ostracism)*: players are left to train on their own and are barred from attending team events.
- *Formal disciplinary action*: players are disciplined and their freedom limited in various ways for perceived failings.
- *Exertion of monetary pressure*: players are fined for behaviour on the field or for other perceived failings.
- *Physical violence*: there have been several examples of physical violence that have been seen in 'fly-on-the-wall' television documentaries. Although, I wish to make it clear that this has not been within my personal experience.
- *Torture*: this may sound rather extreme but I feel that some of the humiliation heaped on players by their managers amounts to nothing less than torture.

In Chapter 5, I referred to 'clarity in authority relations' and 'clarity in the leader's role'; and, defined the true nature of authority as being 'when the leader or manager is able to directly affect the behaviour of a team member if they possess authority with respect to that team member'. But, the real source of authority possessed by a manager or leader lies in the acceptance of its exercise by those who are subject to it. There is another aspect which concerns the degree of clarity and consistency that the manager or leader adopts in the way they exercise their authority. If the manager or leader is quite clear that the way they will manage is by setting boundaries and reinforcing them with the degree of firmness required, there will be no confusion, this will be perceived as caring, thereby pre-empting the need for other team members to behave more and more badly in order to find out just how far they can go. However, if they are inclined to manage by being punitive, sooner or later they will be exposed by their team members as punitive or even sadistic. The more an authority is muddled, the more it will be pressed to show its true colours by those over whom it has authority, they will push and push to see how far they can go.

Personality of the leader

The personality of the manager or leader may have much to do with the way they carry out their role. Where the manager or leader is an insecure person, having made up their mind, they will not change it, since their fear of losing face may be worse than their fear of losing the battle. A good example is that concerning an incident between Glen Hoddle, the (then) England team manager, and Chris Sutton, the Blackburn Rovers striker, who declined to play for an England 'B' Team. Hoddle is on record as having said that because of this incident Sutton would never play for England again. For one reason or another, perhaps following pressure from other influential characters in the game Hoddle said that Sutton could play again, if, as I interpreted his remarks, he were to apologize and beg forgiveness! In other words, to submit utterly and totally to his authority. Whether or not this was so in this case is unknown but in many instances where managers and leaders are acting in a punitive manner it is based on their insecurity. They do not have sufficient confidence to treat other team members as equals, rather, they feel the need to totally dominate them.

At one level we might conclude that people with a high degree of insecurity should not be engaged in management roles. However, we might also recall that all behaviour is learned by achieving our desires and all behaviour is dynamic and changeable: provided, of course, that we have the desire to change our way of behaving. The more we satisfy our desires, the more we learn: the more we learn and the more conditions we control under which our desires can be satisfied. So it is with managers who, initially, because of their own insecurity, find it difficult to act in anything but a punishing or bullying manner. However, with experience they may be able to act with firmness if they have the desire to develop a more mature approach. Where they are successful they will now have control over this type of behaviour. Here we are talking about learning from our experience, a developed awareness that we achieve through reflection. Nevertheless, it still holds true that whatever we know we have learned about, in principle, while satisfying desires.

There is a world of difference between developing discipline of other team members by identification with a manager or leader that they admire—what might be referred to as a 'good authority'—as opposed to other team members having regimentation imposed on them, or sometimes painfully inflicted. As has been pointed out several times in this book, many of the activities of managers or leaders may achieve results which are contrary to those intended. This is one of those activities: forcing discipline on team members is almost certainly going to be counterproductive, even detrimental to what the manager or leader wishes to achieve. As for punishment, this is likely to be no more successful, it may restrain the team member, but it doesn't teach them self-discipline or self-control. If we want to achieve that, we need to adopt a totally different approach.

Management is an emotional game

As we will have discovered throughout the book, whether we like it or not; whether we ignore it or not; management is an emotional game. The vicissitudes of the role can arouse in the manager or leader all sorts of emotions. It is normally when leaders or managers get carried away by the emotions which have either been aroused by other team members behaviour or by their own disappointment —and, they are not self-aware—that they punish other team members. If they are not self-aware it is no good repeating the adage 'own it don't blame it', they will not be able to own it.

Sometimes, of course, they are aware of it and, it would be helpful if they would admit to themselves that this was what they were doing, rather than camouflaging it as a method of instruction. Otherwise they may fool only themselves and not other team members. It is in this sort of situation that rationalization and other defence mechanisms frequently come into play as a means of avoiding the unthinkable.

The most helpful advice I can give in order to prevent yourself from emotionally abusing other team members is that concerning the art of achieving an 'emotional distance', which is essential if we are to be able to take a clearer view of past, present, and future. In all sorts of organizations there will be pressures on managers and leaders to 'get good results'. It is important that they are able to deal with these pressures and that they have the capacity to prevent group and organizational pressures and human failing from distorting or limiting their self-perception. While in the middle of a crisis, an overwhelmed team might well appreciate a manager or leader who is able to remind them of the boundaries that have been agreed and to reinforce them with the required degree of firmness.

Some effects of punishment

In spite of the wide use of punishment by managers and leaders it has to be said that nothing is gained. There is absolutely no benefit to be gained from this sort of behaviour. All that team members learn from punishment is that might makes right. When they have the opportunity they will try to get their own back; thus many team members punish their managers or leaders by acting in ways which are distressing to them. For example, footballers who have been punished will respond by playing out of position or not putting their full effort into a game, or even by reporting sick with a 'niggling' injury. To make things even worse their timing for being injured or for being off-form will frequently be at the most crucial time, so as to punish the manager or leader as much as possible. Frequently, players are asked to play when they have a slight injury, those who are managed in a punitive way are most unlikely to co-operate. Managers and leaders might do well to bear in mind that in all win–lose situations the 'loser' will not be satisfied until they have got their revenge and 'won'. Punishment simply stores up trouble for the future.

Any punishment—physical or emotional—has the effect of setting us against the person who inflicts it on us. And here we must remember that the injury inflicted on feelings may be much more hurtful and last much, much longer than physical pain. Should we have any doubt about this there are continual interactions between managers and leaders and other team members which provide us with all the evidence we need. Take, for example, the hurt feelings that other team members and sometimes managers and leaders experience as children, which have a lasting effect on interactions in their adult lives. One player that I worked with on a one-to-one basis was the son of a professional footballer, who, when he was a child and was trying to emulate his father by playing football, perceived the actions of his father to be humiliating. Later in life, when confronted with an authority figure in the shape of the manager, who was also critical, he unconsciously associated that criticism with his early perceived humiliation, lost all self-esteem and, in effect, became what he perceived his father had suggested—useless. The way that he had dealt with this as a child was to run away from all responsibility and to seek solace in playing in non-competitive situations. Now, in adult life, faced with a loss of self-esteem he responded in the same way—by running away.

Frequently, the manager would rationalize his punitive actions by saying that some players responded to a stick and others to a carrot. It may be true that some team members will seemingly respond to punishment, but while criticism or fear of punishment may restrain us from doing wrong, it does not make us wish to do right. Disregarding this simple fact is the great error into which leaders and managers fall when they rely on these negative means of correction. Of course, every team member will react differently to any punishment, depending on their personality and most of all on the nature of their relationship with the leader or manager, but no punished team member escapes the feeling of degradation. Even in the rough, tough, macho world of football the relationship will be damaged. Although pretending not to mind, so that they can preserve their place in the team, and perhaps while rationalizing madly, the players do mind. One of the results is that the players feel superior to their manager or leader, who has resorted to such crude methods. By way of example, I can recall situations, when, after a bad result, the players had been subjected to a tongue-lashing intended to belittle them. Sometimes, you could actually see players grow in stature, as if to say 'do as you will, I'm above all that, I'm better than you'. The danger is that this attitude, while it neutralizes the feeling of degradation, impairs not only the team members' trust for their manager or leader, but also their ability to respect them.

Most team members resent punishment and the more they admire and respect the managers or leaders, the more they are insulted by such chastisement and disappointed in the wielder of the rod. They trusted them and now they feel they can no longer do so. In this sense we can say that punishment is effective as most of us learn to avoid situations that lead to punishment. However, as we have seen with regard to criminals, it is a very weak deterrent to the person who believes they will not be caught; so the team member who was open in their actions before now learns to hide them. Thus, the team member (referred to in an earlier chapter), who openly stated that he didn't know what he was expected to do and was then so severely abused, did not ask again although he still did not know what he was supposed to do. The more severe the chastisement, the more devious will team members become.

Team members also learn to express remorse when it is expected of them, whether they feel it or not. In reality they may only be sorry that they have been found out and now have to 'face the music'. An example of this behaviour was a young player who was successfully making his mark in the team but had made a couple of blunders that could not be covered. After the game he was pushed and pushed by the assistant manager to admit his mistake. He eventually did so and when it happened next time he showed he had learnt—but all he had learnt was to say sorry. Thus, we should remember that such an expression of regret, extracted under duress, is an essentially worthless statement made to pacify us, or to get the reckoning over with. A further example concerned the goalkeeper, who, after a miserable defeat was lambasted for his failings during the game. After another such defeat, the goalkeeper came into the dressing room after the game and immediately apologized—he had learned that it was better to get the reckoning over with. Of course, what he and the young player had not learned was anything about his and his team mates, possible failings in the game.

Punishment, which by its very nature is always to some degree painful and degrading, is a very traumatic experience, both because of what it entails directly and because it endangers the team members belief in the manager or leader's benevolence, which is the firmest basis for their sense of security. Therefore, any managerial or leadership act which is meant to be a punishment, however mild, will be resented by the team member and the more drastic the punishment, the more severe the indignation it will arouse. Quite clearly no team member is likely to try to emulate or identify with someone they resent, no matter how admirable that person may be in other respects. In my experience of working with the football manager this was certainly true for those players who were punished while others would still retain their trust in the manager. For most players, the experience of their manager in training and other non-playing circumstances was that he was an extremely amiable, knowledgeable and competent professional—the sort of role model that all would seek to emulate. However, come match days the emotion would frequently turn him into a different sort of person who would at times become punitive and be resented by the team members picked out for this treatment.

In this context I feel it is important to add to this by showing that we can all change our behaviour. At one stage, I was working in a one-to-one mode with one of the players who informed me how he had discussed the manager with another team member just after he joined the club. He had said to the other player that the manager seemed a nice man and the other player responded by saying that he was, mostly, but he'd better be careful from time to time. He replied to the effect that he was surprised, and the other player added—'but he's not been so bad since Lionel's been here'. We may conclude that, while we can change, any punishment, no matter how justified in the eyes of the manager and even perhaps those of the team member, interferes with the main goals, namely, that other team members should admire the manager, accept their values, and want to act in a responsible way.

Physical, or any other form of punishment, will often cause permanent psychological injury. But even when it does not it only proves that managers and leaders who are by and large good enough managers and leaders can get away with a lot without doing serious damage to other team members. All in all, it is believed that it is always a mistake to punish a team member; even if it is thought that they deserve it. When punishment has been meted out to team members, they instinctively feel they have been treated unfairly. They may not make those distinctions clearly, or with conscious comprehension, but their feelings are nevertheless very strong. Why do team members react in this way? Primarily, it is because punishment threatens the team member's basic need for attachment to authority figures; or, put another way, the security that rests on them seeing managers and leaders as protectors who will always treat them with respect and value them. They will also feel they have been treated unfairly because it is human nature to resent anyone who has the power to punish us. How can team members possibly feel secure, if their security depends on a person whom they resent?

A very public example of this resentment concerned the Dutch international footballer Van Hooijdonk who had a dispute with his manager that became toxic. He then failed to report for pre-season training with his club (Nottingham Forest) and was subsequently punished with a heavy fine. The indignation that this punishment aroused in the player resulted in his staying away from the club for several weeks. A similar situation arose in the time I was working with the football manager. A newly recruited player openly disagreed with the manager who then punished him by leaving him out of the team. Such was the indignation about this punishment that he never played again. He took his wages until the end of the season when his contract ended and left.

There seems to be a belief in football management that the only way you can gain control over team members is to insist upon total submission which will be gained, if necessary, by humiliation. This extends to other sports such as American Football where this also seems common practice, and to other industries. I suppose this comes from the old military model of 'square bashing' which employed such methods with the intention of gaining total submission from soldiers so that they would obey orders at all times. For soldiering, in the 1900s, where personnel were used as cannon fodder and it was important that they stayed in line, this may have been appropriate, but for footballers (and even modern day soldiers) this is highly inappropriate, as the need is for creativity and self-discipline.

The difference between creating learning opportunities for team members as a desirable means of influencing behaviour, or regulating aspects of their behaviour and 'teaching' them by chastisement, may seem small or irrelevant to a manager or leader who is convinced that the purpose of their punishment is to teach other team members to act better in the future. But, as far as the team member is concerned, the difference is enormous. If other team members can feel that the manager or leader's intention is to make things good for them, even if they don't agree with the correction or prohibition, they still know deep down that the manager or leader means well; nothing blurs their view of the manager or leader as their main supporter. In many situations the manager or leader who punishes team members, will think that they are doing so to protect them against doing things which may have adverse consequences for them. The manager or leader may believe they are protecting them from themselves, but other team members will feel differently.

If the manager or leader were to really think about it before they punished a team member they would probably never punish because they lacked the objectivity and emotional distance which are the primary attributes of a dispenser of justice. This notion of emotional 'distance' was raised earlier and the reader will recall that when we are not able to maintain a distance from the group, when we become overwhelmed by the emotion, we are rather like an engaged telephone, our perceptual process is not working because new input from our sense organs is simply not getting through. We are purely reacting to our emotionality and can in no way be objective. Indeed, I feel that it is reasonable to say that in many of the instances where a manager or leader feels the need to punish, it is because they are emotionally aroused.

Where team members are managed in a punishing way, the manager or leader is relying on fear; put another way they are bullies. If a manager or leader has established control through fear, the frightened team members, not daring to speak, are left with the conflict. They cannot confront the manager or leader because they fear recriminations such as being ostracised or whatever consequences may have been threatened. But if they say nothing at all, they are left with their angry and frightened feelings. Left in this state, they may become lethargic, feel that they are paralysed to act and suffer an extreme sense of hopelessness. Controlling anger is exhausting to cope with and the knock-on effect requires consider-able emotional energy. As was stated in Chapter 2, we only have a certain amount of mental energy and where we use a good deal in controlling and coping with this sort of situation, it means we have less to pursue other desires. As a result, the enthusiasm of team members is inhibited, and this in turn affects their capacity to work. Also associated with being a victim of aggression may be feelings of worthlessness. The victim takes into themselves the role ascribed to them; but often hidden away, are feelings of revenge. A part of them will be saying 'They're not going to get away with it. Some day they will pay'.

Surely, we might say, being aware of the wholly negative consequences of punishment there isn't a manager or leader in the world who will want to continue in this way. If all that punishment achieves is team members with such a low opinion of themselves and such a low mental energy to apply to their work that the manager or leader is only getting a fraction of their worth, then surely, all will realize that there has to be a better way. Unfortunately, this is another example of where we don't learn by reading books, in this sort of circumstance we need to learn from our experience. For some managers and leaders, this sort of behaviour has been a way of life for many years. By self-reflection it is possible for them to identify the ways in which they treat other team members which are not helpful to either themselves or their team. For some, this may be sufficient to develop self-awareness and self-control so that they manage in a different way. Others may require the assistance of talking, in confidence, to a consultant such as myself who can offer advice and understanding to help them help themselves.

Getting results through other people

The foregoing has detailed and clarified many of the negative behaviours associated with punishment. But it seems that the problem of getting team members to do what has been agreed, is central to the issue of 'getting things done through other people'. So, let's look further and take as a starting point the need to accept that other team members are rarely convinced that something is wrong simply because their manager or leader says it is so. Where it becomes wrong for them is because they wish to be cared for by their leaders or managers, to be thought well of by them. Since the best way to ensure that they are cared for, in the short run, is to do what the leader or manager approves of and in the long run to become like them, they identify with their values. This identification is thus the result of caring and admiring one's leaders or managers, not of being punished by them.

As has been stated previously, the only really effective discipline is self-discipline. This will best be achieved by team members who are motivated by an inner desire to act commendably in order to do well in their own eyes, according to their own values, so that they may feel good about themselves. Self-discipline is based on values which team members have internalized because they admired and wanted to emulate people such as the manager who lived by them—for in this way they hope that they will be esteemed by these significant others.

Self-discipline is part of our internal values, that is, part of our conscious. It is not much of a conscience that tells us not to do wrong because we might get punished. The effective conscience motivates us to do right because we know that otherwise we will suffer all the pain and depression of feeling bad about ourselves. So, in the final analysis, we can reliably say that we will only do right in order to prevent the pangs of conscience—to feel good about ourselves, not to avoid punishment. It is internal chastisement that will ultimately have the greatest effect upon discipline. Conscience is developed from internalizing the values of important role models.

While it is our inner feelings about ourselves which are all-important in this regard, there are also some external ingredients which support our ability to respect ourselves. These include the wish to gain or preserve the esteem of others whose opinion we value. In football, these may include the manager or leader, team mates, and perhaps the supporters. But, of course, the reverse also applies and if we do not value their positive view of us, then what they think is unimportant. They have no power to influence our behaviour, even if they have the power to chastise us. In football, we see examples of this on many, many occasions.

The typical scenario is that of an autocratic manager, who will take up an appointment at a new club and, in the short-term get good results. However, as time goes by, respect and esteem for this bully will rapidly vanish to the extent that they now have no power, no authority. To other team members, the manager or leader is no longer of any consequence and they have no influence whatsoever. Once in a while circumstances will arise, perhaps a local derby, where the team members will be motivated to succeed for their own satisfaction, but otherwise they will simply not care. All the team members will do is to try to avoid being punished and this they will achieve by acting like the 'nodding dogs' we see in cars, never openly disagreeing and never openly 'breaking the rules'. Sooner or later, the manager will get the sack, frequently blaming the lack of quality of 'his' team members as a reason for the lack of success. Sadly, many owners of football clubs are unable to see beyond these words and continue to employ these bullying failures.

If we want our team to be disciplined and committed to achieving shared aims they will do so if they have internalized values of hard work, persistence, and forbearance of pain. Thus, it is only self-respect that can be counted on to prevent us or other team members from doing as we desire. If this fails to restrain us, then our conduct will simply depend on our calculation of the possible consequences. That is to say, we then live by a situational morality that changes with the conditions of the moment, both managers and other team members go for the least difficult option. Frequently this will be the 'quick fix' and we all know that this is going to lead to failure. If we want to be successful we all need to work hard and to continue to work hard in spite of continual setbacks. This requires a morality securely anchored in the deepest layers of our personality. Thus, when it comes to discipline, the goal of the manager or leader ought to be aimed at increasing the self-respect of other team members and making it so strong and resilient that it will, at all times, deter them from looking for easy options or from doing wrong.

It cannot be emphasized strongly enough, that whatever team members do, at the moment of action it seems right to them, no matter how spurious their reasons or self-deceiving their evaluation of the situation. Sometimes they take a chance that doesn't come off but more likely they make a decision that happens to be the wrong decision—a genuine mistake. Therefore, when we reprimand them, we ought also to make clear that we are persuaded they acted as they did only because they thought it was justified. This approach is the only one which will safeguard their self-respect and permit them to give us a positive hearing. In effect, we need to see their behaviour as neither bad nor good, neither black nor white, but grey. Because they make a mistake or do things in a way which does not meet with our ideas or wishes, it does not make them bad people. Although we may be annoyed at the action taken collectively by the team or by an individual team member, we should remember Freud's warning: the voice of reason may be insistent, but it is very soft, whereas the clamour of the emotions is often overwhelmingly loud, so loud as to block out all other voices and this is especially so in team dynamics.

The clamour of the emotions

The 'clamour of the emotions' may affect not so much what we do, but the way that we do it. This point was made in the last chapter in regard to giving feedback. I cannot think of many more important managerial skills than that of giving feedback to team members. On many occasions it requires the highest degree of self-control and self-awareness if we are not to allow emotions, such as anger, to poison the whole interaction in a way which prevents learning and development. The manager or leader needs to carefully cultivate the voice of reason and make it attractive to team members so that although it is soft, it will nevertheless get a hearing. Shouting at team members will not get us very far. They may be shocked into obedience, but they—and we—know that they are not hearing the voice of reason. The task of the manager is to create an environment in which reason can be heard and heeded. This, is paramount to the success of all managers because if they are not capable of self-control, they are not likely to speak with this soft voice of reason and if team members are fearful of their manager's displeasure or of actual punishment, they will be in no position to listen to this soft voice.

None of us is perfect and we all have desires to break the rules from time to time. I guess there are not many reading this book who will not have broken the speed limit or other traffic regulations on frequent occasions even though we are aware of the potential dangers. If we want to understand this state of mind, then we have to imagine how we would feel or act—or actually do act—when we are in the grip of the desire to do something against the rules that can easily be done and does no damage to anybody else. No matter that what they did may have been dangerous and no matter how they rationalized that they acted this way because they felt it was justified. Take for example, the player who makes a tackle from behind, knowing it is against the rules of the game, with the result that they get booked by the referee. From the manager or leader's perspective this may seem like reckless undisciplined behaviour that has cost the team in some way. However, our own views may not be important what is required is an awareness of the other, the team member. Listening to and understanding the 'other' perspective will provide a way for future development.

Telling team members that that they have done wrong, particularly in an angry and disappointed tone, deflates their self-respect and diminishes their respect for us and with it their need to act in ways that will gain our approval. On the other hand, listening to them, understanding their justification for their actions and then telling them that we are convinced that had they known the likely results of what they did they never would have done it, increases their self-respect and their respect for us, with all that this entails. It is the wish to be cared for that induces them to do right in the present. As they begin to act in a more mature fashion their self-respect will motivate them to act in a responsible way.

For many involved in the macho world of teams this may seem like a soft option. But I feel quite sure that the many managers and leaders who have adopted such an approach would testify that it is constant hard work. It is easy to let off steam and to spill out the first thing that comes into your mind. As one of the footballers I was working with said, 'It's easy to be autocratic, it requires no skills, it just comes naturally'. To manage in a self-controlled manner requires a good deal of effort and self-discipline over a long period of time. This is far from being easy. Nevertheless, nothing that has been said should be understood as suggesting, even for a moment, that managers or leaders should not reprimand team members when they do something that they believe is wrong, nor to suggest that they can never be annoyed with them. Any manager or leader who cares deeply about other team members will also at times feel strongly about the ways in which team members are behaving. Even the kindest and best intentioned manager or leader will sometimes become exasperated. The difference between the good enough and the not so good manager or leader in such situations is that the first has a degree of self-awareness and realizes that their irritation usually has more to do with themselves than with whatever the team member did and that giving in to it benefits no one. The second believes that their anger is due only to another team member and that they therefore have every right to act on it. You may recall the slogan, 'own it, don't blame it'.

It is in everyone's interest if we can keep in mind that when we are angry, we don't reason very well, we are unable to proceed on the basis of a balanced judgement. In the same way, other team members cannot listen receptively to what the manager or leader has to say, when they are responding to their emotions rather than to their reasons. Even if we try to suppress our anger and speak judiciously, they will nonetheless sense our repressed emotions and react to them, they will pick up the non-verbal cues, rather than listening to our words. Pretending we're calm when we're boiling inside and would like nothing better than to boil over openly teaches our team members that we are dishonest with ourselves— exactly the type of behaviour which is detrimental to the instilling of discipline.

The trouble is that often, just because we hate to disappoint other team members, we fail to experience empathy for what they feel when we have to deny them something they want. We want them to accept and understand our reasons at a time when their emotional involvement precludes this. In the early days the manager would try to deal with issues immediately, even during a match, when the emotion was at its highest and when it was preventing team members from thinking clearly. Had the manager accepted the player's disappointment or anger and waited until the next day to discuss the situation with them, he would have found that the team members' self-perception was now alive and self-control was such that the issues could be discussed in a constructive manner. In such a case it is much better to wait. This was one of the behaviours developed by the manager which he used to good effect. It would seem that time is a good healer—of emotions.

Should we never punish?

I have little doubt that many managers will be asking, 'Should, we never punish team members? Is there never a time or circumstance when it is appropriate to do so? What about those managers and leaders who, reflecting back on their childhood or playing days, are convinced that punishment did them a lot of good? And when, as children or players, we ourselves were chastised, did we not sometimes feel that it cleared the air and that, much as we disliked the experience, it had some value? If our experience was that of being punished there is every chance that we will also be convinced that punishment is appropriate and perhaps necessary behaviour. It is thus, that bullied children become bullying parents or bullied team members become bullying managers. But does this make it right or helpful? My purpose here is not to debate the relative morality of punishment. Rather, it is to analyse the conditions which instil in a team member the desire to be a well-disciplined team player. If we can do this, then there will be no need to think of punishment. From this we can conclude that chastisement has no merits, but we can go further than this and say that punishing team members is always undesirable.

That having been said, there are times when a team member has done something seriously wrong and the manager or leader gets very upset, when there is a possibility that punishment may occasionally clear the air. Almost certainly the manager or leader, by acting upon their anger and anxiety, will find some sort of relief. Subsequently when they are freed of their upsetting emotion, they may feel bad about having punished the team member, perhaps even a bit guilty, but they may feel more positive about their team member after they have discharged these negative feelings. For their part, team members need no longer feel guilty about what they have done, since in the eyes of the manager or leader they have paid the penalty, even though team members usually view the penalty as more severe than was warranted by their misdeeds. Both manager or leader and other team member, free of the emotions which stood between them, can feel that peace has been restored. Sometimes working in the emotive atmosphere of the football club it seemed that some sort of discharge of emotions was necessary before issues could be dealt with in a positive way.

So, what do we do?

So, let's return to the problem of what a manager or leader is to do to prevent indiscipline in other team members. Ideally, letting team members know our disappointment should be an effective restraint, but I doubt that this will always suffice. In some instances the only real solution may be to amicably part company with the team member. I would stress amicably to explain that I am not suggesting that this activity is to be regarded as punitive. In the instance concerning Van Hooijdonk, referred to above, the circumstances became toxic because the player was punished. Faced with the disappointment of not knowing how to resolve the problem, anxiety is bound to be high and the situation will call for the highest level of self-control. If, the desire of the manager is to find a suitable resolution to the difficult problem they are facing the chances are they will maintain their self-control and succeed. However, if the desire of the manager is to punish the other team member for not being submissive they will continue to be filled with toxic anxiety and the aims will not be achieved.

I cannot stress often enough that team development works best if the team members are not only very deeply and positively impressed by the person and competence of the manager or leader, but also wish to remain in their good graces because of the affection they feel for them, because their team members respect them and want to be respected by their managers or leaders. That is why, when given half a chance, those team members who have been managed in a caring and respected way will do all that is possible, within reason, to retain the respect of their manager or leader and fear nothing more than to lose them as a protector. It is not difficult to imagine that when this position is reached team members will be highly committed and would be prepared to run through brick walls for their manager or leader. If we are looking for the holy grail of leadership this must be about as close as we can get to it.

The desire for attachment is so strong that when our words are not enough, when telling other team members to mend their ways is ineffective, then it may be the case that the threat of a limited and momentary weakening of our care and affection is the only sound method to impress on them that they had better conform to our request—otherwise we will no longer be able to think of them so highly. Therefore, when showing disappointment is not sufficient to induce other team members to mend their ways, managers or leaders may convincingly impress upon other team members that losing their affection is a real danger. Our words and actions may be simply symbolic, nevertheless they will clearly convey to other team members that they are in danger of losing our attention. Team members who get this message will correct their behaviour for their own reasons to secure the desired advantage—the manager or leader's permanently undisturbed affection—in the future.

The way to do this is to remove the team member from our presence for a short while (or *vice versa*). We may send them away to cool down and think about the situation for a while, or we may ourselves withdraw to our own office. Here, physical distance stands for emotional distance and it is a symbol that speaks to the team member's conscious and unconscious at the same time; this is why it is so effective. The purpose of sending the team member out of the manager or leader's presence must never be to punish them, but only to permit both manager or leader and team member to gain distance from what has happened, to cool off, to reconsider. It is the fear of desertion which, as likely as not, deeply impresses the team member.

Separation anxiety is probably the earliest and most basic human anxiety. In the case of an infant it might lead to death. Anything that rekindles this anxiety is experienced as a threat; hence, as long as a team member—however dimly—realizes that their very existence is in danger if their prime caretaker deserts them, they will respond to this real, implied, or imagined threat with feelings of anxiety. Even though they are old enough to know that their life is not threatened, they will respond with feelings of dejection because they nevertheless to some degree still feel as if it were. The difference is that at this older age the fear is not of physical but of emotional deprivation. The emotional relief and often the true happiness manager or leader and team member experience, when after their short separation, they are again reunited will enhance their relationship.

This sort of behaviour will only work well if the underlying motive of the manager or leader is not a desire to punish the team member, but a wish not to become so angered by his misbehaviour that anger may lead to a more serious disruption of their basically mutually respecting relation. Managers or leaders who wish to punish and hurt other team members are able to use any opportunity to do so. One method is that of withdrawal. They can fool themselves that they are not acting out their hostile feelings, but only want to correct the team member. Such managers and leaders punish a team member by not talking to them for days and even weeks. This can arouse such anxiety in them that not only does their relation to their manager or leader become seriously damaged—but also the team member's personality.

Praise

The 'good enough manager' or leader will avoid punishing other team members and will make every effort to have their criticisms of other team members overbalanced by praising them whenever this is appropriate: deserved praise feels so much better to both of them. Praise is effective, not because we are seen as good judges of objective values, but because it is a statement of our strong positive emotions, of our joy and pleasure in other team members doing well. Our response to team members' misbehaviour should also be mainly emotional, expressing our feelings rather than our objective judgements. In praise we come emotionally close to other team members and often also physically, too—by, for example, embracing them—and they understand this.

The opposite reaction is the consequence of our disappointment in other team members. We have every right to feel disappointed, but our disappointment gives us no right to punish. Other team members know this; this is why they resent us punishing them yet modify their behaviour to undo our disappointment. When they know we care for them, our disappointment in their misbehaviour is understandable to them. By the same token, their care for us is their reason for fearing our disappointment. Thus praise—a symbol of an increase in our respect and affection—and temporary withdrawal of affection are the two best ways to influence team members forming a mature approach to their work.

It is only the example of our own good behaviour that will induce our team members to make such behaviour part of their behaviour—and only then if we are open about it and neither force our values on them nor expect them to be able to emulate our examples before their own development makes them ready to do so. We must accept it as understandable and not be disappointed in them, if occasionally they fall into error; and we must at all times retain our conviction of their inherent goodness, acknowledging that it just takes time for our example to come to full fruition, as it did in our own lives.

The more we realize, through our constant reflection, how true this was for us, the better it will be for them and for us and the easier and smoother will be their development. We must also be equally honest and open about our emotions, showing through our behaviour how deeply we care about other team members without necessarily always telling them that we do, although this too has its place. We must believe that caring has its best effect through the ways we respond to their needs and help them with their difficulties. When we are disappointed in them, letting them know this also has its place in our relations, provided we don't become critical and punishing, but convey our disappointment through keeping or increasing our distance, because in truth we can't be very close to them when we don't feel like it. Every manager or leader would do well to remember the words of Shakespeare, 'They that have power to hurt and will do none ... they rightly do inherit heaven's graces'.

As with any other aspect of managing and leading teams, if you really want to know about punishment, reflect on situations in your own life when you have been punished and get in touch with your feelings. I have little doubt that your experience will confirm all that has been written in this chapter. Without reference to your feelings you may well find yourself rationalizing your current actions as a manager or leader. You won't learn just by reading this book, you need to apply the text and understand it in an emotional way.

In the next chapter, the last, I shall continue to challenge some of the predominant approaches to leadership by stressing those aspects of the role which I consider are important if you are to get results through other people.

CHAPTER EIGHT

Leadership re-defined

I have defined 'management' as, 'getting things done through other people'; and 'leadership' as, 'attempts on the part of the leader (influencer) to affect (influence) the behaviour of a follower' (or as I would have it, joiner). I have not sought to draw any further distinction because I take the view that leadership is an integral part of management. What I want to do now in this chapter, is to explore some of the existing notions of leadership. It will be clear that the total effect of nearly everything that has been written in this book is a challenge to the macho concept of leadership, characterized as:

- one where the leader takes all the important decisions and gallantly leads 'his' team into battle, be that a physical or metaphorical battle; and
- one where the manager is in total control of everything that occurs and that their views and desires are the only ones that count.

It would be silly to suggest that existing views of leadership are without value. Naturally, there will be times when it is totally appropriate for the manager to lead from the front by making decisions for the team. However, I am going to challenge the notion that this sort of leadership, which is predominantly regarded as the norm, is far from being what is desirable leadership and that what is required is a very different approach.

It is suggested that the most important way that a manager or leader can 'attempt to influence and to affect desired behaviour of other team members' is to provide the sort of environment for all team members that will encourage them to develop as autonomous individuals. What constitutes the right sort of environment, how this is achieved, what benefits this will achieve and why, are some of the main topics of this chapter. For the moment, though, I shall concentrate on the manager or leader and suggest that those much envied and admired, so-called 'charismatic leaders', are those who provide the sort of environment that encourages other team members to admire and respect them and to seek to emulate them. This role model is then internalized by other team members who adopt the same sort of values modelled by their leaders. In this way they internalize the very values that result in them wanting to be committed team members.

As part of the process of learning about leadership we need to understand why it is that team members so willingly identify with such leaders. Many reasons have been referred to throughout the book. For example:

- the need, at first a necessity in infant life, for attachment to authority figures;
- the need to develop a basic trust in the leader based on experience which shows them worthy of that trust; and
- the need to know that they will not be 'let down'.

Those much admired managers and leaders referred to above, provide positive responses for other team members on all these counts. But, I would suggest, they also follow such managers and leaders because:

- those leaders have a high level of self-awareness—especially an awareness of their emotions.

This enables them, in turn, to access the emotions of others. They are capable of 'feeling into' other team members—or put another way, they are capable of a high degree of empathy.

When team members say that their manager or leader under-stands them, they don't just mean that the manager or leader understands what they say or what they mean—a cognitive understanding. Team members also mean that their manager or leader understands them and treats them as real and complete human beings, that is, the manager or leader also understands their feelings or emotions. Team members want to be treated as people who have:

- desires to be creative;
- to be able to think;
- to be valued;
- to participate in making decisions; and,
- to be autonomous individuals who are not dependent on others for the way their working lives are organized. But, most especially;
- they want to be treated as people with feelings or emotions, people who experience love and affection, anger and frustra-tion, lethargy and excitement, boredom and pain.

If a manager or leader is not able to get in touch with and understand their own feelings there is little chance that they will be capable of 'feeling into' other team members. Adopting the style of leadership frequently portrayed as heroic and brave will almost inevitably involve a hard hearted approach where rationalization or denial of all sorts of feelings will come into play—this is why we need to adopt a different concept of leadership. One which embraces the notion of 'reflect and respect'.

Authority, responsibility and accountability

In Chapter 5, authority was defined as 'that which within a definite area may allow, disallow or insist upon change, with or without any further references'. From this definition you will have gathered that authority was a neutral term. This is so, but it does mean that the person (or persons) with authority, here the manager or leader, has the responsibility to do that which is required by the terms of that authority. Other team members may share these responsibilities from time to time but no one else has the specific authority for this responsibility and if they don't do it, no one will ask why. As the manager or leader they have this authority and they are accountable. If the team do not achieve a certain level of performance, others may ask the manager or leader to explain why. For example, part of the authority of the manager or leader in football will involve the development of team members and the gaining of their commitment to achieving the aims of the organization. Naturally, the manager or leader cannot achieve this on their own, they will have to delegate tasks to other staff members. But, if they are not successful they will have to answer the question 'why'.

An important responsibility of the manager or leader, then, is to provide the sort of leadership that will encourage both leadership and commitment of other team members in the service of the task, be that task winning football matches or manufacturing widgets. This is what has previously been referred to as 'managerial authority', which refers to that part of the leader's authority that has been delegated to them by the institution they work in.

'Leadership authority' is very different and refers to that aspect of the manager or leader's authority that is derived from the recognition of other team members that they have the capacity to carry out the task. This sort of authority should not be seen to be confined to a designated leader or manager but to all team members. The ideal situation is that all team members will engage in a leadership role and will be trying to effect the behaviour of other team members in all manner of ways, not least, in the area of inspiring them to win. This point was well recognized by the football manager who frequently said that what he wanted was a team of eleven leaders. This will not come about unless the manager or leader adopts the sort of approach that treats all team members as autonomous beings who are able and want to contribute to the success of the team in a meaningful way.

Teams or single-leader work groups

This aspect of teams is helpfully commented upon by Katzenbach and Santamaria (1999), who distinguish between 'teams' and 'single-leader work groups'. The latter are defined as relying entirely on their formal leaders for purpose, goals, motivation, and assignments; each member being accountable solely to the leader. It is, they say, this sort of group which is erroneously called a team. A real 'team', by contrast draws its motivation more from its mission and goals than from its leader. Team members work together as peers and hold one another accountable for the team's performance and results. In a real team, no individual can win or lose; only the team can succeed or fail. This view is shared here and I would like to stress that it is the real 'team' that is referred to throughout this book.

There can be little doubt that the 'single-leader work group' demotivates team members and undermines the effective performance of team members. Yet, this is the predominant set up at most football clubs and many other organizations. The manager is the one who hires and fires and makes the decisions for most other things as well. Things are beginning to change and managers are now having to come to terms with new ways of managing because the players have much greater power. By and large, they are now much better educated and most especially, they have vastly greater earning power as a result of the money available in the industry. However, while managers may be changing, they are doing so slowly and grudgingly and with little or no development of the skills required in this changing environment. This is personified by Bobby Robson the ex-England manager who, when interviewed for the Daily Telegraph (7th August 1999), stated, 'Players have become a bit powerful now. I think it's the money. How do you frighten players who are on £2 million a year? In days gone by you had some control. It seems now that's disappeared'. It would appear that what he's saying is that there is only one way to control players— that is, by frightening them or by bullying them. This simply is not true. As was explained in the last chapter, discipline can best be achieved by self-control.

The manager or leader who antagonizes other team members or who threatens or bullies them may achieve short-term results, but in the long-term they will be doomed to failure when the team members start seeking revenge. An example of the sort of results we can expect from failing to provide a work environment that encourages leadership and commitment by other team members is referred to by Bowen (1999), who while relating to the uncertainty brought about by such factors as downsizing, changing technology, and the charge to 'do more with less' refers to 'work rage'. He explains that this phenomenon can be experienced in the form of sabotage either by direct damage to machinery or through computer viruses. In addition, he points out that charges of discrimination processed through grievance or litigation are rising and suggests that each can be seen as a way of team members gaining revenge.

In these sort of circumstances, which are becoming more and more frequent, how can we possibly say that the current mode of leadership is appropriate? I believe that the current position is indefensible and that leadership has to change and change quickly. None of us respond positively to bullying, uncaring, or untrustworthy leaders or managers. Even the least self-aware among the readers will be able to recall the loathsome feelings they had for those who treated them in this way. They will also recall how they set out individually and collectively to get their revenge. I should, therefore, be preaching to the converted. Fine, I hear the reader say, but what am I to do instead? What is this different concept of leadership that I need to develop? Throughout the book I have made a great deal of the need for self-awareness and self-control. I believe that this and the provision of the right sort of environment lie at the heart of the different concept.

Self-awareness of emotions

Before looking at the manager's role in regard to the provision of what will be referred to as a 'facilitating environment', I first need to clarify some of the issues concerning self-awareness. I shall start with the notion that the self is the organizing function within the individual and the function by means of which one human being can relate to another. No matter what our human experiences are they always go beyond our particular methods of understanding at any given moment. There is no methodology that will provide a complete and satisfactory explanation of our behaviour and the best way that we can gain an understanding of our identity as a self is to look into our experience. As human beings we can reflect on some past experience and can picture ourselves as doing something and we can then also experience the feelings that we had when we were actually doing whatever it was.

By reflecting on previous experience we gain a greater depth of self-awareness. Above-all we can understand the emotions attached to our behaviour. The greater the awareness the greater control we have over our behaviour. Take for example the common experience of driving a car. The less aware you are of how to drive a car, or of the traffic conditions you are driving through, the more tense you are, the more anxiety you will experience and the firmer hold you will keep of yourself. But, on the other hand, the more experienced you are as a driver and the more conscious you are of the traffic conditions and of what you need to do in emergencies, the more you will be able to relax at the wheel, the less anxiety you will experience and you will have more of a sense of control. You will have the awareness that it is you who are doing the driving, that it is you in control.

As with any other activity, driving a car is not just an activity, it also involves thinking and feeling. If we were to limit our reflection to thought only, we would ignore a huge part of our experience. Many readers will be familiar with the extreme feelings associated with road rage. How could we possibly say that driving a car only concerns thought? Clearly it involves varying degrees of feelings as does management and leadership. Failing to recognize the part that emotion is playing in any work activity, and telling a team member to think about what they are doing when they are overwhelmed by feelings of anger will be of little value. What is required is contact at a feelings level.

Self-awareness expands the control we have over our lives and with that expanded power comes the capacity to let ourselves go. The more self-awareness we have, the more spontaneous and creative we can be at the same time. For those who have spent a great deal of their lives denying that they have feelings this is going to be a difficult, but far from impossible, task. In achieving self-awareness, most people will need to start back at the beginning and rediscover their feelings. We should not be surprised that many people only have a general acquaintance with what they feel. For some, their connection with their feelings is about as far removed as if they were at the end of a long distance telephone. If, as a manager or leader, you persist in the belief that you are always expected to be in control and to show no emotion other than that such as anger which supports your hard-man image this will remain the case. It seems clear that much of the management and leadership styles adopted in a wide range of organizations to date have simply resulted in the deliberate denial of our feelings.

How can football managers understand the doubts and anxieties of a young—or not so young—footballer if they themselves are not open to the experience of their own feelings? How can football managers communicate their feelings about the way the team have performed in a match when they cannot access those feelings? Doubtless this is why many managers and leaders find it so very hard to praise their team members. And, conversely, why they frequently express anger. In discovering our feelings it is important that the individual manager or leader gains an understanding of the experience that it is *they* who are doing the feeling. That they are the active one's who own the feelings they are experiencing. This carries with it a directness and immediacy of feeling and the individual experiences the feelings on all levels of themselves. The more self-awareness a manager or leader has the more alive they are. Self-awareness brings with it the experience that it is 'I', the acting one, who is the subject of what is occurring. We might say that they feel with a heightened aliveness.

As managers and leaders we are frequently trying to understand other team members' behaviour and are constantly making interpretations of that behaviour. Indeed, the ability to make such interpretations reasonably accurately is a necessary social skill. Yet, this constantly practised skill can be exceedingly difficult, because every direct and immediate experience of feeling and desiring is spontaneous and unique. That is to say, the desiring and feeling are uniquely part of that particular situation at that particular time and place. As was stated in Chapter 1, the manager or leader cannot prepare for these unique eventualities, they have to interpret them there and then. Even when we think we have the time to prepare, such as when we have arranged a formal meeting by appointment, we frequently find that unpredicted feelings enter into the relationship.

To be able to respond in a helpful way, in what are sometimes highly complex situations, it is important that the manager or leader be aware of their own feelings so that they do not stand in the way of them really getting to know the other team members. If they are not so aware, they may be preoccupied:

- by their own feelings—especially negative feelings such as cynicism; or
- by their own reactions to what other team members say; or
- by showing how clever they are.

These considerations will overshadow the relationship and distort their perceptions and reactions. If the manager or leader's feelings can be worked over by self-reflection and self-understanding, they will be freer to observe, listen, take in, and understand what is going on here and now. Faced with any experience, the emotional learning that life has given us, such as the memory of a past disastrous relationship, sends signals that streamline our decision-making process by eliminating some options and highlighting others at the outset. In this way the emotions are involved in reasoning—as is the thinking brain.

Most intriguing for understanding the power of feelings in mental life are those moments of impassioned action that we later regret, once the dust has settled. These situations develop when we set our perceptions against our internal store of memory and— mainly unconsciously—ask the following sort of questions.

- Is this something I hate?
- Something that hurts me? or,
- Something I fear?

If the answer to any of these questions is 'yes' we are most likely to respond by eliminating these options. Part of our internal store of memory consists of the interactions of life's earliest years where we developed a set of emotional lessons based on the attunement and upsets in the contacts between infant and various caretakers. These may now be triggered again in later life by the current unpleasant experience.

For example, a manager facing defeat in an important match may experience strong feelings of disappointment. Such is the anxiety that it evokes the memory of a similar situation in their childhood when they experienced the same feelings after failing an examination at school. On that occasion, they dealt with their feelings by pretending (rationalizing) that it didn't matter. Now, they will adopt the same approach. This was something they did not like and their perceptive process told them that they should treat it by invoking the previously used coping mechanism. Our passions when well exercised, have wisdom, they guide our thinking, our values, our survival. But they can easily go awry and all too often do so. The problem is not with emotionality, but with a balance of the appropriateness of emotion and its expression. When it comes to shaping our decisions and our actions, feeling counts every bit as much—and often more—than thought. A view of management and leadership that ignores the power of emotions is, sadly, short-sighted.

There is much evidence that people who are emotionally adept—who know and manage their own feelings well, and who read and deal effectively with other people's feelings—are at an advantage in any domain of life such as picking up the unspoken rules that govern success in organizational politics. People with well developed emotional skills are also more likely to be content and effective in their lives, mastering the habits of mind that foster their own productivity. These people master abilities such as:

- being able to motivate themselves;
- being able to persist in the face of frustrations;
- being able to control impulse and delay gratification;
- being able to regulate their moods and to keep distress from swamping their ability to think; and
- being able to empathize and to hope.

Conversely, people who cannot marshal some control over their emotional life fight internal battles that sabotage their ability for focused work and clear thought (Golemen, 1995).

It is helpful to see the manager or leader's role either in terms of 'interpersonal activity' which concerns the ability to understand other people; what motivates them, how they work, how to work co-operatively with them; or in terms of 'intrapersonal activity' which concerns the ability to understand the same things about themselves. For managers and leaders it is a capacity to form an accurate awareness of themselves and to be able to use that awareness to operate effectively in life. It is also the capacity to discern and respond appropriately to the moods, temperaments, motivations, and desires of other people. The key to self-awareness is to access your own feelings and the ability to discriminate among them and draw upon them to guide behaviour.

Having an awareness of your own feelings as they occur is the (considerable) difference between being murderously enraged at someone and having the self-reflective thought 'I am feeling angry'—even as you are enraged. This awareness of emotions is the fundamental emotional competence on which other competencies, such as emotional self control, build. Without self-awareness we may simply act out our feelings by lashing out at one or more of the other team members (blaming not owning). My experience of working with the football manager has shown that while it is not easy for someone to develop their self-awareness it is certainly possible. What made it more difficult in this particular case was that other team members, being aware of the manager's past behaviour, would try to make him angry in a way that would enable them to deny their own anger.

Where other team members are able to use the manager or leader as a conduit for all their anger, they may feel a degree of comfort. However, the more serious issue, here, is that they will rob themselves of their anger. And, where the manager or leader, because of their lack of self-awareness, colludes with the other team members by taking in their anger, they will be robbing the team of a valuable asset. In terms of motivation and task performance, team members need to be angry from time to time, they need to get in touch with their anger and frustration about not achieving their desires, in order to summon up the energy to confront the problems presented. If they are able to deny their own anger they will act like a team of 'pussy cats'.

There is a danger that self-awareness can lead to anxiety and to the subsequent use of one or other of the defence mechanisms referred to in Chapter 4. For example, we might tell ourselves 'I shouldn't be thinking this way' or 'Don't think about it'. At times, this sort of denial is not at all helpful, especially when it continues over a period of time. What is more productive is when we are aware of the anger and take the option of not just acting on it but the added option to try to let go. Feelings are a wonderful source of information and inspiration and are used to good advantage in guiding our behaviour.

A good example is an experience I had of consulting to a change process in a large organization. Here, the clients were overwhelmed by the enormity of the problem they faced. They expressed feelings of inadequacy and fears of failure. So strong were these feelings that they acted to sabotage any clear thought and because of this they were totally unable to work at the task. In one sense this was not helpful, but when considered from the perspective of feelings this was possibly the best available information they could have. When they were able to access their feelings and to gain an understanding and control of their experience they were also able to gain an under-standing of what it would be like for others engaged in the change process. By relating to the valuable experience of their own emotions they were able to guide their thinking about how they would help others. This sort of experience is available to all managers and leaders who have sufficient self-awareness. It may be particularly helpful in the football context in the period prior to a match, as a means of providing an indication of the emotional state of team members, at a time when it is still not too late to do something about it.

Our goal should not be emotional suppression but balance. Every feeling has its value and significance. A life without passion would be a dull wasteland of neutrality, cut off and isolated from the richness of life itself. What is required is appropriate emotion—feeling propor-tionate to circumstance. When emotions are too muted they create dullness and distance. Managers or leaders who are experienced by other team members as 'cold fish' do not inspire; rather, they appear uncaring and uninspiring. Equally, when managers or leaders are experienced by other team members as 'raving lunatics' they will be regarded in precisely the same way. It is only when feelings are owned and expressed in an appropriate and proportionate way by managers and leaders that they will be regarded as inspiring. The first step is self-awareness, catching the worrisome episodes as near their beginning as possible—ideally, as soon as, or just after, the fleeting image triggers our anxiety. To be effective, we need to constantly monitor the cues we receive for anxiety.

Self-awareness, phantasies and relatedness

Another way of talking about the ideas and feelings with which we invest in any new situation is to say that we have phantasies about

it, about ourselves, about others, about the nature of the relationship and the relationship between others. By phantasies I mean
mental concepts not based on reality. This requires that managers
and leaders not only need to understand relationships with team
members, but also their relatedness to those other people. That is,
the way that emotions and phantasies affect the way they relate to
other team members. Where managers or leaders are experiencing
negative feelings about another team member, such as feeling angry
with them or not trusting them, this will effect the way they relate to
them. This is also likely to be the case for other team members who
may develop negative phantasies about the manager or leader. For
example, they may phantasize that the manager or leader 'does not
care about others' or 'that the manager or leader is angry with them
because they disagreed with them in the last meeting'. The reality
may be somewhat different, but in such cases, the likely outcome is
that the other team members will not have any desire to
communicate with the manager or leader for fear of the results.

Developing this theme, it will be helpful to remind ourselves of
the distinction between those relationships that are predominantly
based on unconscious displacements from early life and those that
are primarily reactions to the real attitudes and behaviour of the
present day person. A relationship of the latter type, as it occurs
between manager and team member, is based on the team
member's conscious appreciation of the manager as he really is,
which may be called a 'reality relationship'. It differs from what I
have referred to as a 'phantasy-relationship' which occurs where the
team member unconsciously projects onto the manager a potent
figure of his early childhood.

In most situations, reality factors, that is, the real situation and
the real attitude of the manager are the determining ones in
establishing the quality of the team member—manager or leader
relation. The team members feelings toward the manager are fairly
directly caused, are conscious, and are subject to relatively easy
control. Phantasy-relationships, on the other hand, although they
may be currently stimulated, are remotely caused, are largely
unconscious, and require considerably more skill for their control.
At first sight this sort of relationship may seem difficult to
understand and one could easily forgive the reader for saying that
they have got by in life thus far without thinking about such

matters, so why start now! In the next paragraph, I shall try to explain why there are very good reasons why all managers and leaders need to understand these sort of dynamics.

Because of the nature of the manager or leader's role, this sort of experience is unavoidable. Being in a position where they have authority for other team members this helps to recreate, to some extent, in the minds of other team members, a dependency situation analogous to their infancy. It thus tends to reactivate their characteristic ways of handling problems which were developed at that time. As an infant sought help from their parents, or as a child asked for help from their teacher, so a team member seeks help from their manager. Even a request for something as simple as an afternoon off places the team member in the position of seeking a favourable response from the manager or leader—a person in authority. When the help sought is more extensive than this, the feeling of dependency is proportionately greater. In such circumstances, this is almost certain to trigger off, what are technically called 'transference' feelings, to this new situation of their infantile feelings and attitudes. In ordinary language all that this means is, as the term implies, that the team member transfers feelings and attitudes that were first associated with an earlier authority figure onto a current authority figure. Part of this 'transference' will be positive, corresponding to the love the team member felt for the parental figure, part of it will be negative, corresponding to the fear the team member had of anyone possessing power over their destiny.

Throughout the book I have provided examples of this sort of relationship. One that I referred to earlier concerned a young footballer whose father had left the family home when he was a young boy. As a result of this painful experience he formed the view that he could not trust his father who he perceived had let him down. His way of dealing with this situation was to cut himself off from his father and to not communicate with him. Faced with the authority of the football manager it recreated the previous dependency situation and recreated the same feelings and his way of dealing with them. The manager, at that time being unaware of such dynamics and finding the player unresponsive to his efforts to help him, saw him as unintelligent and other staff members spoke of him and treated him as 'thick'. Fortunately, I was able to help in this instance and a reality relationship developed between the player and the manager which resulted in the team member becoming more of a complete person, using his intelligence, and flourishing.

Often transference feelings are not direct projections of a parent or other childhood figure onto the manager or leader. In the course of the team member's life they may have projected this momentous early figure onto a number of other people such as teachers, acquaintances, employers, and so on. Where this is the case, the projection onto the manager may then be from one of these later persons, or derivatives as they are called. In the successive transfers that have occurred, the original figure may have become modified or even quite distorted.

Thus, the manager may become the recipient of the feelings that another team member currently has toward another manager or coach from his past, as well as, or instead of, those he had in childhood toward a parent. When another team member's problem is an emotional one, requiring for its solution a modification of their own attitudes, the so-called transference tends to develop more rapidly. Such team members are less likely to be able to respond to the reality factors in their situation including the actual attitude of their manager—they will be so emotional that they may not be capable of self-perception. And, of course, this will also apply to the manager or leader who does not have a sufficient degree of self-awareness.

Self-awareness and coping

For all of us, emotional life is in a constant state of flux; we are constantly bombarded by internal and external stimuli which produce continually changing moods and feeling states. Those anxieties that arise from within may be sparked off by physical stress, painful events, and upsetting experiences. The ability of managers, leaders, or other team members to cope with these occurrences depends on inner resources and their availability at that particular moment. A team member may actually rise to a crisis by greater effort and discover unexpected strengths. Alternatively they may already be strained to the utmost and any additional burden becomes too much. It is likely that there is a potential breaking point for even the most stable team member.

How we cope with anxiety is strongly connected to having an

understanding of these constantly changing states of emotion which highlights the need for and the benefit that can be derived from a trusting relationship between the manager and other team members. Frequently a team member that is suffering extreme doubts and anxieties will be looking for someone to help them with their pain. By making themselves available the manager can provide an outlet and act as a receiver for the excessive anxiety with which the team member cannot cope. In doing so, it will give the team member the opportunity for the more mature part of them to come to the fore and recover whatever ability they have to understand, work over, and eventually handle the painful situation, instead of acting and thinking defensively. In some instances this might take time, in which case it might be helpful for the manager to refer the team member to someone who has the ability to be patient, thoughtful, and capable of containing the emotional pain.

While working with the team manager there were three occasions when I was able to fill this role and then to work with the team member and the manager to help to establish a reality relationship which he and the team members concerned could develop. However, I am left wondering how many other young players at other clubs have either been forced into submission only for them to rebel at a later stage; or, are thrown out onto the scrap heap being regarded as having an 'attitude' problem. One of my earliest field notes reminds me that football is a physically and emotionally painful experience. I am, frankly, amazed that football clubs (and other sports clubs) do not employ consultants such as myself to look after the emotional well-being of team members, especially as they are such valuable commodities.

One of the manager's first concerns for other team members has to be the establishment of a positive reality relationship. This done, the manager or leader may find that the other team members are getting sufficient support from conscious confidence and security, that they can explore the many issues when they arise. I shall return to this theme below while developing the notion of a facilitating environment.

A facilitating environment

A facilitating environment will depend on many factors and can only ever be regarded as a 'good enough' environment. However, there are certain principles that can be followed which will result in the sort of environment first described by Winnicott (1965b). In order to explain what is meant by this term we need to see it in the original Winnicottian context of infant development and to build on some of the notions already referred to throughout the book. Winnicott informs us that infant development does not occur unless the circumstances are good enough. A facilitating environment is first absolutely and then relatively important, and the course of development can be described in terms of absolute dependence, relative dependence, and towards independence.

It is not possible to say what is a good enough holding environment, but we can say that it is made possible by the mother doing the right thing at the right time, that is, when the baby is ready for it. She provides the context in which development takes place. There is never complete integration—the individual and the environment are interdependent. There is no emotional or physical survival of an infant without environment, reliable holding has to be a feature of the environment if the infant is to survive. The need for mental support, psychological and emotional, continues in adult life, especially when there is anxiety. Similarly, we cannot say precisely what is not a good enough holding environment but we do know that if this process does not take place effectively, the baby tends to take in or to introject not a comforting, progressive experience—but what Bion has called a nameless dread, severe contentless anxiety.

In the same way that the maternal holding environment effects the development of maturity in the infant, so the holding environment provided by the manager or leader will affect the existence or otherwise of maturity. Where the members of an organization, or part of an organization, have a basic trust and perceive the holding environment as good enough, there will exist a state of maturity. Where, however, the reverse applies, there may exist a state akin to infantile dependence. That is, they will be overwhelmed by their identification with the team, will not be capable of experiencing their own personality, and will not be able to influence others.

What we are concerned with is the environmental provision which is well adapted to the needs of the individual at any one particular moment. In other words, this is the same subject as that of maternal care, which changes according to the age of the infant, and which meets the early development of the infant and also the infant's reaching out towards independence. This way of looking at life may be particularly suited to the study of healthy development. The psychology with which we are concerned here takes maturity to be synonymous with health. This way of reasoning uses the concept of maturity equated with psychiatric health. It could be said that the mature adult is able to identify themselves with environmental groups or institutions, and to do so without loss of a sense of personal going-on-being, and without too great a sacrifice of spontaneous impulse.

For the infant and it is postulated, for the members of a team, the quality of the holding environment is vital. There is a need to develop a sense of security where they will carry around an expectation that they will not be 'let down'. In the holding environment provided by the manager or leader the quality of conditions needs to be the same as in the maternal holding environment if it is to be regarded as a 'facilitating environment', that is one which is healthy in the sense of there being maturity: one in which there will be progression. If other team members are to express themselves in a creative, spontaneous way; if they are not to be overwhelmed by anxiety; if they are to have the confidence to overcome setbacks and still pursue their desires; the manager or leader needs to accept the responsibility for ensuring and developing a facilitating environment.

For footballers, as for those in other industries, this is essential. Footballers will, the manager hopes, identify with the team as a group but they will not be lost or overwhelmed by this identification, rather, they will retain their individual personality and ability to influence others. During the process of maternal holding, much can occur that will effect the process of movement from infantile dependence to maturity, there is a possibility for failure at every point. This will also be the case regarding the manager or leader in their attempts to provide a facilitating environment for other team members. Fortunately, our growth to maturity does not depend on having perfect mothers; they only have to be good enough. The good enough mother responds automatically in a complex manner. Rather like the manager or leader, the mother cannot find out what to do from books or from anyone else when her baby spontaneously reaches out towards her in gesture and action. In a manner similar to that which I used to describe the so-called charismatic manager or leader, the good enough mother is attuned to the baby both psychologically and emotionally. This is what is required if we are to provide a facilitating environment.

Power and leadership in a facilitating environment

In Chapter 5 when referring to authority I explained that although a manager or leader may be delegated authority for team performance, what they can actually do is mitigated by the team members. In the context of a 'facilitating environment' it may be useful to reconsider this topic by drawing attention to the distinction between power and leadership. Power may be described as a 'leader's influence potential'. However, even though an individual may possess considerable power in relationship to another, for a number of reasons they may not be able to use all the power available to them. A leadership act simply reflects that portion of the power available to an individual that they choose to employ at the time. Because a team member is in a position of power, be that position power or expertise, it does not necessarily mean that they have power. We also need to consider the inter-relatedness with the other team members—the followers or joiners. The needs, attitudes, values, and feelings of other team members will determine the kind of stimulus produced by the leader to which the followers or joiners will respond.

Basic trust in a facilitating environment

The manager or leader has an important role to play if there is to be an environment where there is sufficient trust for other team members to begin to satisfy their needs for self-esteem by participating in the planning, organizing, and controlling of their own tasks. The various needs of team members, such as growth, belonging, self-esteem, recognition, and self-actualization, can only be met where there is a mature situation. That is, a situation where team members are able to be themselves and to understand and experience other people as distinct individuals who are separate and perhaps different from themselves and to be able to take part in co-operative relationships with these differentiated team members. It is the role of the manager or leader to ensure that such a mature situation exists.

If we are able to reflect upon the situation where the manager or leader is relying on threats, fear and punishment to get things done through other people, we will realize that other team members are simply being treated as an extension of the manager or leader. They might equally be viewed as robots which are programmed to carry out the desires and wishes of just one person—the manager or leader. This type of management does not treat other team members as distinct individuals who are separate and perhaps different. On the contrary it denies them that right and respect. All it achieves is a dependence on the manager or leader which leads to immaturity on the part of the other team members, who now cannot perform to the best of their ability. This is a crazy situation for any manager or leader who is trying to get results through other people.

Trust in interpersonal relationships is essential if full and open communication is to occur in a team An open non-manipulative sharing of information is required for the effective solving of work problems. This all sounds simple, but as is the position in the maternal holding environment, trust does not exist automatically, it has to be developed from experience. In the work situation, much will depend on the sort of facilitating environment that is developed by the manager or leader. Work orientations, which are based on the manipulation of other team members, generate widespread distrust at all levels. This widespread distrust of the leader or manager by other team members is one of the initial problems encountered in any team. Trust is exceedingly difficult to come by and very easy to lose.

On many occasions where there are problems or difficulties other team members are frequently well aware of the failings of the team and will have a good idea of what is wrong. And, if asked they would probably say, 'I could have told them we were going to lose' or something similar. Why, then, don't they tell the team manager or leader? Why don't they share this vital information? In most cases it will be because, in the team members' perception the manager or leader wouldn't have listened! In the team members' view the only thing the manager or leader wanted to hear was a confirmation of their own views. For a team member to provide a contrary view is not what the manager or leader wanted to hear. Worse still, they will also fear the consequences of being the bearer of bad news. They fear that the leader or manager will scapegoat them and write them off as a whinger or as a poor team player.

Where there is a tendency towards an authoritarian or bureaucratic style of management or leadership the rigid control structure moulds team members so that the holding environment is experienced as capricious and lacking in orderly structure and in cause and effect relationships. Consequently, team members feel there is little chance or hope of changing anything in their environment and are therefore not open to observations and information that would lead to improvement. On the contrary, they adopt forms of behaviour that seem appropriate to them under the conditions that they perceive are imposed upon them by their environment: these forms of behaviour may well be anti-task.

An example of this sort of behaviour is reported by the ex-England Manager, Terry Venables, who, at that particular time, was a player with Chelsea. Venables explains how there was a fundamental difference of opinion between the manager (Tommy Docherty) and the players about the way they should approach an important European game. In the event, the players ignored their manager and decided how they were going to play. As Venables states, the whole team felt much more secure about protecting their lead, by playing the way they wanted (Venables and Hanson, 1994). In this instance, the behaviour was not anti-task, but it was certainly anti-manager and not without considerable risk.

Sadly, as is frequently the response in these circumstances, rather than try to develop a strategy for changing fundamental attitudes and practices in order to achieve the conditions for progression; the more typical approach by managers and leaders is to seek more leverage for their power based, paternalistic tactics of bargaining, manipulation, intimidation, deception, legalistic manoeuvring, brinkmanship, conciliation, defamation, capitulation, and appeasement. Of course, these tactics only serve to reinforce the lack of basic trust and make the prospects of developing co-operative relations even more remote. The result is an immature situation where there is little chance if any of progression.

Maturity/immaturity in a facilitating
environment

Where a team is seen as immature, this is not a neutral position. On the contrary, it may be seen as synonymous with being 'unhealthy'. Who is going to risk the chance of being different, thinking differently, rejecting favourite assumptions, when one is certain of being punished for being wrong or for questioning the team manager or leader's view. Fear of failure creates a defensiveness that is the enemy of both learning and creativity. The behaviour of team members, which for them is rational, will be that which they feel is appropriate under the conditions that they perceive are imposed on them by their environment. Should they not perceive it as 'good enough' and not have a basic trust; if there is not a sense of security around an expectation that they will not be 'let down'; it will block the development of team members.

Thus, not for the first time, we can see how a manager or leader's intended actions can have an opposite effect on other team members, from that intended. All attempts to intimidate and humiliate team members into submission will only result in non-co-operative relations, and, instead of desires for achievement, they will develop desires for revenge which will result in non-achievement of task. We have seen, in Chapter 4, how frustration of team members who have not been able to satisfy their desires leads to regression or the adoption of all manner of defence mechanisms. Frustration may occur when a barrier exists between the team members and their goals. If they are unable to overcome the barrier or are unable to find a substitute or alternative goal and are unwilling to give up on satisfying the desire, they will become frustrated. Seemingly irrational behaviour may occur in several forms when the blockage to goal accomplishment continues and frustration develops. Frustration may increase to the extent that the team member may become engaged in aggressive behaviour which can lead to destructive behaviour, such as hostility and hitting out. If possible, team members will direct their aggression against the person that they feel is the cause of their frustration. Often, however, this will not be possible, they cannot attack the cause of their frustration—the manager or leader—directly and they may look for a scapegoat as a target for their hostility.

Scapegoating

The phenomenon of scapegoat formation is simply a manifestation of the displacement of aggressive impulses upon an individual or a team. Reference to the origin of the term 'scapegoat' explains the process. In ancient times family members would tie pieces of cloth containing descriptions of unwanted thoughts and behaviours onto a goat who would then be driven out into the wilderness: the hoped for result being that the unwanted thoughts and behaviours would go with the goat and not return. Scapegoating occurs most often when the expression of these impulses against the substitute person seems fraught with less imagined or real danger than their direct expression. Thus the manager or leader may feel angry with the whole team, but will not have the confidence to take them all on so they will displace the anger onto a substitute, usually one of the team members who will not fight back. Again, such behaviour by a manager or leader can only lead to the perception of the team members that the holding environment is not good enough and thus they resort to less mature, infantile like behaviour.

Aggression and dissatisfaction

Aggression is only one way in which frustrated behaviour can be shown. Other forms of frustrated behaviour include those already referred to in Chapter 4 such as rationalization, and regression, or of fixation, and resignation, which may develop if pressures continue and increase. Rationalization simply means making excuses. For example, a team member might blame someone else for their inability to accomplish a goal; this might be another team member, the referee, or even an inanimate object such as the weather. Regression is simply not acting one's age. A person who cannot start their car and kicks it is demonstrating regression and so is a manager who throws a temper tantrum when they are annoyed and frustrated. Fixation occurs when a person continues to exhibit the same behaviour pattern over and over again, although experience has shown that it can accomplish nothing. Resignation or apathy occurs after prolonged frustration when people lose hope of accomplishing their goal(s) in a particular situation and want to withdraw from the reality and the source of their frustration.

Where the desires of team members are thwarted their development becomes distorted and they may respond by blocking the team
from achieving objectives; they may become resistant, antagonistic,
or unco-operative. There may be occasions when such behaviour is
open and confrontational, however, it is much more likely that it will
be subtle and covert. In football it may find expression in a missed
tackle, a feigned injury, verbal abuse at the referee, and all manner of
behaviours that work to the detriment of the manager or leader. The
important point to bear in mind is that such behaviour is a
consequence not a cause, the team members adopt forms of
behaviour they feel are appropriate to them under the circumstances
they perceive are imposed on them by their holding environment.

A child confronted with a difficult situation may recourse to a
temper tantrum; on the other hand, by acquiring certain skills a
person can retain self-control even in difficult situations. The real
problem arises when we feel ourselves threatened but have little
control over the activities posing the threat. It is when we feel we
cannot influence the most important things that happen to us, when
they seem to follow the dictates of some inexorable power, that we
give up trying to learn how to act on, or change them. In the most
general sense, job satisfaction is a pleasurable or positive emotional
state resulting from the appraisal of one's job experiences. This
positive assessment or feeling seems to occur when work is
congruent with the individual's needs and values. Where there is
no such congruence, where your values and needs do not match
your work, there is a high likelihood that you will not only
experience dissatisfaction but perhaps disaffection as well.

Knowledge can be used as a stimulus to approach the 'not
knowing', allowing us to put up with ignorance as a basic condition
for achieving mental development. The word 'learning' undoubtedly denotes change of some kind. To 'not learn' means to stay in a
state of sameness. If sameness is preserved, time must stop in its
tracks. Thus, time is the destroyer of sameness, things do not remain
the same. Provided that we allow sufficient time for the recovery of
self-control, knowledge will permit further development. Time also
implies hope, If things can be different, they may also be better.
However, by the use of phantasy we may attempt to stop time in its
tracks. Without time there is no hope but also no disappointment
nor the fear that things might even get worse.

Hope and optimism

A basic need of all team members is for 'esteem'—both self-esteem and recognition from others. Most people have a need for a high evaluation of themselves that is firmly based on reality—recognition and respect from others; especially significant others. We are in constant need of reassurance, although at the same time the sense which makes it possible for us to worry about what may happen, also makes it possible to postpone the satisfaction of present needs and put up with current discomforts in the expectation of future rewards. This is a state of mind that we refer to as hope. Hope offers more than a bit of comfort in an anxiety ridden world, it plays a surprisingly potent role in life, offering an advantage in realms as diverse as school achievement and bearing up in onerous jobs. It is more than the sunny view that everything will turn out all right. It has been defined by Snyder (1991) as 'belief that you have both the will and the way to accomplish your goals, whatever they may be'.

As with hope, optimism is a state of mind that means having a strong expectation that, in general, things will turn out all right in life, despite setbacks and frustrations. Optimism is an attitude that helps team members avoid falling into apathy, hopelessness, or depression in the face of tough going. While the pessimistic team member's feelings lead to despair the optimistic team member's feelings will be bright and hopeful. Where team members have a high evaluation of themselves—a high self-esteem—they will have the self-belief that they have mastery over the events of their lives and can meet challenges as they come up.

Desire for competence

Another of the mainsprings of action in all team members is a desire for competence. Competence implies control over environmental factors both physical and social. People with this motive do not wish to wait passively for things to happen; they want to be able to manipulate their environment and make things happen. The competence motive reveals itself in adults as a desire for job mastery and professional growth. Developing a competency of any kind strengthens the sense of self-esteem, making a team member more willing to take risks and seek out more demanding challenges. Team members who have a high evaluation of themselves are able to bounce back from failures; they approach things in terms of how to handle them rather than worrying about what can go wrong.

If these needs are to be met, the conditions required are very much the same as those required in the maternal holding environment. In a facilitating environment team members can respond in responsible and productive ways to an environment in which they are given an opportunity to grow and mature. A self-actualizing man or woman is an individual behaving at his or her most productive level. An individual is most likely to behave in self-actualizing ways if the culture in which they work is characterized by openness, trust, a willingness to confront conflictual issues, and if they have challenging goals.

A facilitating environment will ensure that the anxiety of venturing into the unknown, the process by which team members develop new skills and ways of behaving, is not fundamentally disruptive. Any change will involve a loss, it will mean a change from the comfortable, routine, known way of doing things. A giving up of things taken for granted. All change will result in some level of anxiety. Where the right sort of environment exists the anxiety can be dominated just because the thread of continuity has not been broken and can always be given a reassuring tug. Spontaneous growth follows from the consolidation of familiar patterns of expectation. A facilitating environment will provide the consistency, confirmation, and continuity that helps team members make sense of their world: it will both hold them and let go of them.

Application of a facilitating environment

When the manager or leader offers security they do two things at once. On the one hand, because of their help other team members are safe from the unexpected, from innumerable unwelcome intrusions, and from a world that is at times not known or understood. On the other hand, other team members are protected by the manager or leader from their own impulses and from the effects that these impulses might produce. For example, by providing support and encouragement to other team members even when they are experiencing what may be regarded as the 'most rotten luck', will shield them and keep them in touch with reality. It will also protect them from their impulses to phantasize that there is a jinx on them or something of the sort.

Perhaps the most outstanding and most continuously operative of all team members' needs is that for emotional response from other team members. I use the term emotional response advisedly, since the eliciting of mere behavioural responses may leave this need quite unsatisfied. We all know what it's like to be alone in a crowd and we all know what it's like to be dealt with by someone who is acting like a 'cold fish'. It is this need for a response and especially for praise, which provides team members with their main stimulus to socially acceptable behaviour. One of the reasons why team members abide by the values of their teams is because they desire approval.

Containing mental pain

One of the most valuable things a manager or leader can do is to listen to other team members and to verbalize the individual team member's anxiety and concerns. By doing so, they will show that they are capable of accepting such feelings. This will convey a message to the team member that their manager cares; that they can bear to look at the team member's anxiety without being afraid of it and of seeking ways to avoid it. The manager or leader is someone who can feel pain and not break down under it and this gives the team member hope of this anxiety being tolerable. It also indicates that this may be a way of finding a solution. In adopting this approach the manager or leader has demonstrated that they are treating the team member as a whole person who is capable, with the manager or leader's help, of resolving this painful situation.

Listening

Listening promotes a feeling on the part of the team member that their problem is being shared, that someone who is genuinely interested in their welfare is helping to work to a satisfactory solution of it. This feeling is symbolized by the manager or leader's frequent use of the term 'we' in discussing the situation with them. The feeling of sharing itself mitigates the burden and eases the tasks that must be undertaken in working toward a solution. This feeling of sharing by the manager or leader serves to reinforce the self-esteem of the team member and with this support they are better able to bear frustration for the sake of future benefit—they develop hope.

Put another way, the team member experiences this situation as being held by the manager. This is the role that Donald Winnicott (1965b) referred to, where the mother needs to hold the infant both physically and emotionally. This holding Winnicott says, 'facilitates' the child's mental development because it allows a time span in which to learn to cope with their anxieties. In like manner, the team member will also experience anxious situations and in these situations the manager or leader can provide the sort of holding environment that will facilitate the team member's return to a less anxious state by providing an opportunity for the team member to learn to cope with their anxieties.

A dynamic process goes on if a receptive person is able to listen, understand and contain mental pain. Wilfred Bion (1962) shed some light on this process when he suggested that the team member finding anxiety, aggression or despair accepted and contained, is enabled at a feeling level, to realize that someone—here the manager or leader—capable of living with these feared or rejected aspects of themselves, does in fact exist. The manager or leader has experienced them, not been overwhelmed, on the contrary has coped with them, they therefore become less frightening and the team member is therefore able to cope.

Where, however, the manager or leader has insufficient self-control and is unable to accept the team member's feelings without being overwhelmed by them, they will not be able to provide support to the team member. Failure to respond appropriately leads to a feeling that aggression, depression or terror cannot be borne by the other person. The team member continues to feel that it is an omnipotently powerful force that cannot be circumscribed or bound. It comes to be experienced as an endless dread. If no resolution is apparent the team member may deal with this ghastly experience by repression. This of course means that it has not gone away, but will influence the team member's future behaviour from the unconscious.

The manager can also help the team member regarding the containment of anxiety by helping them to think about, to clarify, and to differentiate a vague feeling and to link it to what is meaningful by naming it and thus to modulate the pain. It is a sort of caring for team members which fulfils a function whereby there is a sort of mental digesting which translates the unendurable distress into something more defined, thus making it safer to experience. It is much the same as the doctor examining a team member and diagnosing the symptom of a physical pain. Once the team member knows what the diagnosis is, be that a torn muscle, a cartilage or a fractured bone, it will be a great relief. Instead of experiencing a general doom they will now be able to understand what it is about, and start to find ways of getting better.

Holding doubt and fear of the unknown

As a consultant and a manager there have been occasions when I have been thanked by a team member or manager for a very helpful discussion in a situation where I felt I had not really done anything. Normally in such circumstances a team member or manager has become stuck over something and as a result of talking with me, they have begun to sort it out, with the result that they can go away and make changes. All I have seemingly done is to listen attentively and with understanding. Perhaps I have shown an appreciation of the difficult situation the other party was in, or not agreed to blame someone else. I might also have asked a relevant question here and there that may have helped to clarify the issue.

What I, in fact did, was to provide an opportunity for the other party to be listened to, one where they were able to listen to their own thoughts, to explore, and to look for clues. This is not an easy activity for the other person as it will raise a certain amount of anxiety: they have to face not knowing and this brings with it the fear of becoming confused and finding no answer, of being lost in doubt and despair. By providing a holding environment where the fears are contained and showing that I am not omnipotently knowing either, it makes it possible for the team member to accomplish a task which they cannot do on their own. This is a role which is frequently carried out by all managers and leaders, and sometimes by other team members, and one which is invaluable to all.

Containing conflict

In Chapter 4, reference was made to the conflict which may be experienced by a team member, mainly internally, or by acting out in his relationships with other team members, or a mixture of both. Here the manager needs to act as someone who will contain and hold the team together. By providing a good enough holding environment it becomes safe for the team members concerned to air their disputes and grievances, to express their hostility and explore the assumptions they have made about each other, without feeling that the team is likely to break up. Communication, exploration, and understanding at a reality-based level may thus be established.

The need here is to ensure that team members are not incited to indulge in immature attitudes. The work required of the manager or leader lies in the tolerance of the expression of feelings in words and thoughts and to a very limited extent in behaviour. The manager or leader should be working in alliance with the mature, reality-based parts of the team members and the infantile modes of thought and feelings will be the subjects which are brought out for review, to be understood and worked on. In teams, the different parts of the personality of the various individual team members, such as loving and hating, idealization and persecution, omnipotence and help-lessness, responsible and irresponsible, careful or careless will all be in existence and will from time to time come to the fore. By being aware that these different aspects of the personality all form part of the whole, the manager or leader by tolerating such conflict that is produced by their co-existence and continuing to care for the whole group, in spite of its bad aspects, will make it easier for team members to deal with the conflict within themselves and so function better in their relationships with each other. Just because someone is guilty of bad behaviour doesn't make them a bad person.

Containing anger and helplessness

A different degree of holding operates when a team member uses the manager in order to get rid of an unwanted part of himself. In such cases the team member will behave in a way that produces helplessness and suffering in the manager. For example, where in the past a player has constantly experienced rejection, he may react by treating the manager in like manner. In one such case, a team member who was regarded as talented had been left out of the side on several occasions over the past couple of years. When a new manager arrived he said that he wanted to play his part and was keen to do well. Before the next match the team member arrived late and in the next few matches displayed a difficult attitude. The manager felt helpless, angry, and frustrated because he felt that he had been reasonable and given this team member every chance. Here we can see that the feelings experienced by the manager are a repetition, or mirroring, of the team member's feelings. It seems that what in fact was happening was that the team member was projecting into the manager those feelings that he could not tolerate, feelings of rejection. These are not easy circumstances for managers or leaders, but if they are to retain a valuable team member they need to provide a holding environment that will take the full impact of the team member's anger, retain their self-control, and then take up the anxiety and not the defence to it.

When a team member's problems are primarily due to external factors, they are likely to be conscious of them and to have very little resistance to discussing them with a receptive listener. When, however, emotional factors complicate their problems, it is likely that other team members will transfer their problems onto the manager or leader. In these circumstances, team members are less fully aware, or perhaps quite unconscious, of the existence or nature of their personality difficulties and of their relation to their reality problem. It is rather like psycho–somatic illness where the pain is experienced as real, but the cause is not physical. The team member cannot talk about them directly because they are to a considerable degree unaware of them. And even so far as they are dimly conscious of them, the same resistance that operates to keep them from becoming more fully and clearly aware of them serve to inhibit their talking about them.

I cannot stress strongly enough the fact that the manager would serve no helpful purpose by relating to the team member their suspicions that the problems lay in early life. They will best operate at the conscious level, or at most, the pre-conscious level, not trying to unearth and bring to consciousness the deeply unconscious emotions of the team member. Much of the effective power of working with the team member results from the parental role, with which the team member's emotions often endow the manager. The manager or leader in the role of parent surrogate is able to give needed additional courage and strength to the team member. As with a child, a team member confident of the manager's trust, will face difficult problems and new experiences unflinchingly, whereas one dominated by anxiety will cower away from the new and seek security in the old. A team member who is supported by their confidence in the strengths of the manager will be willing to give up their old and worn patterns of behaviour which have proved futile for the solution of their problems and dare to attack it by new and more hopeful methods.

Just as the child's affection for their parents makes them willing to try their suggestions, so their attachment to the manager renders a team member amenable to suggestions from them. So effective, indeed, is this force, that the manager must exercise caution if they are to avoid exploiting the dependency by overguiding the team member. Often, however, a team member is at the end of their resources with regard to their problem and a manager can provide a necessary aid by calling attention to a number of courses of action between which the team member can then choose. Suggestion in this sense, far from controlling the team member, acts instead to enlarge the breadth of their choice and consequently their freedom of choice.

Concluding remarks

Seeing the role of leader as one who works hard to develop a facilitating environment, one where all team members can act in a mature way and thus express themselves to their full ability, is rather different from the 'over the top and at them' role so frequently portrayed in other books. I would suggest that the latter approach requires little more than a degree of bravery—which admittedly, is a valuable asset for any manager—but hardly sufficient on its own to get results through other people.

Developing yourself in role, so that you are capable of providing a role model for other team members, requires the acquisition of many other skills. The starting point for the development of these skills is yourself. Our desires guide and manifest themselves in our behaviour. Thus, all behaviour is the result of us gaining control over our desires by which we basically mean, learning how to like or to appreciate something. This is how we come to know about the world. Unless we have the desire; unless we view self-awareness as something we want; we shall not begin to achieve it. If we do not have the desire; if we do not view emotional maturity as something we want; we shall not achieve it. Unless we have the desire to change the way we currently manage; we shall not achieve it. Unless we have the desire to treat all team members as equals; we shall not achieve it. What is more, unless we have those desires, we shall be most unlikely to get the best possible results through other people; we shall not begin to develop an achieving team. Those who are brave enough to have the desire will find the way.

At the start of the book I stated that the reader might find this book uncomfortable reading. Some of you may have experienced feelings of discomfort and uncertainty as a result of the many challenges to the concepts and values of significant managers and leaders that you have internalized and which have guided your actions and behaviour over the years. For some of you, it may seem that almost everything you stand for has been challenged and for others a great deal of what you stand for. All I ask is that you reflect for a moment and feel what it was and perhaps is like to be a member in a team (and here I use the word loosely), where someone is appointed the leader and then proceeds to deny you the opportunity to even relate to any of the concepts and values that you have internalized.

AFTERWORD

Football has provided us with a unique opportunity to study the complicated and emotional interactions between manager or leader and other team members. When working with the football team there was little that went on without my knowledge and, being a human activity without the complications of machinery or other technology, it exposed and made the human dynamics available for examination in an exceedingly rich way. That both football and management are emotional games is hardly contestable. For both the manager or leader and other team members, emotional involvement is seldom a choice and all team members are likely to be subject to high's and low's of emotion as a result of situational events. It is, therefore, helpful if all team members can develop a level of self-awareness that helps them understand their emotions and gain a degree of self-control. I would suggest that for the manager or leader, this is imperative.

This leads me to an important aspect that I have, thus far, barely touched upon: that concerning personal change. Let me start from the notion that all learning involves some degree of loss. We learn every minute of every day and most of this learning is in the nature of a minor modification to our existing knowledge, which does not represent a huge change and subsequent loss of previous knowledge. For example, in football, a team member may, as a result of a desire for growth, learn a modified way of kicking the ball or of tackling an opponent. This is not earth shattering stuff, but the player will now lose his previous knowledge in favour of the new. Such is the nature of our activity as human beings that we are engaged in a dynamic process, one where we are constantly changing.

However, loss and change can sometimes present us with considerable difficulties. Developing a level of self-awareness will be an achievement in itself, but will not necessarily result in the desired level of self-control. An example concerns a client I was working with on a one-to-one basis who over a period of time developed a high degree of self-awareness but when she became overwhelmed by her emotions would revert to past ways of dealing with matters—ways that she hoped she had dispensed with. For the woman concerned this caused considerable frustration that she had not been able to lose her past so easily. This example provides a timely warning that self-reflection and self-awareness are only starting points, the individual needs to work hard at the process of change. To try to explain the process for the client I used the following example, which I have since used on other occasions with other clients.

I asked her to think of her motor car and about the length of time she had owned it and, about how long she had owned the previous model. It turned out that she had owned her previous car for some three years and had taken possession of the current one some six months earlier. I then asked her to consider what happened when she faced an emergency in her car. After much thought she laughed and said, 'I turn on the windscreen wipers instead of the indicators'. We then explored why this was and she realized that she had reverted to previous learned behaviour connected to her last car. Put another way, we could say that emotionality had caused her to react in a previously learned way. Basically, it is no different with any other form of learned behaviour and, while my client was frustrated at her 'lapses' into past behaviour, she realized that other personal changes were far more complicated than driving a car and to change them might take time and determination. The life we have learned to drive is infinitely more complicated than the cars which we learn to drive; but, the same principle applies, it is a dynamic process which is perfectly capable of change.

Nevertheless, we all have our blind spots and have all developed our individual coping mechanisms which can make it difficult for us to become aware of some of our learned behaviour. The problem is that being a manager or leader in any organization can be an extremely lonely position. The increasing demand for greater efficiency and effectiveness in a constantly changing environment means that, from time to time, all leaders and managers experience situations that bother them professionally and personally. Quite often such situations are experienced around issues of leadership and authority. The result can mean an adverse effect on the performance of not only the individual manager or leader but also of those working with them and ultimately the whole organization.

The difficulty is, who can the leader or manager turn to? In theory it should be possible to try to resolve the problem with a variety of people. However, the many reasons that make it such a lonely position, may also inhibit the leader or manager from seeking advice in these quarters. For example, a football manager may feel that it is not appropriate to go to other team members, or to the Chairman or other Board members, as this may result in a loss of confidence. Thus, the very circumstances of the problem are frequently the reason for its perpetuation. I take the view that these are not normally individual problems that can be solved by, for example, the leader or manager attending a course. Rather, they are organizational problems and the individual leader or manager is required to be seen as a person-in-role in an organizational system. Thus any attempt at gaining a greater understanding of the situation needs to take into consideration the wider organizational system. This can best be achieved not by the importation of 'new' knowledge but by a better understanding of the 'current' or experiential knowledge.

The sort of confidential consultancy provided to help the manager referred to in this book, supports the manager or leader in a process of development. Managers and leaders need someone neutral to talk about the issues in their work that bother them. The material for work is the client's experiences in their own working situation. That is, the manager or leader's perceptions, thoughts, feelings, images, and described behaviour of interactions with those they relate to day by day. Working with this material the consultant seeks to enable clients to develop their understanding of themselves by learning how to analyse, and modify, the way in which they interpret their organizational roles.

Let me now return to the important notion of leadership. It seems clear that there are many different roles that leaders have to take if they are to be truly effective. Among these are:

- being an exemplary role model;
- setting boundaries for creative activities by all team members;
- developing long term goals, and setting a vision; and
- ensuring that the various functions are aligned.

Above all, though, I would suggest that the key leadership role of any manager or leader is that of:

- providing an environment that encourages leadership by all team members.

The mind set that we adopt in our approach to managing and leading teams will have much bearing on how we take up our role. For example, if as a manager or leader, we approach our task with the view that it is 'our' team and the players or team members are 'our' players; we are likely to end up, not with a team, but with a single leader work group. A single leader tends to treat others in the work group as extensions of themselves. And, in this world we end up in a situation where:

- no one but the leader has thoughts and ideas;
- no one but the leader makes decisions;
- no one but the leader takes responsibility for results; and
- no one but the leader is allowed to express their emotions.

This provides an environment where even the strongest characters are likely to suffer stress and anxiety. An environment where self-esteem and motivation of team members will be at their lowest. If we want to 'get results through other people', this seems to be the least likely way to achieve our aims.

Throughout the book, I have not only tried to present a different approach but have also tried to model a different approach. I would hope that, long before now, you will have noticed that when referring to managers and leaders, I have avoided the use of expressions relating to 'their' ownership of teams. Rather, I have taken an inclusive approach whereby I refer to 'the manager or leader and other team members'. I have also sought to avoid using the term 'follower' because this tends to be interpreted as 'the' leader and 'their' followers. This is slightly more difficult because whichever team member provides leadership they must use power to get their new ideas across and they need people to join them in that endeavour, or to follow them. I would suggest that for all members of teams, it may help, when you have an idea that you want to put forward, to think of your peers in the team as 'joiners', rather than 'followers'.

If we take up the role of managing and leading a team with a mindset that takes an inclusive approach whereby we view others as individuals who are partners in the team, we will treat them in a very different way. In this world we end up in a situation where:

- all team members (including the leader) can develop their thoughts and ideas;
- all team members (including the leader) can contribute to and make decisions;
- all team members (including the leader) will be accountable and take responsibility for results;
- all team members (including the leader) will be allowed to express their emotions; and
- all are autonomous beings with brains and emotions of their own.

In this sort of environment, even the weakest characters will develop the mental strength and 'attitude' to approach the task with confidence. This is likely to be an environment where self-esteem and motivation of all team members will be at their highest. If we want to 'get results through other people', this seems to be the most likely way to achieve our aims.

This applies to members of teams in all manner of locations and, while the scenario for many of the situations described has been the interesting world of football, I should not want this book to be seen as being solely concerned with management and leadership in the football setting. Everything referred to will be equally applicable to the management and leadership of any team in any industry or calling. Naturally, there will be differences in circumstances but the effects of emotion on the various participants will still be the same. It doesn't matter whether it's a football club where the manager and chairman are vying for authority; or a hospital where consultants and managers are vying for authority. The end result, in both situations, will be confusion and stress for those team members who are subject to this confusion and tug of loyalty. The highs and lows of emotion will occur in all organizations, which may result in a lack of perception that can have drastic consequences for those concerned. And, if managers and leaders, in any setting, are not capable of developing the notion of 'emotional distance' they may become overwhelmed by the emotion and incapable of providing leadership to the other team members at their moment of need.

More specifically, football has also provided us with data regarding the sort of problems that other industries may face in managing the so-called 'knowledge workers'. In football, where team members feel that their skills are not appreciated or valued according to the individual's self-estimation, the player concerned will simply ask for a transfer to another club. In such circumstances a really sophisticated and mature style of management is required. One where the manager or leader will maintain control of their emotions even when filled with anxiety and frustration. Even though the team member may be acting in a disturbing and uncontrolled manner and doubtless seeking to make the manager or leader react in a way that will justify the behaviour they are adopting.

'Knowledge workers' in other industries will soon be behaving in the same manner and other industries will have to develop more sophisticated management and leadership skills. As we have seen in football, where managers try to act in the old authoritarian and bullying manner players simply walk out and justify their walking out by claiming that they have done so because they have been treated badly. That is not to say that every situation will be resolved to the satisfaction of the manager's desires. As in football, 'knowledge workers', are valuable commodities and others will always be willing to pay more for their services than their current employer can afford to pay. That is the way of the world with any commodity that is in short supply. However, by retaining self-control managers can at least negotiate in a reality-based manner and thereby ensure that they get the best possible deal for their organization.

Coming to a conclusion, I am aware that in one sense, this exploration of the management and leadership of teams remains unfinished. This book has dealt with issues that relate to those aspects of management and leadership that concern individual dynamics and behaviour which are constantly complicated by the multiple desires of various team members. But, there are other issues concerning group dynamics and group behaviour such as the basic assumption behaviour first referred to by Wilfred Bion (1961), that have not been explored here. I don't think that this in any way detracts from the value of the book; but, I feel it right to point out to the reader that this is not the end of the journey. Perhaps this other material will be the subject of a future volume.

REFERENCES

Alexander, P. (1965). *William Shakespeare: The Complete Works*, (p. 237, Sonnet 94). London: Collins.

Anzieu, D. (1989). *The Skin Ego*. London: Yale University Press.

Bateson, G. (1979). *Mind and Nature*. New York: Dutton.

Bettleheim, B. (1988). *A Good Enough Parent*. London: Pan Books.

Bion, W. R. (1961). *Experiences in Groups*. London: Tavistock.

Bion, W. R. (1962). *Learning from Experience*. London: Heinemann.

Bowen, R. B. (1999). Managing in a cauldron: today's angry workplace. In: *Harvard Management Update*, (pp. 1–7) February.

Erikson, E. H. (1950). *Childhood and Society*. New York: Norton.

Fairbairn, W. R. D. (1952). *Psychoanalytic Studies of the Personality*. London: Routledge & Kegan Paul.

Fiedler, F. E. (1967). *A Theory of Leadership Effectiveness*. New York: McGraw-Hill.

Francis, T. (1987). *Clough a Biography*. London: Stanley Paul.

Freud, S. (1926). *Inhibitions, Symptoms and Anxiety. S.E.*, 10. Harmondsworth: Penguin.

Goleman, D. (1995). *Emotional Intelligence*. New York: Bantam Books.

Guntrip, H. (1971). *Psychoanalytic Theory, Therapy and the Self*. New York: Basic Books.

Katzenback, J. R., & Santamaria, J. A. (1999). Firing up the front line. *Harvard Business Review*, 77(3): 107–117.

Kernberg, O. (1966). Structural derivatives of object relationships. *International Journal of Psycho-analysis*, 47, 236–253.

Klein, M. (1975). *Love, Guilt and Reparation and Other Works*. London: Virago.

Klein, M. (1975). *Envy and Gratitude and Other Works*. London: Virago.

Lawrence, P. R. & Lorsch, J. W. (1967). *Organisation and Environment*. Boston: Harvard Business School.

Miller, E. J. (1985). Organisational development and industrial democracy: a current case study. In: E. J. Miller (Ed.), *Task and Organisation*. London: John Wiley.

Pitt-Aitken, T., & Ellis, A. T. (1989). *Loss of the Good Authority*. London: Viking.

Skynner, R. (1989). In: J. R. Schlapobersky (Ed.), *Institutes and How to Survive Them*. London: Tavistock/Routledge.

Snyder, C. R. (1991). The will and the ways: development and validation of an individual-differences measure of hope. *Journal of Personality and Social Psychology*, 60(4): 579.

Stapley, L. F. (1996). *The Personality of The Organisation: A Psycho-dynamic Explanation of Culture And Change*. London: Free Association.

Stein, M. (2000). After Eden; envy and the defences against anxiety paradigm. *Human Relations*, 54(2): 193–211.

Tannenbaum, R., Weschler, I. R., & Massarik, F. (1961). *Leadership and Organisation*. New York: McGraw Hill.

Toman, W. (1960). *Psychoanalytic Theory of Motivation*. London: Pergamon Press.

Venables, T., & Hanson, N. (1994). *Venables the Autobiography*. Harmondsworth, England: Penguin.

Winnicott, D. W. (1965a). *The Family and Individual Development*. London: Tavistock.

Winnicott, D. W. (1965b). *The Maturational Process and the Facilitating Environment*. New York: International Universities Press.

INDEX